TURNING POINTS in a DIFFERENT LIFE

BY TED BOYNTON

Ted Boynton

and

Mary

Cover Photo by Author
Mary at the helm of our
Yacht "Mary Constance."

ISBN: 1479220981
ISBN 13: 9781479220984

Dedication

For Mary

While these memoirs are mine and written in the first person, from the day that Mary and I met on a fateful Christmas afternoon, they really are "our memoirs." Since that day, it has always been "Mary and Ted."

Introduction

Life is full of "what ifs." Repeatedly my life has reached turning points. I ask myself, "If I had taken this branch, instead of the other, how would my life have been different?" Some of the turns seemed to be a direct result of our decisions, but other changes seem to have been imposed on us by other people, or by fate, or, as I have come to believe, direction from a higher power, from God.

My daughter Beth says that I am a storyteller. Perhaps this is true, but if I am, it is because of the different life that my wife Mary and I have led. I have told stories about when we were fighting a gale in the middle of the Atlantic. Or about the time that we had an explosion in our motorhome while parked in a cemetery. Perhaps it was about my "divinely inspired," unsuccessful, screwball decision to buy a very large sailboat and head for the West Indies. Or perhaps about flying over the Himalayan Mountains, photographing the rugged terrain below through an open door.

I have always been an avid amateur photographer and tend to see the world as if looking through a camera lens. I have never considered myself a writer, but through the years, when we have shown our pictures or described our life, people have said, "You ought to write a book."

In the following pages I will write about our "different life" and about the major turning points that directed us to our adventures. I had several sources of information to refresh my memory. My mother kept all the letters I ever wrote to her, as well as a number of very interesting family letters which I did not write.

I still have my flight logs from World War II. I also was able to find some very helpful information about my time in India, flying over the hump, in American Airlines archives.

Mary and I have produced 45-minute sound slideshows, one for each year of our ocean travel. I still have the scripts for these nine productions. We never kept a narrative-type ship's log, only using our log for navigation details. Fortunately, Mary kept a daily journal of all our sailing adventures. Without her journals and her remarkable memory, which persists to this day, I would have been unable to write these memoirs.

CHAPTER 1

The Early Days

Fate decided to have me raised in an upper-middle-class family. My mother and father enjoyed a successful marriage for more than 50 years, setting us a wonderful example. My wife Mary and I recently celebrated our 68th wedding anniversary.

I was born in Buffalo, New York on March 18, 1921, one day after my mother's 21st birthday. She had eloped from college and, perhaps to placate her dismayed father, I was later named after him: Edwin Matthews Boynton. From my birth, they called me Teddy. Later I became Ted, a name I use to this day.

Following my father's different jobs, we moved to a Chicago suburb where I have my first childhood memory. I tried to shoot squirrels with a toy wooden gun.

Our final move was to the Cleveland suburb of Shaker Heights, Ohio. In spite of the Great Depression, I enjoyed a privileged childhood. By this time my father was working for the Curtis Publishing Company, publisher of the *Saturday Evening Post, Ladies' Home Journal,* and other magazines. He started as an advertising salesman for the *Post* and spent his business life in the Cleveland office, ending up as a regional vice president.

I'm not going to spend much time reminiscing about my childhood, except to say that I was told many times by teachers and parents that I wasn't living up to my capabilities. In my grade school years, we moved to a larger house in a fancier neighborhood and a better school where I continued to "not live up to expectations."

By now I had two brothers. Bob, three years younger than I, was an excellent, highly motivated student. The youngest brother, Doug, was well on his way to becoming a juvenile delinquent.

A turning point occurred the summer before I entered high school. My father was a third-generation graduate of Amherst College and was anxious for me to become the fourth generation. It was obvious, with my grades and attitude, that I was not on the right track, so he enrolled me at Western Reserve Academy, a highly structured, private, college preparatory boarding school. There my study habits would be monitored and controlled.

Fate interrupted his plans. In late summer I had my tonsils removed, not an unusual procedure in those days. The day after surgery, I awoke with sharp pains in my stomach and the doctor discovered that I had a very high white blood cell count. He diagnosed my symptoms as acute appendicitis, and I had my second operation that day. There was nothing wrong with my appendix, but he removed it anyway. He did discover a small duodenal ulcer near the same location. Recovery was much slower in those days, and I was put on a soft diet. As a result, I missed the enrollment period for Western Reserve Academy. This was a life-changing event! I will never know what would have happened had I attended that school and gone on to an Ivy League college.

My father still had Ivy League plans for me and I found myself enrolled as a day student in University School, another private college prep school. US, as it was called,

was located within walking distance of my house. I was still without supervision. I continued to not live up to everyone's expectations for three more years.

I was unhappy at US. In order to find a place in the student body, one had to be a jock, studious, or wealthy. I didn't fit into any category and convinced my father to let me transfer to Shaker Heights High School for my senior year.

I was much happier there, and my grades soared enough to gain admission to Antioch College in Yellow Springs, Ohio. I suspect that, in those depression years, just having enough money would have sufficed. I went because my parents expected me to and I had nothing else to do. I started college in the fall of 1939.

While waiting for college, two friends and I drove in my car from Cleveland through New England into Canada, where we visited Québec City and Montréal, then through Ontario and back home. Perhaps the high point of the trip was watching the famous Dionne Quintuplets through a one-way screen. I loved the trip and already my love of travel was showing itself.

Antioch was a very liberal college and advanced for its time. It had a student council which was very active in college policy making. We had an honor system which allowed us to pick up our exams and complete them anywhere. It really worked. I actually flunked a math exam because I couldn't remember a formula which was in a book right on my desk. After their first year, girls didn't have any curfew rules; men never did. Faculty were selected for their actual teaching ability and were very close to the students.

Antioch was a cooperative college. One semester each year, students were required to earn graduation credits by working at jobs off campus. Antioch's personnel department secured these for us and we received a minimum wage.

One semester, I worked at the Underwood Typewriter factory in Bridgeport, Connecticut, in the parts department, where my supervisor was a little tyrant who cured me of any desire to be involved in any kind of manufacturing. The job did have one great feature; its location was close enough to New York City that, along with other co-op students, I was able to enjoy several weekends in Greenwich Village. We left immediately after work and stayed up almost all night visiting jazz nightclubs and after-hours jam sessions. We crammed ourselves into other co-op students' tiny New York apartments for what little sleep we did get. We returned to work tired, happy, and in some cases hung over. I didn't learn anything about manufacturing but learned a lot about Greenwich Village nightlife and jazz.

I also spent time as a mailroom clerk in an advertising agency in Cleveland and commuted to work from my home. I did learn how advertising agencies function because I delivered mail to every department and people were very willing to tell me what they were doing. This information proved helpful in later years.

Totally without motivation, I managed a two-point scholastic average, enough to keep me in school. My attention, however, was not focused on studies; it was centered on one girl, Cora. Our romance blossomed during the two years that she was at Antioch. Looking back now, I believe she must have worked hard to keep her attention focused on her studies.

Cora was a good student and knew why she was in college because neither of her parents had had that educational opportunity. They lived on Long Island and her mother worked in Manhattan as an office manager. Her father was a timid little man totally dominated by his wife, as was Cora. Her mother withdrew her from Antioch at the end of her second year to care for her younger brother, who was recovering from a serious case of rheumatic fever. I believe another reason was to get Cora away from me.

At the Carson Pirie Scott department store in Chicago, I worked as a sales clerk in the basement store. I learned to operate a cash register, and my sales were good enough to earn me a promotion to manager of the men's jacket department. I learned to fold jackets and display them properly after shoppers had gone through the department, scattering jackets behind them. Retailing did not appeal to me but I had my own tenement apartment, complete with bedbugs. Cora was working in Chicago. During that time, Cora and I had agreed to be married at some later time. It was not a formal engagement; no ring was involved.

At the end of this work period, Cora returned home by way of Cleveland. We traveled by train and spent a memorable night in a Pullman upper berth. After a short visit to my parents' home, she went on to New York. I learned much later that my mother was concerned about Cora because she bossed me around too much.

Our unofficial engagement ended less than a year later, with a letter from Cora, which I received while working in Bridgeport, in January 1942. This was an eventful year for me! Looking back now, the letter showed quite remarkable insight and maturity. She pointed out that I did not seem to have any direction in my life and that I never seemed to finish anything that I started; I was too immature to consider undertaking marriage. It was a kind and definite message breaking off our relationship. I later discovered that Cora and I had had separate meetings with the collage dean, who told each of us that we were not ready for the responsibilities of marriage.

This was another turning point. Everything Cora said about me was true. My mother also showed remarkable insight, considering that she had never met Cora's parents. Cora was already showing signs of following in her mother's footsteps as a dominating woman. I would have resisted her bossing because of my own background. In addition, Cora would have had great difficulty coping with my restless nature. The marriage probably would not have lasted, or at least would have been an unhappy one. The letter calling off our relationship was not a surprise to me and actually gave me a sense of relief. I was free.

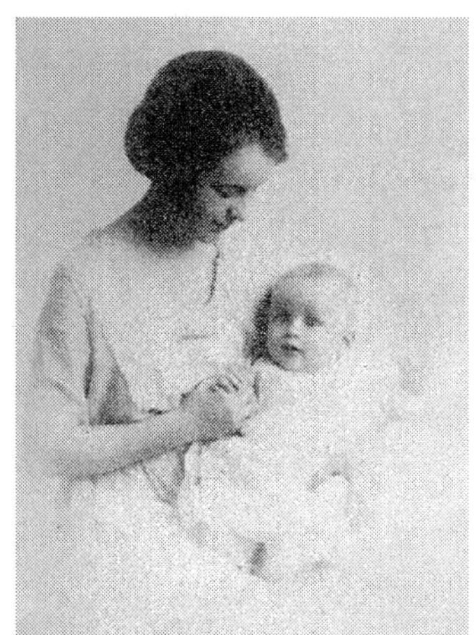

My Mother and Me

Ted Age 5

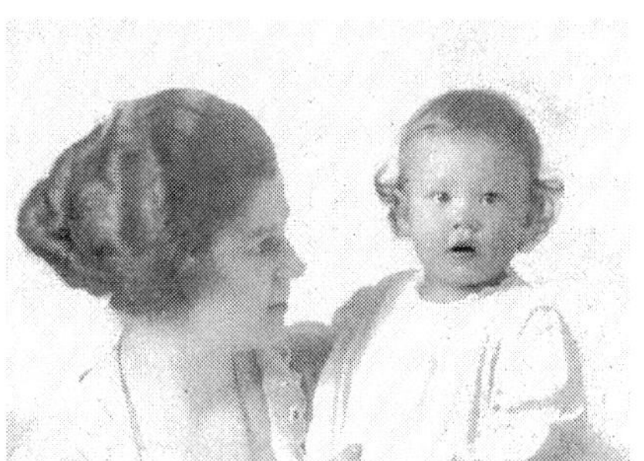

Mary and Her Mother

Maary Age 5

The First House in Shaker Heights

The House Wher I Grew Up
in Shaker Heights

Team Portrait US in the background

Antioch College Towers

Shaker Heights High School

High School Graduation Portrait

Our Crew in Casablanca

This Is To Identify EDWIN MATTHEWS BOYNTON

who has been certificated as an airman by the Civil Aeronautics Administration and whose signature appears hereon.

Signature Civil Aeronautics Representative

Signature Fingerprinting Officer

Place of birth BUFFALO N Y

Date of birth 3/18/21

Color eyes BLUE hair BLONDE

Weight 145 lb. Ht. 5 ft. 8 3/4 in.

My Airman's Identification

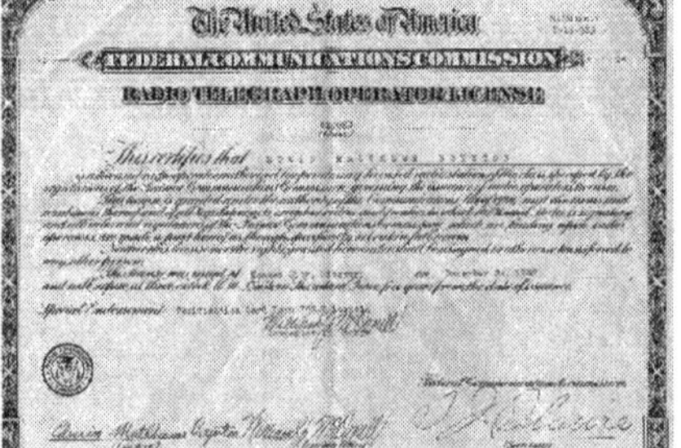

The United States of America

FEDERAL COMMUNICATIONS COMMISSION

RADIO TELEGRAPH OPERATOR LICENSE

This certifies that

My Telegraph License

CHAPTER 2

Pearl Harbor

On December 7, 1941, several of us were in the third floor lounge of our off-campus dorm when an announcement interrupted the music we were listening to and an excited voice told us that the Japanese had bombed Pearl Harbor. None of us knew where Pearl Harbor was, but very shortly, everyone in the world knew it was located in Hawaii.

We kept listening as President Roosevelt declared war on Japan. This was a turning point in my life and in the lives of every man of draft age. The military service needs for men changed dramatically, and suddenly draft classification numbers dominated our lives. Eventually every male between 18 and 45 was registered and eligible for induction. My draft board classified me 1-A. This meant that I was eligible for induction and had no deferment excuse. I knew that Antioch College had sent a notification to my draft board that I was enrolled there. I suspect that, with my academic record, they didn't suggest my deferment.

When the government held the national conscription lottery, I drew a high number. That meant that I was not likely to be called up for some time. My concern was not entering the service; almost all of us wanted to help win the war. Rather, it was about which service branch. I most definitely didn't want to be a foot soldier. I had heard my Dad's stories about his experiences in World War I. An Amherst graduate, he ended up laying railroad tracks in France, and he had volunteered to serve! World War II induction practices were more sophisticated, but I wanted to be certain how I best could serve my country. No slogging through mud for me. I thought I deserved to be an officer. As everyone had pointed out, I was just drifting in college. The war was my salvation! No more school; I would help win the war!

CHAPTER 3

Service

For some time after the war started, men still had the option of selecting the branch of the service they preferred upon enlisting. I decided that I wanted to be a naval aviator. I traveled to Columbus, Ohio, where the naval recruiting center was located. I passed all of their initial tests with little difficulty. My physical examination went well, until a final test. I was seated in a revolving chair with my head down and my eyes closed and revolved rapidly. When directed, I sat up with my eyes still closed. I canted to one side. Then they rotated me in the other direction and I sat up leaning to the other side. They repeated this procedure several times. They informed me that I had failed my equilibrium test, which indicated that I might lose my orientation in close maneuvering situations. The test also indicated that I might be subject to seasickness. I did feel a little queasy as a result of taking the test several times, so I couldn't argue with them. It's ironic that after thousands of hours sailing in all kinds of seas, I have never been seasick.

I really wanted to serve my country, was hurt by my rejection as a candidate, and told them so. One of the officers said I should try the Army Air Corps just down the hall, as they didn't give that test. The Army Air Corps recruiters were much more enthusiastic. They gave me their series of tests and a physical, and I passed. I would go through basic training, then flight school, and end up a second lieutenant with my wings as an aviator. It all sounded so simple to me, but there was one hitch. Because the Army was so short of training facilities and aircraft, I probably would not be called up for several months. I wanted to win the war, right then, and I most certainly didn't want to stay in college. I decided to defer my decision to enlist.

This was another fork in the road. Had I been able to enter naval aviation, I might not be writing this now. Most early naval pilots never returned home. Fatalities for early Army pilot trainees were also alarming.

That spring, my final semester at Antioch ended and I moved home. Once again, fate stepped in; this time it was my father. He was not at all happy about my Army Air Corps decision. He had a business friend who had rejoined the Army as a major. His job was supervising the Army recruiting station in Cleveland. Dad arranged to have me talk with him as a friend. At this point, I really wanted to be in the service as soon as possible, but not as a foot soldier. The major suggested several possibilities to get on a track that should to lead to a commission. One of these really interested me. He said that the Army was very much in need of trained radio operators and that anyone with a commercial radio operator's license would almost certainly be sent to officer's training school to become a Signal Corps officer. He suggested that since I had some time before I would be drafted, I consider going to a radio training school and try to get qualified as a commercial radio operator. He even suggested a radio school in Kansas City, Missouri, which was already training servicemen.

Midland Radio School accepted my application. In early May 1942 I arrived in Kansas City, two weeks before my courses would start. I registered at the school and secured a dorm room. With time on my hands, I decided to hitchhike to Mexico. I assured my parents that if I couldn't complete the trip in time, I would always keep sufficient money to take a bus back to make my school deadline.

I already had a lot of hitchhiking experience. One summer, while still in high school, I traveled to northern Ontario to join my uncle at a fishing camp. On one leg of my trip, a nice young couple had squeezed me into the front seat between them. After quite a few miles on the road, we rounded a slow speed curve in their old Ford coupe and ran, head on, into another old car. When the effect of the immediate impact wore off, all three of us appeared unhurt. Then, while we sat there gathering ourselves together, I felt warm liquid flowing from my head. I had a moment of panic until I discovered the hot liquid was coffee from a broken thermos bottle on the shelf behind me. The driver of the other car was all right too. A number of cars stopped at the accident scene. When I asked one of the drivers, he was willing to take me on the next leg of my journey.

I had also hitchhiked between Cleveland and Antioch College in southern Ohio several times. I can't imagine making these trips today; times were different then, before so many superhighways. I always enjoyed the experience because of all the interesting people I met.

My trip to Mexico was a great success. My first day, I picked up a ride with a man who was going all the way to Houston, Texas. From there I hitched to Galveston because I wanted to see the Gulf of Mexico. I saw my first palm trees. I returned to Houston with a young man about my own age, who had been the third mate on a steamer which was sunk by a U-boat just off Haiti. He said the U-boat fired two torpedoes and missed, then subsequently surfaced and sank their ship with gunfire. All but one of the crew survived, and were spotted in their life rafts by a naval patrol boat and picked up after 30 hours at sea.

From Houston I caught a ride with a man who worked for a small independent oil producing company which was drilling a wildcat oil well nearby. We detoured on our way to Laredo, Texas to visit a ranch where he was trying to lease their oil rights. This gave me the opportunity to see miles and miles of cactus, small brush, and several rattlesnakes. I came much too close to a rattlesnake when I bent down to pick up something from the ground and looked up to see a coiled rattler about five feet away. I backed off quickly and a ranch hand dispatched the snake with a club.

In Laredo I learned that there was going to be a bullfight in Monterrey, Mexico the next day. Mexico was preparing for the celebration of Cinco de Mayo, hence the bullfight. I had always wanted to see this spectacle, so I took a very crowded bus to Monterrey. There I discovered the hotels were jam packed because, of all things, an International Rotary Convention was in town. I managed to get a very small room somehow.

I can't recall how I was lucky enough to meet a young American my own age who had lived all his life in Mexico and was fluent in Spanish and English. That night he took me to his father's country club, where we attended a dance. I found that upper-class Mexicans danced just as we did, except that many of my partners didn't speak any English. He also helped me to get tickets to the bullfight, where I sat in the cheap seats on the sunny side of the arena. I was fascinated by the pageantry of the occasion but couldn't get very excited when the matador finally dispatched the sad, blood-soaked bull. Once was enough for me! I hitchhiked back to Kansas City and arrived in plenty of time to start my classes at Midland Radio School.

The goal was for us to pass the examinations for our commercial licenses. The school allowed us to proceed at our own pace in taking federal license examinations. This was a great advantage for me because I was able to advance quickly. For the first time in my scholastic career, I concentrated on my studies. We learned how to send and receive Morse code, and to touch-type well. We also studied the construction and maintenance of radio receivers and transmitters. When my code speed had advanced enough and I had learned enough theory, I took and passed my Class B Amateur Operator License examination. I was the first in my class to do so.

I wrote the following to my parents in a letter dated August 11, 1942:

Dear Mother and Dad,

Well, I have some wonderful news for you; it looks as though I am going to be hired by American Airlines. Last Friday the whole class filled out applications and were interviewed by American Airlines officials. We were told, at the time, that only a few of us would be picked. Today, Mr. Mossman called about eight of us into his office and told us that we had been selected. We filled out our official application blanks today, now before our final acceptance, it is just a matter of routine, physical examinations etc.

The arrangement with American is ideal. I will continue in school for about five more months, American wants us to have our licenses if possible. We will receive approximately one hundred dollars a month plus our tuition. This salary is to be fixed by the government for all airlines sometime in the near future. We will be in a special class which will teach American Airlines procedure rather than the more general procedure we are now getting.

When we leave Midland, we will go on as ground station operators for a period of about two months to receive practical training. Then we will go on as regular flight operators. American Airlines fly the North Atlantic, from some place in either the United States or Canada, to some place in England or Scotland. It is a military secret and besides I don't know. Our pay will probably be somewhere between two hundred and three hundred dollars a month. This pay will also be fixed by the Army for all the airlines.

When on duty as a flight operator I will wear an Army officer's uniform with special insignia and second lieutenant's bars. All our expenses will be paid while we are out of the country and we will be housed in officer's barracks.

I imagine that I will be on the payroll by the end of this month. This will mean that I will be able to start paying you back the money that you have put out so far and also that I will be able to start buying defense bonds. I have felt guilty because I have been unable to do this before now.

Love, Ted

This was certainly one of the most important turning points in my life. I would be flying with highly skilled airline pilots in airplanes maintained by very skilled ground mechanics. By Christmas of 1942 I had passed both of my Federal Telephone and Telegraph Radio licenses. After that, all I did was study airline abbreviations and procedures. I expected to be sent to an American Airlines location where I would act as a ground station radio operator. Several of my classmates departed to different cities. However, I just stayed in Kansas City. It was a boring time because, with my licenses, I didn't need to study radio anymore and you can only memorize so many abbreviations.

I even considered enlisting in some branch of the military but discovered that now I was classified 2-B as an "essential war worker." I could have resigned my job with American, in which case I would have been drafted immediately with no choice of where I would go. I wasn't that bored!

I never did go to a ground station. In February I was sent to Chicago, where I participated in training flights and I was finally in the air. An excerpt from a letter to my parents describes what we were doing.

I have twenty hours of flying time in my log book now, last week I averaged three hours a day in the air for six days and figure I covered over three thousand miles, practically all of it right around Chicago within fifty miles of the airport. We started out flying with instructors and have since graduated into flying local trips around the airport alone. I took one trip to Minneapolis and back which was very interesting and added another state to my list. We had a very slight leak in an oil line on one of the motors so we landed for about an hour. Northwest Airlines co-operates very closely with American, so they did our repair work. Airline captains refuse to fly these planes unless they are certain that they are in perfect condition. The mechanic on the ground said we could have flown five thousand miles with that motor and it wouldn't have given us any trouble. Our captains just will not fly with even the tiniest thing wrong.

Minneapolis has a very nice modern airport with a brand new administration building. I operated the radio coming back and one of the other fellows operated it going down, so I had a chance to watch the scenery and the navigator. I will be going on more of these trips in the future. They are much more interesting than the routine trips around the field.

I haven't told you much about the actual work I do, so here goes. The planes on which we fly have two transmitters and a number of receivers (this is between you and me stuff). One of the transmitters has a rather short range and the captain uses it for working the control towers and airways range stations. The other transmitter is much more powerful and is used for working our company stations and sometimes Army stations. Most of our operations here are run on a regular airline basis and most of our contacts are with company stations.

Airplane radio contacts fall into two types, those to do with landing, taking off, and maneuvering in the immediate vicinity of the airport, and those to do with ATC clearances, position reports, weather transmission and reception and so forth. The Captain handles all of the first type on his small transmitter, and while I have to copy and log all of his contacts, my main job lies with the second type of contacts. In order to fly on any of the airways connecting practically all the cities in the United States, a plane must be cleared to fly by the Airways Traffic Control. This government agency is responsible for keeping planes separated in the air. The ATC has various centers whichcontrol various areas. When we pass from one area into another, we must get a clearance from the next ATC; this is obtained through AAL company stations as a rule. In addition, the plane must report over various checkpoints along the route; I make these reports to the company. I am also responsible for seeing that the radio equipment on the plane is in good condition before we leave the ground, but I don't have to do any maintenance; we have maintenance men for that. I have to able to make emergency repairs in the air if necessary.

An excerpt from a letter dated Chicago, March 8, 1943:
I have been checked out and I am now officially a Flight Radio Officer (FRO) with more than seventy-five hours of flying time. My raise in pay was effective the first of this month. We found out that we are officially based in New York. This means that we are on expenses here, and have been since the day we arrived, this includes room and board, laundry, cleaning, taxi fares, etc., and we are expected to spend that much!! I don't see how I could possibly do it with wildest kind of padding of the expense account. Imagine, that brings my present income to about $400.00 a month.

A letter from Chicago, dated April 8, 1943:

I have flown every day since I arrived back from home. Among the places I have gone are Minneapolis, Omaha, Iowa City, Detroit, Cleveland, St. Louis, Tulsa, Erie, Fargo. Some of these places I have visited several times. Since I last saw you, I passed over our house again two nights ago on the way to Erie. I have one hundred and seventy hours of flying time.

I won't be here in Chicago much longer. Practically all the others have gone to New York for the final phase of their training. I will be joining them as soon as my passport arrives. I sent for it two weeks ago and it takes anywhere from ten days to a month to get one. I don't know how long our training will be, probably a couple of weeks to a month and then we will be going south. I think that I would have gone on with the others anyhow if they hadn't needed two or three of us here to train new FRO's. They have just brought in several experienced FRO's who have been on foreign duty, to do the teaching so they don't need me any longer.

This is my day off and so I am going out to the airport. We have just had a new ground station installed to handle the contacts with our Army planes down here. It is going on the air today and I guess I will operate it for a while.

Don't worry about my leaving without letting you know. I will write as soon as I find out when I am going.

A letter from Forest Hills, Long Island, New York, dated April 25, 1943:

We had a very sudden change in our plans and two of us caught the train with about two hours notice. They wanted us here so that we could start Navigation School Monday morning. Some of the fellows are all set to go on foreign flights now. I think it will be some time before we leave the country though. You will receive another offering in the form of clothes via express very soon, Mother. I am trying to streamline my luggage to a "pick it up and go" amount.

A Letter from the Forest Hills Inn dated May 14, 1943:
Dear Mother and Dad,

Well at last some fairly definite news. I am now through with my formal radio training, I was graduated from school last Friday. I am definitely going north, probably within the next week; we will make at least one trip all the way across to Scotland, probably not more than one. We will then be returned to New York and then on down to the Southern run. Their plan is to have us checked out on both runs as quickly as possible and then turn us out alone.

I will go in C-54's which are the largest and best four engine planes being manufactured in mass production exclusively for transport purposes. They are truly superb airplanes. Our radio operator's position is very well designed, as is the rest of the plane. We have a large comfortable chair, just behind the Captain's position and the equipment is all located within easy reach. There is one large room in the plane, considerably larger than our breakfast room at home which is used for nothing but storing gasoline, the plane carries more than two thousand gallons of gas.

We were issued all our government flying equipment which includes afine pilot's bag for carrying clothing, a light weight summer flying jacket, a sweater, and winter flying equipment.

This winter equipment is even superior to that which we used in Chicago. It consists of a parka, complete with a hood with fluffy fur lining, just the kind that you have seen Arctic explorers wearing in pictures. We have trousers lined with fleece, and fleece lined boots which come up to the knee. All this equipment is white leather trimmed with brown, very sporty, funny stuff to be talking about with summer in the air.

Please try not to worry as little as you can about what I am doing. American Airlines hasn't lost a single radio operator in all the time that they have been flying and they don't intend to. I will let you know when I am going and will write often while I am gone, but remember that mail delivery from northern remote bases is often extremely slow. I may be kept in these bases much of the time I am gone.

According to my log book, I made two round trip check flights on the north Atlantic route. My first left on May 27, 1943; the second departed on June 1. We flew from LaGuardia Field to a base in Prestwick, Maine, or to one in Goose Bay or Stevensville, Labrador. Our next stop was often at BW-1, a base located in a fjord in Greenland, then on to Iceland and finally Prestwick, Scotland. At many of these stops, we laid over until we could continue in the later crew's airplane on the next leg of the trip. There were very strict regulations about the number of hours we could fly before we had to rest.

I wrote the following letter dated June 14, 1943 from Forest Hills:

I have been checked out on the Northern Route. I am scheduled to go south. There are seven or eight to go out before me so that I won't get out for at least two weeks. I will probably be out for at least two months, perhaps more. I am rather sorry that I'm not going north but the Southern experience will stand me in good stead later.

On July 5, still in Forest Hills, I wrote the following:
Dear Mother and Dad,

It now looks as though I will be leaving here on about the tenth. A new system has been set up on the southern run. It will mean that I will be gone about forty-five days. It looks as though I will stay on the southern run for the rest of the summer, perhaps longer. It looks as though I may have a student operator go south with me. This has me a little worried because most of the remaining student operators are top notch radio operators, who have been on company ground circuits. I'll feel a little silly if I have to check someone like that. If I do I will just put the cards on the table and let the other fellow operate half the time, he could probably teach me a lot.

Since I wrote last I have been briefed on the southern run. Briefing consists of the entire crew getting together with an instructor who is well acquainted with the route. He goes over just about everything imaginable from clothes, housing facilities, radio facilities, to emergency procedures. In our case, it took about three hours. We will be briefed again on any changes when we get to Florida.

Saturday morning, bright and early, we went out to a Long Island yacht club for "ditching procedure." Two crews went along. Ditching, or leaving an airplane when it is on the water, is not as simple as it might sound. When we arrived at the club in our special limousine, we all donned our bathing suits and then the fun began. We all gathered around on the grass and had a lecture on life rafts. The instructor had three different kinds already inflated and launched on the grass. There are three kinds which we might have to use, the three man, five man and the seven man. The latter is new, it will eventually be installed on our planes because it has more room per man, and is more seaworthy.

Each raft is a self-contained unit and contains all the supplies necessary to keep the specified number of men alive for some time. As usual, the Airlines have gone into the project much more thoroughly than the Army or the Navy, and as a result, our rafts are better equipped, at American's own expense. Most of the changes have resulted from ideas coming from two sources. The first, from men who have survived days at sea in life rafts and secondly from a group of airline men who spent a week in life rafts and actually found out from first hand what should be added or changed.

Probably the one most important item on life rafts is water. Through tests, they have discovered that the average man can stay conscious on as little as two ounces of water a day. Of course, with this small amount it is impossible to assimilate food. As you have probably read in the papers the Navy has developed a water purifying system in which chemicals dissolve out the salts in ocean water. American has developed a similar process which is even better and takes up less room. These are being manufactured now and will be in our rafts very shortly. Rafts also carry emergency rations of water in cans and emergency field rations of food, but on an extended trip, the main source of food would be fish. The new fishing kit which we have is very effective. Experience has shown that in tropical climes, fish often gather around the raft. In addition to food, water and fishing equipment, there is a hand air pump, a large tarpaulin which will cover the entire boat and a smaller one for catching rain. There is a sea anchor which activates automatically in the water when the raft is launched. Numerous other items include a bailing bucket, three paddles, a sail, and other equipment including flashlights, flare guns, compass and a Bible. A five man raft with all of its equipment makes a bundle about the size of a large duffle bag.

After the lecture was finished, we went down to the water with two five man rafts, just as they would be found on board the plane. We all donned "Mae West" inflatable rubber life preservers which inflate with two of the little carbon dioxide siphon bottle chargers. American built a platform which is just about the right height, eight feet off the water; so we abandoned our mythical airplane. The captain and first officer are in charge of launching the life rafts; the navigator and flight engineer are in charge of getting them to the door. My job is to throw the emergency transmitter into the water; it floats. Launching a raft is very simple; one man throws it into the water while the other holds on to the rip-cord. The boats inflated in less than thirty seconds. As soon as the raft was launched, we pulled the cords on our may-west life preservers and jumped into the water, it was cold. I swam after the transmitter and immediately found that I had thrown it too far. Swimming in a maywest is not too easy. By the time I got back to the raft, several members of the crew were already aboard. There is quite a trick to getting into a life raft wearing a "Mae West" which catches on the side of the boat in just the wrong way.

Once we were in the boat, we assembled our paddles, hoisted our sail and sailed out into the harbor. By the time the other fellows had completed this, I had the emergency transmitter ready to go. It has a kite which supports the antenna and a balloon when there isn't any wind. Of course, I didn't do any transmitting but I could have. After this, we spent about an hour practicing capsizing and righting the raft, and got quite expert at climbing in and out.

The morning was very well spent, in my estimation, now I believe that I would know about what to do in a real emergency. If we were carrying passengers and were forced down at sea, it would be important that every member of the crew be well prepared, because one of us would be in charge of each seated person.

There were a couple of things I didn't tell my parents about, however. When our instructor demonstrated launching the life rafts, twice they didn't inflate when he tossed them into the water, and instead just floated there in a big lump. He explained that they had been used and repacked many times and probably someone goofed the last time. On a lighter note, shortly after we completed our chores on the raft, some very attractive young women on a very nice yacht called to us. We paddled over, climbed aboard and had a cold beer with our bathing-suit-clad hostesses. The rest of the trainees had been ashore for some time before we eventually arrived.

Now I knew that we were to be flying the southern route. We had a two-hour check-out flight on the new aircraft from LaGuardia Airport to LaGuardia Airport. We would be flying in C-87's, B-24 Liberator bombers built by Consolidated Aircraft which had been converted to cargo planes. They had high wings, with four supercharged engines and distinctive dual tails.

In the conversion, the bomb bay doors were removed and windows were added in the cargo bay. A larger door was installed to facilitate loading. Folding bucket seats could be placed on each side of the cargo bay. Gun turrets and the glassed-in bombardier's compartment, in the nose of the plane, were removed and another small cargo space was created. A heavier weight-bearing floor was installed in the cargo bay, which could carry 20 to 25 passengers or 12,000 pounds of cargo.

These airplanes were certainly not the pilot's favorite! Ernest K. Gann, in his book *Fate is the Hunter,* said, "They were an evil bastard contraption, nothing like the relatively efficient B-24 except in appearance." They had clumsy flight controls and frequent engine problems. The C-87 did not climb well when heavily loaded. The auxiliary fuel tanks were linked by improvised and often leaky fuel lines that crisscrossed the crew compartment. We often smelled gasoline fumes. The Davis wing design could not handle in-flight icing conditioning well. Gann wrote, "C-87's...could not carry enough ice to chill a highball."

However, we all felt that these planes could fly with more things wrong with them than any other aircraft in existence.

I imagine, though, that we all had to feel that way. After the almost luxurious crew quarters on the C-54's, the C-87's seemed cramped, extremely noisy and poorly heated. Our captains and flight engineers were very particular about how the cargo was loaded; the planes were not tolerant of shifting or improper loads. Most of us were happily unaware of many of these faults when we left for South America.

> This letter from Biloxi, Mississippi was dated July 1943:
> *Dear Mother and Dad,*
>
> *No doubt, you are in a great state of confusion as to my activities by now and I can't do much to straighten you out.*
>
> *To go back to the day I sent you a telegram saying I was going south.* [The telegram was in a prearranged code.] *I did go, and got about two-thirds of the way before we turned back. They simply needed a crew to take a plane back. I arrived back in New York four days after I had departed. I was told that I would be going right out again so I decided it would just be better to let you think that I had gone right down, so I didn't write.*
>
> *Then this special trip was called, as to the purpose and destination of this trip, I can tell you nothing and I would appreciate it very much if you wouldn't tell that I am taking it. If you have mentioned it to anyone just tell them that it has been cancelled and I have gone south. Please don't worry, and for gosh sakes, don't breathe a word to anyone about this trip. It is extremely important that you remember this.*
>
> *All my love, Ted*

The purpose of the trip was to deliver a captured, disassembled fighter plane to Australia. The American Airlines C-54 was the only plane that was capable of carrying such a large load. We were on the schedule to go out next. However, no one on our crew made the trip. Little by little, each of us was replaced by more senior personnel. The chief pilot displaced our captain, our copilot was replaced by a ranking captain, and so forth. I was replaced by the chief FRO (Flight Radio Officer). It took me more than 50 years to visit the South Pacific!

When we finally left for our trip south, we were once again detoured in order to take our plane for some necessary refitting. During the next nine days, we flew from New York to Biloxi, Mississippi, then to Mobile, Alabama, to Macon, Georgia and finally to Miami. Our airplane received four new engines and new landing gear, among other things for this trip. We would later learn the reason for this extra maintenance.

From Miami, we finally flew south to Borinquen Field in Puerto Rico, then on to Atkinson Field in British Guiana, near Georgetown. Next, we flew to Belem, Brazil and finally to Natal, Brazil, where we were to be based. Surprisingly, the longest nonstop flight we made during this period was from New York to Biloxi, 1132 nautical miles, which took us six and a half hours.

The Natal airport was a busy ferry waypoint for bombers as well as being a base for our Air Transport Command flights to Accra in Africa. Our flights took us from Natal to Ascension Island, then on to Accra, located in the British colony of the Gold Coast, now called Ghana.

Probably no other air base used by the Air Transport Command was of more importance than Ascension Island. It was located on only 34 square miles of volcanic rock. Its position was halfway between the bulge of South America and Africa. In peacetime, Ascension Island was a British cable station and had a normal population of about 165 cable-company employees. The maximum sustainable population on the island was set by its limited water supply. Negotiations were opened with the British early in 1942 for use of the island as an airport. Britain readily agreed.

By March 1942 an American Army force, consisting of coast artillery, quartermaster, signal corps, hospital, Army airways communications, and other units, was on its way to the island to begin construction work. Unloading the supplies, machinery, and construction materials from three freighters was no easy job. Ascension had no proper harbor, and a projecting shelf of volcanic rock prevented ocean-going vessels from making a close approach to shore. Supplies had to be unloaded onto a barge or a lighter to be taken ashore. Construction work was under way by April 13, and less than three months later, on July 10, 1942, the 6000-foot runway was open for traffic. Meanwhile, the task force had also constructed underground gasoline storage tanks, roads, barracks, a hospital, a unit for distilling sea water, and an electrical plant.

Ascension Island was a dismal place to be stationed. There was nothing there but the airbase. The single runway was built on flattened volcanic rock. There were only two directions to take off and land. We stopped only long enough to refuel, to get the weather forecasts for the next leg of our trip, and sometimes to have a meal. I remember one time when someone on the base had seen a rabbit. This was an exciting event and I was told about it several times. We sometimes carried mail on our plane, and the airport tower usually asked our pilots if we had any on board. If we did, an airport jeep met us to pick it up as soon as we parked. One time we were having a meal at the mess hall when a GI approached our table. He asked if we were the crew that had brought the mail. When we said yes, he said, "I haven't gotten a letter in almost two weeks and this is what you brought me." He produced a notice of induction from his draft board! We all, including the GI, had a good laugh.

The city of Natal, Brazil had little to offer crews except ice cream and a flourishing whorehouse which offered the only place in town to get a drink and a local meal. I ate some ice cream and had a meal in the other establishment, where we had to check in with an American MP. Our names were recorded, and when we returned to the base, we were forced to undergo a prophylactic procedure regardless of our protestations that we hadn't visited "the girls." I didn't eat any more meals there. Our quarters at the base were spartan but satisfactory.

I was surprised, when I looked in my flight logbook, to discover that in March I made only two round trips. After we arrived in Africa, we waited for a following crew and took their plane back to Brazil. This method was mandated by the number of flying hours we were allowed in a given period. If any weather or mechanical delays occurred on the next flight, we just had to wait until they arrived. Still, according to my flight log book, I was in the air 59 hours and 33 minutes in August.

This is a letter dated August 1943:

Dear Mother and Dad,

Your letter of the tenth arrived today after a series of apparent mishaps. It had previously arrived here and been sent back to New York. Dad's letter of the 18th arrived a couple of days ago, so I have been supplied with lots of news. I am writing this from the base hospital which I expect to be leaving very soon. I picked up a case of bronchitis three days ago and ran a fever for a couple of days. I am well on the way to recovery now and should be out tomorrow or the next day. It has been a rather interesting experience. They certainly do take good care of you here. I had chest X-rays, blood tests and a urinalysis, all in quick succession, they don't leave anything to chance. Of course, none of them showed anything wrong. Since I wrote last, I have taken another trip, quite uneventful as far as the ride itself was concerned. [This was a trip to Accra.] We hired a dilapidated 1938 Ford and drove about sixty miles into the bush country. About the only change was that the natives' costumes got more and more absurd—a pair of shabby khaki shorts and a beautiful silk hat, etc. The vegetation was wild but not as thick as that of South America. There were some very large trees, probably thirty feet in diameter, one hundred feet tall and huge at the base.

I took quite a few color pictures on the trip. I certainly hope that they come out all right; the light wasn't too good because the sun kept going in and out of the clouds. Color film has to be exposed carefully.

I guess the pictures were a failure because I have no recollection of them. Only a short time after I wrote the letter to my parents, our crew was advised that we had been selected to fly to India to be part of a project labeled 7-A. We would be flying from India to China over the Himalayan Mountains, the "Hump."

We left Accra on September 1, 1943. One thousand nautical miles, and five and three-quarter hours later, we arrived at Maiduguri, a British air base in northeastern Nigeria. Next, we flew for eight and a half hours, and 1319 nm, to Khartoum, in what was then the Egyptian Sudan. From Khartoum we flew to an airbase located in what was then the Crown Colony of Aden, located on the eastern approaches to the Red Sea. Next, with one other stop, we flew 1700 nm to Karachi, India which is now in Pakistan, then on to Agra, and finally arriving in Tezpur, India at 5:38 p.m. on September 7, 1943. Tezpur was located in Assam province, near the Burma border. This was to be the base for our flights over the Himalayan Mountains into China. Crossing India was unusual because at various stopping points, with their changing time zones, we arrived when breakfast was being served three stops in a row.

After we had landed in Tezpur while taxiing behind a jeep to an assigned location, we saw several C-46 cargo planes lined up with bashed-in noses. We learned later that the army had sent these planes, with little proper instruction, for use by the green Army pilots who previously had been flying C-47's (the military version of the civilian DC-3). The two aircraft had different landing gear configurations, and when the pilots applied the brakes, as they had been previously doing, the C-46's nosed over.

My Uniform

Doug, Merchant Marine-Ted ATC-Bob Navy

Consolidated C87

Ground Crew at Tezpur

Douglas C54

We wore these ID's on the Back
of our Flight Jacket

CHAPTER 4

The "Hump"

Two days after we arrived, we made our first round trip over the Hump. Our operation 7-A, an American Airlines designation, was unique and is well described in the following. It is reprinted from *Flight Deck,* a publication for employees of the airline:

Project 7-A on the Hump
Ex-CBI Roundup
March 1982 Issue
By Lewis C. Burwell, Jr.

American Answers FDR's Call When President Roosevelt called for help during WW2, American Airlines answered. This is the story of AA personnel's cooperation in improving the Hump airlift in 1943.

At the GSW Flight Academy, located along the long corridor that runs from the Classroom Building to the Health Maintenance area, is a short stretch of abbreviated AA history. On the west wall, adjacent to the Student Service Center lobby, you'll see such things as the President's Trophy, the Flight Academy dedication plaque, the Wright Brothers Memorial Trophy, the Air Mail Flyer's Medal of Honor displayed and the Distinguished Service Award plaques. On the east wall hangs one single plaque, approximately 9" x 18", upon which is inscribed the names of six men. Preceding these names is this brief note: "This plaque has been dedicated by the members of

Project 7-A to those men who paid the supreme sacrifice in service to their country." If that seems an unusual statement to be made concerning employees of a civil airline it's because circumstances surrounding Project 7-A were, themselves, highly unusual. That relatively small plaque, with its reference to a project that occupied only a four-month period in American Airlines' history, nevertheless represents an intense dedication of energy and skills under very difficult circumstances. It further represents a significant contribution to the success of the allied effort in the China-Burma-India Theatre during WW2.

For the benefit of our new crewmembers, let it be noted that during WW2 American Airlines turned over nearly half its fleet, along with appropriate support personnel, to the Air Transport Command. ATC was, in effect, a worldwide military airline, and was operated primarily by specially assigned airline personnel mobilized for the purpose of supporting the total war effort.

We'll leave the precise details leading up to Project 7-A to the historians. For our purposes, it should be sufficient to note that the year was 1943, and it was a time when Japanese forces had cut off the Burma Road supply line, drastically affecting Chinese military operations in the area east of Burma. While the U.S. had promised to bring in essential material by military airlift, this operation was being handled by inexperienced people and was not going well. General Claire Chennault's 14th Air Force, which had been providing invaluable tactical support to Chinese and American forces, was spending too much time on the ground for lack of fuel and munitions. Madame Chiang Kai-shek came to this country to address the Senate, making it clear that unless the airlift could be improved, China would fall to the enemy.

Not about to let this happen, President Roosevelt called in his advisors to seek a way to assure the needed improvements. When it was suggested that the expertise of the airlines be brought in to solve the problem, the reaction was quick, was affirmative, and was followed by only one qualifying thought. FDR, so the story goes, asked for the call to go specifically to American Airlines. That call went out almost immediately.

On July 18, 1943, American Airlines was informed that the President of the United States, together with General H. H. Arnold of the Army Air Force, was ordering the diversion of 10 four-engine C-87 transports (converted B-24's) and approximately 150 men from our Air Transport Command South Atlantic operation, and that these aircraft and personnel were to proceed with all haste to an undisclosed base in northeast India. For this special assignment, this contingent was to obtain sufficient equipment, supplies and spare parts to support a 90-day operation. The necessity for secrecy allowed only limited initial information as a basis for planning. The operation was to be known only as Project 7-A. Arrival time in India was to be as close to yesterday as possible.

On July 19, plans went into high gear. Coincidentally a group of AA people had just concluded a series of meetings in New York for the purpose of increasing the ATC operations in Brazil. Pressed into duty on Project 7-A, these men went immediately into the process of acquiring essential supplies in Miami and then went on to Natal, Brazil, to select personnel. It was in Natal that they opened sealed orders and got down to the business of making final decisions.

By this stage of the war our people in the Air Transport Command had gathered considerable experience on the military way of doing business—experience which was about to pay dividends. When told that spare engines were no problem because India was "full of them," the 7-A leaders instantly had all new engines hung on the assigned aircraft. Though they were scheduled to operate for only 90 days, from a base with "existing facilities," they planned beyond that, amassing equipment and supplies drawn from all directions. On the basis of much needed foresight, they begged, borrowed and otherwise obtained nearly every spare C-87 part from Brazil and arranged to gather more enroute to their assigned destination.

The Project 7-A orders disclosed that the mission ahead would involve flying supplies from India into China across the Himalayas, that formidable barrier affectionately called the "Hump." Flying over this obstacle would have to be done at 20,000 to 25,000 feet, which is why the C-87 was selected. Its 14-cylinder P&W 1830 engines were equipped with turbo superchargers which could significantly boost their 1200 horsepower for high altitude work and heavy gross weight take-offs.

To be a self-sufficient operation, Project 7-A's manning requirements had to include pilots, flight engineers, navigators, flight radio officers, ground mechanics and station personnel. The process of selecting those who would go needed to consider both experience and youth. In selecting Captains, for example, the process began at the bottom of the seniority list because it was felt that the younger men would be better able to endure the anticipated hardships. Additionally, a large group of more senior Captains volunteered their services, thereby providing invaluable experience and a recognized element of stability. With regard to choosing maintenance personnel, most of our people had only minimal experience on C-87's, and no formal training. But they were pro's led by pro's and, as time was to tell, they and all other members of Project

7-A would perform expertly and exceptionally under very adverse conditions. All knew they were being confronted with a challenge that had to be met. All went with the sole purpose of meeting it. Along with the Army personnel, they went right to work. The first order of business was the unceremonious eviction of the present occupants of their prospective quarters—numerous goats, cows and associated "litter." While the necessities were quickly established it would be some time before any semblance of amenities would exist. Yet in spite of these initial developments, the next day, August 2, saw the operation of 7-A's first "Hump" crossing—Captain Toby Hunt at the controls. Thereafter, each day saw the arrival of additional aircraft, personnel and equipment, all pressed into immediate service. The essential tonnage moving into China increased rapidly. The primary cargo was gasoline and bombs. These C-87's were, in effect, flying bombs, operating in conditions that at best were described as terrible. The monsoons kept the countryside around the airport in a state that looked "like the Mississippi Delta in flood."

Over the "Hump", weather conditions were the worst in the world. On "normal" days, there was severe turbulence and severe icing, spiced generously by severe updrafts and downdrafts. There was nothing like the Trans-Atlantic operation our crews had come from.

The "Hump" routes flown were across a secondary chain of the Himalayas. In clear weather, it was possible to fly a short southerly route at 11,000 to 12,000 feet. More often, due either to weather or Japanese aircraft, it was necessary to fly a longer northerly route operating at 20,000 to 25,000 foot altitudes on instruments. The wreckage of numerous Air Force C-47's on the peaks below were often visible reminders that the territory could be very unforgiving.

For the ground operations, weather was hardly any better. Maintenance was carried out with little protection from the elements, crude work stands, and little or no lighting for night work. Rain was ever-present, temperatures always well over a hundred. Mildew everywhere. Food spoiled before one's eye. Men slept naked under mosquito netting, waking up as tired as when they went to bed. But the work went on.

When morale suffered, there were always those who could lift it up. There were visits by Brig. Gen. C. R. Smith, and on a few occasions, visits by old friend "Red" Clark, then an Army Colonel at a nearby base. There was excellent organization among the men to keep the social processes going. Exercise programs benefited the body. Competitive sports with Army personnel produced comradery, shared beer rations, vastly benefited spirits. And though food was a major problem, trips returning from China eventually began bringing back fresh vegetables and eggs, bringing incalculable benefits to the total being. Excellent leadership and sound discipline prevailed. While no day was routine, there were some typical patterns.

J. D. "Ted" Lewis, a major figure in the operation, documented this "typical day": Call assigned crews at 5 a.m., get them in a truck, haul them through the mud to breakfast, then to the airport. Mechanics are getting the engines warmed up ... "It's raining! It's dark! It's hot! The clouds are 500 feet or lower, the visibility not too good ..." Someone in a jeep drives up and down the runway. They chase the cattle off the runway proper and make sure that water in the low spots on the steel mat is not over 9" deep. "Meantime, the pilot gets his clearance which consists of permission to fly to China. No up-to-date weather information and no forecast." A manifest is provided to show that the plane has no passengers.

The load consists of 1,000 gallons of aviation gasoline in drums, six 500-lb. bombs and several cases of bomb-detonating fuses. The manifest also shows that there is sufficient gasoline in the tanks to go to China and back without refueling and that the take-off will be made at maximum allowable gross weight—65,000 pounds.

The crews are soaking wet. They get aboard, taxi out, run up their engines and then take off down the runway, which is lighted with gasoline-burning smudge pots. Within a couple of minutes, they are on instruments and climbing to get on top or up to 20,000 feet to make a crossing on instruments. Soon it gets cold—wet clothes don't help—Arctic flying suits are put on—oxygen masks are worn. An occasional glimpse through the clouds shows the "Hump" not too far below.

On the afternoon of July 24, just six days after receiving the initial order, the final pieces fell into place and the 7-A group was ready to launch. By nightfall, the first aircraft departed Natal, its ultimate destination an obscure point in the Assam Valley of northeast India called Tezpur. Its scheduled arrival date was August 1, 1943. In command was Captain E. S. "Toby" Hunt.

As scheduled, the first aircraft arrived on August 1, only to find that their "facilities" were as yet unprepared. An Army unit based at Tezpur was to have done the job; having not expected the new residents to arrive so soon, nothing was yet accomplished. So Project 7-A's first contingent, tired from flying halfway around the world, hungry, afflicted with dysentery and suddenly soaked by the enveloping monsoons, found themselves without usable living quarters, mess capabilities, and any form of sanitary facilities. An inauspicious beginning.

At the China terminal, an instrument descent is normal; a drop down from say 18,000 feet to the airport level of over 6,000 feet, bearing in mind that the descent is in a valley so fly it on straight courses and with careful timing. At Kunming, a truck loaded with coolies gets the plane unloaded. The pilot and crew get coffee and another clearance to return to India—one hour on the ground!

The manifest shows passengers now. An army truck drives up to the plane. In it are 40 small, thinly clad conscript Chinese who carry a couple cups of rice and chopsticks as baggage. They are herded aboard—no seats—no warm clothes—no oxygen in the cabin. On the trip back, they sit huddled on the cold metal floor and seem to pass out because of altitude. They look dead. Upon arrival in India, they are awake again, half frozen; only saying a word or two. They realize they are back on earth. Their talk speeds up to a rattling chatter as they are again herded into a truck which will take them to a training camp where they will learn to fight the Jap.

From three to six such trips were made each day while maintenance was performed on the remaining aircraft. The only factors limiting the availability of aircraft were lack of engine replacements, spare parts and the fact that too little maintenance equipment and personnel precluded round the clock activities.

Every able hand gave unstintingly of themselves and many among them dedicated much spare time to the training of Army personnel who would sustain the airlift operation once Project 7-A was terminated. A number of Captains undertook a program of training for Army pilots in which they instructed on C-87 transition, route familiarization and other work that was of great benefit to the Army in extending their operations on the India-China route. All this work was done because each officer felt that if they could impart even a small part of their own experience to the younger Army pilots, many lives could be saved as well as many valuable airplanes and cargoes. All time devoted to this was over and above the time required to carry out the normal duties of Project 7-A, which meant that many of the Captains sacrificed rest periods in order to help out.

As indicated by the Flight Academy plaque, Project 7-A was twice struck by tragedy, the first occurring in the rainy pre-dawn hours of August 23. That morning three planes taxied out for take-off. Number 1 took off and flew away. Number 2 took off and Number 3 was just ready to leave when a burst of flame was seen through the rain. It was straight down the runway and looked like gasoline burning. A jeep rushed to the end of the runway and on through mud to a half mile beyond. Number 2 plane lay scattered through the cane-brakes afire. An engine had failed on take-off. Dead were: Harry T. Charleton, Captain; Robert H. Dietze, First Officer; Joseph Smith, Flight Engineer; John E. Keating, Navigator; Robert E. Davis, Radio Operator.

Tragedy's second blow was struck on November 18, days before the 90-day operation (which had then been extended for a month) was to have wound down. Aircraft 111675 under the command of Captain Toby Hunt departed at 0830 local time, bound for Kunming, China, with a heavy load of small arms ammunition. Captain Hunt's return trip was to be his 66th, a Project 7-A record. As it turned out, no landing was possible in Kunming due to weather. Two attempts were made without breaking out at minimum altitude. The decision to return to India was thwarted by one engine failing, a second unable to develop full power, and a cargo that the crew was unable to jettison. All but the Captain bailed out. He rode on in an effort to save the aircraft, losing his life in the process. He made his 66th "Hump" crossing in a magnificent hand-hewn, pagoda-like coffin, and was buried in India beside his five AA compatriots and members of General Chennault's "Flying Tigers" group.

There were other close calls. Weather played a part. Increased Japanese action at the end of the monsoons played a part. One aircraft was destroyed on the ground due to suspected sabotage. There were numerous displays of extreme courage and skills, but no further loss of life. The operation began winding down in late November, its mission well accomplished. Air Force crews were ably prepared to continue the work and would, in fact, go on to perform remarkably. A major Allied offensive begun in 1944 (one which would eventually return Burma to British forces) would be supplied entirely by RAF and U.S. Air Force transports. Chennault's 14th Air Force, supplied entirely by air, would go on to compile a brilliant record. Not only had our people participated in the launching of an operation, they had been instrumental in proving a military technique.

After the final Project 7-A "Hump" crossing was logged on November 28, the records credited American Airlines personnel with having flown 1,075 trips and carrying over 5,000,000 lbs. of cargo under tremendously adverse conditions. In reverence, we've mentioned the names of those who made the supreme sacrifice in the effort. As appropriate as it would be to mention all other participants, space will not permit it. Let it be noted, however, that all contributed to a very proud moment in American Airlines history. This brief narrative scarcely begins to tell their complete story. But let this final point be made: WW2 it is said, revealed the real potential of the transport plane. It might therefore be concluded that Project 7-A also served to establish an important standard for an industry.

My logbook tells me that I made 16 round trips over the Hump, which means that I crossed the Himalayan Mountains

32 times. I had flown to India with Captain Ray Mix. Where possible the airline liked to keep the same people together on a crew. Ray had a mercurial personality, but somehow I was able to cope with his occasional burst of temper when things were not going right. He seemed to like my work and me. Ray was a very good pilot, and several times his quick responses kept us from very serious trouble.

Several flights stay in my mind. On one, our captain handed off the takeoff to the first officer, who forgot momentarily that he was flying the plane and not handling the landing gear retraction. Our plane started to descend, and by the time the captain grabbed the wheel and pulled it back, we just skimmed through the tops of a bamboo thicket. When we arrived at Kunming, we found bamboo twigs in our landing gear.

High-altitude winds over the mountains were very fickle and very strong. On some trips they would be blowing from the east and other times from the west. We had no reliable weather forecasts. Our destination had a radio beacon, but without a method to determine drift, a plane could end up making a large curve while still heading directly toward the beacon. In those days, the only way of determining drift was by observing a point on the ground or a celestial fix. Often this was impossible because our navigator couldn't see the sky or the ground.

On one trip, the winds shifted and we did not realize that we had been blown way off course toward the higher mountains. A momentary break in the clouds below us revealed a river that our navigator was able to recognize and to use to plot a new course, which saved us from possible disaster. Perhaps that break in the clouds was another turning point for all of us.

Another time we were flying on instruments. I had just received a message that the Kunming airport approaches were below minimum, and suddenly a tunnel of clear visibility, all the way to the ground, appeared below us. Ray dove into it in very sharp turns. We quickly dropped about 8000 feet and landed safely. Our planes were not pressurized, and I suffered a large blood blister on my eardrum from the sudden increase in pressure.

A letter dated India, September 14, 1943 written to my parents:

> *It will probably take a long time for this letter to reach you, and I imagine my letter from the states explaining and my Brazilian letter giving you my APO should have arrived. I certainly hope so.*
>
> *I have discovered exactly where Uncle Frank is stationed and I think my chances are very good that I will see him before I leave. I missed him by just about two weeks. He has a rather important job, from the sounds of it. I have talked to an Army officer who came over with him and seems to know him quite well. He is going to do his best to get us together. Our quarters are much less primitive than I expected them to be. The food is extremely plain, but I don't mind that as much as some of the other fellows. I miss good milk, fresh salads etc., but I take vitamins every day which should replace these items.*
>
> *I had a fairly good stock of cigarettes when I left which should last me while I am here. We even get a ration of beer every once in a while. Candy is scarce but we get a little once in a while.*

My trip over was extremely interesting and I will have some tales to tell. I have seen one of the wonders of the world, only six more to go.

This country is much more modernized than I had expected. There are extreme contrasts, however; an old fashioned ox cart and a modern motor truck side by side; an Indian in a white linen suit talking to another Indian wearing a sari.

I am studying navigation in a class sponsored by the navigators and starting today, I am going to teach code to some of the navigators. I can take a shot with an octant and plot it by now. By the time I leave here, I should be a fairly decent navigator. It is a very interesting subject.

We are located near a small town here which has very little to offer except ice cream sodas; that's something though. The prices here are exorbitant to us and very cheap to the Indians. Everyone in India seems to think that all Americans are millionaires. I suppose we are, compared to eighty percent of the population. We see very little of the tension that is supposed to exist here. This is probably because we can't speak their language. Language is a terrific barrier to understanding between people. One natural reaction is to think that the other person is dumb.

Before I leave here, I will probably have a chance to see some of the larger cities of India. This should be very interesting. It is interesting to observe others' reactions; it has been just the reverse. Most of the fellows just want to get back to the States and stay. I want to see much more of the world. Perhaps I will have my chance, who knows. I still haven't seen anywhere I would rather live though.

Well I seem to have exhausted my topic of conversations so I'll close now and write again soon.

Love, Ted

The wonder of the world I referred to was the Taj Mahal. We laid over long enough to visit this famous shrine. Uncle Frank was my father's roommate in college. My father met my mother at Frank's wedding. My mother was the sister of the bride. As a result, they had a close relationship though the years.

My uncle at this time was an army major stationed in Guilin, China, as the intelligence officer for that region. On a memorable trip across the Hump, not mentioned in my logbook, I was able to "deadhead" on an American flight to Kunming and then catch a ride in an Army plane to Guilin, where I visited my uncle. Guilin had been a small town until the rapid advance of the Japanese in Burma had driven more than one million refugees to take refuge there.

My uncle was always happiest when in uniform. He had billeted himself in a very nice house and acquired a lovely Chinese mistress. By the time I arrived, he had acquired a standing with the social set. He took me to a fancy party where we were served a delicious seven-course Chinese dinner. At this time, many of the refugees were surviving on less than a bowl of rice a day. Before the dinner, he introduced me to a very lovely lady who, he informed me later, was a Japanese spy. She had asked me several questions about my service, which I avoided or to which I was able to give misdirecting answers.

Today, Guilin is a popular tourist destination because of the unusual huge conical outcroppings of limestone, studded with caves, which rise beside the Li River. At the time of my visit, one large cave served as a Chinese Army facility for monitoring Japanese aircraft. A large map was spread out on a table, studded with small flags indicating the location of enemy planes. I was amazed to learn that this information was collected by hundreds of spotters in enemy territory, who then forwarded it by hand signals from spotter to spotter. I returned to Tezpur in time to join my crew for our next flight.

We came to have considerable distaste for the Chinese Nationalist government. While officially the government was headed by Chiang Kai-shek, many of the provincial warlords had considerable power. The Nationalist government was corrupt and, we came to believe, held little regard for the people.

Here are a few examples. Chungking airport was being extended when we first arrived there. Thousands of Chinese peasants, mostly women, were working on the project. They were carrying large rocks in baskets on their head to other peasants seated cross-legged pounding them into gravel with hammers. The work continued without stop, regardless of weather, when there was any light in the sky. Many of these peasants were very lightly clad and, as far as I could see, had no protection from cold or heat, rain or shine.

When we left our plane in Kunming, we always had a Chinese armed guard watching it. One time one of the guards on another plane fell asleep while on duty. A Chinese officer took him away and executed him.

During this time the Chinese were cornered by the Japanese. Therefore every bit of material we flew was precious. A "coolie" unloading one of our airplanes accidentally dropped a large package which broke open disclosing its contents, Parker 51 ballpoint pens.

Later, after the monsoon rains had stopped, one crew flew over an area in China where they saw hundreds of trucks parked, row upon row. The Nationalists were storing them to use against the Chinese Communists.

One very important trip, for me, occurred when several of us who were interested in photography were able to put together a crew that wanted to make a low-level crossing over the Himalayan Mountains. We were able to fly through the mountains several times at a fairly low altitude. We were able to temporarily open our cargo door wide enough to give us a clear view. I was fortunate to have saved several rolls of Kodachrome slide film. So I took some wonderful pictures of the snow-capped mountains and of a small village located in a valley 12,000 feet above sea level. This was territory that the *National Geographic* didn't reach until many years later. I had no idea then, but this trip was going to lead to perhaps the most important change in my life.

We left Tezpur for home on November 30, three months after we arrived, and reached our home port, LaGuardia Field, on December 5. After I returned, I was placed in a navigation class.

CHAPTER 5

Courtship

I was given a leave to go home for Christmas. I brought my Himalayan pictures with me. My mother invited the Orr family for supper and to see my slides. I was never able to thank my mother enough for being responsible for the most important turning point in my life. The Orrs' daughter Mary came with them. Something life-changing happened that night because, after the Orrs had left, I told my 15-year-old brother that Mary was the girl I was going to marry.

Mary and I had nine dates in the short time I had left before returning to New York. We found in each other wonderful things that filled the holes in our lives. Suddenly our lives had meaning and direction. I don't remember much about these dates. We had a very chaste time together, but I remember taking Mary to a movie and having the almost electric sensation when, in the dark, she reached over and put her hand in mine. By the time I left to fly back to work, we were in love with each other. From that time until this day, it has always been "Mary and Ted."

I think it is important to step back and try to explain where our lives were at that point in time. I still had no sense of what I was going to do or where I wanted to go after the war ended. With the exception of my time in radio school, I really had never excelled at anything.

Mary's life had been much the same. Her parents took her out of public school and enrolled her in Hathaway Brown

School, an excellent girls' college prep school. She was driven to school and back by another girl's chauffeur, so that she really never had any chance to make friends at Hathaway Brown. At the end of her first year, her parents were told that she really didn't belong there. The Orrs lived in Euclid, Ohio, a largely industrial Cleveland suburb. This was necessary because her lawyer father served as the city solicitor and was required to live there. They had a very nice home on a pleasant street, but the school system reflected the nature of the city. Mary's parents then made arrangements for her to attend Shaw High School in East Cleveland. She went to school on the streetcar.

After high school, Mary was sent to Lake Erie College, an excellent women's school. While there, like me, her social life with boys from Western Reserve College and Case Tech was more important than studies. After two years, her parents were informed that she would be better off in a school which would train her for a useful occupation.

After a period trying several different jobs, she had a life-changing experience and decided she needed to walk a different path. She asked her parents to send her to a school in St. Louis, Missouri which taught young women the skills required to become an executive secretary.

As Mary tells it, she brought her old self with her to St. Louis. The city was within "weekend distance" of three military camps. Her brother, who was stationed at one of the camps, often brought his friends to St. Louis with him. In spite of her good intentions, in the time that she was there she was asked to leave two boarding houses because she was a bad influence on her roommates. Four months later, at Christmas break, she was told to pack her things because she wasn't coming back.

Mary arrived back home two days before Christmas. Until after Christmas, her parents said very little to her about her return home from school. On December 26 they sat her down and said that they were not going to pay for any more schooling. They told her that she had better look for a job. She could live at home as long as she paid room and board. Furthermore, they wanted her to talk to a psychologist friend. That was how things stood, that very night when we met at my house to see my pictures.

We had met before, when Mary was 14 and I was 15. Our family, the Orrs, and another family together rented a large cottage for a weekend at Cook Forest State Park, located in a beautiful stand of huge virgin trees on land that had never been developed. I think there were nine children on this expedition. Some of the youngest children slept on cots with their parents. The rest of us slept on a large screened porch.

Mary and I spent the entire weekend together. We walked in the woods and talked late into the night. There was something between us even then. We met again at another outing at Lake Lucerne, an artificial lake development where my parents owned a lot. I took Mary for a ride in my canoe. I don't remember anything else about this brief encounter.

To return to our courtship, it continued by mail with letters almost every day. We saved all of our letters. In fact, in the last few days, Mary and I have been reading them to each other again. I do not plan to reproduce them here because I feel that they are so very personal to us. The amazing thing to me, all these years later, is how many of the things we dreamed about together have come true. We were so meant to be together that we even had similar dreams.

A letter written January 24, 1944 from the Forest Hills Inn in New York:

Dear Mother and Dad,

The fact that I talked to Dad, on the phone the other night, I should say a week ago, has made the time that I have been away from home seem much shorter. I still haven't had any definite word about the future although there have been some rather concrete sounding rumors running around which make me believe that I won't be going down south. I rather expect to hear something definite in the near future.

Did I tell you that Pete and I found an apartment which I think we are going to rent? It is just downstairs and around the corner from here. It has four rooms with sleeping capacity for three. [We would share it with two others.] *It was formerly a superintendent's apartment and is on the basement level. The living room windows open out on a very pretty court.*

Pete and I have also taken up a hobby, we decided that we needed something concrete and constructive to occupy our time so we bought the necessary equipment to develop and enlarge our own film. Pete just bought a camera very much the same as mine. We spent four or five afternoons last week combing the camera stores. He wanted one exactly like mine, but that particular model has more than doubled in value since I got mine. I could sell it today for four hundred dollars. It seems that I have what is probably the best lens of its type on the market.

By the way, while I think of it, Dad, could you write Uncle Gris and ask him if he could provide insurance coverage for my camera equipment. I would want a policy which would cover it both inside and outside the United States. I have considerable other equipment besides just the camera, including an exposure meter, flash gun, telephoto lens and filters. I would like to insure the whole lot if possible.

Mary and I have been corresponding at about the rate of three letters a week, which is good for me. She writes a very good letter and I am improving my speed. I haven't spent more than fifteen minutes on this letter so far. I rather hope that I can swing a little deal with the authorities and get a weekend off in the near future. If I can, I'll hop a plane and be home for a few days. I know it seems silly to be trying to get home so soon after I left but I'm very anxious to see Mary again before I start flying. As soon as they put me on schedule, I won't be able to leave New York. This idea is just in its formative stage, however, and I haven't even suggested it to Mr. Smith. I will keep you posted. That's about all the news I can think of at present, I'll write again soon.

Love, Ted

I actually didn't start flying again until the 19th of February. The problem was that not enough pilots had been certified by American Airlines to fly the newer and improved version of the C-54A. The airlines are very careful about this. The fact that we were involved in the war and flying military planes and routes didn't change their established policies at all. Until they thought a captain was fully familiar with all the flying characteristics and idiosyncrasies of the aircraft, he was not allowed to take command.

CHAPTER 6

Engagment

I must have telephoned or sent a telegram to Mary, saying that I was going to be able to spend three days at home, although no record exists. Mary was training to be a Girl Scout leader in downtown Cleveland. I picked her up at Scout headquarters on February 1, 1944. We went to a local bar to celebrate our reunion. I was babbling on about the wonderful things we could do in the future when Mary stopped me and asked if I was proposing. I immediately said "Yes," and she said "Good." We were engaged to be married! We informed my parents, who were very pleased; after all, my mother had arranged our meeting. That night we went to Mary's home and I asked her father's permission. He seemed happy to say yes. Mary's mother was equally happy.

The next day Mary and I selected her ring, a very pretty diamond solitaire. Then, of course, we had to visit each other's parents to show off the ring. My only memory of the rest of that time is very dim. I do recall that we went to a church to express our gratitude and ask for guidance. We were so much in love and every moment together was precious. It was very difficult to say goodbye because we had no idea of when we would see each other again, but we reminded ourselves how much more fortunate we were than most military couples because we would probably be able to live together while I flew.

A letter dated February 14, 1944:

I've gone and done it again, here it is well over a week since I left home and I am just getting around to writing. I have quite a lot of definite news. I have been assigned to the northern run and I think that I will get out on my first trip Friday or Saturday of this week.

I will go with a senior FRO [Flight Radio Officer] *on my first trip, for a route check. From that time on, I will go alone. Now two FRO's are assigned to one crew. This means that I will alternate every other trip with another fellow. As soon as enough captains are checked out on C-54's we will be assigned singly. The fellows assigned singly right now are doing too much flying. Ralph Kron had one hundred and thirty hours last month and has seventy now for this month and is going out again, tomorrow. Dana* [Pete] *got back from a four day trip the other day. While he was out, he averaged ten hours flying a day and went to bed only twice.*

With relief captains on the crews now, the trips will go much faster. The trips vary in length a great deal depending where they go. I think that I mentioned while I was home, that we sometimes come back by way of the Azores and Bermuda, please under no circumstances mention this to anyone.

I flew about four hours yesterday on a test hop in a most interesting airplane. It is a regular C-54 but has more special equipment than almost any plane imaginable. It is being used to test new devices. We had about ten engineers on board, all working on special radio equipment, two from RCA two from Sperry another from American Airlines. I had a chance to see the radio altimeter or absolute altimeter in action. This altimeter tells the correct height above the ground and is unaffected by varying air pressure. Flying at a constant altitude you can see the hills go by on the ground. They also had a Flux Compass. This compass developed by Sperry has the stability of a gyro compass (a regular compass is affected by climbing or descending) but doesn't have to be reset like a regular gyro compass. There were several other remarkable devices operating on the Radar principle which will do unbelievable things. I wish I could tell you about them. This plane has extra radio compasses, and extra transmitters. I had a fascinating day.

I had a nice letter from Joan [my first cousin] a few days ago telling me about her marriage plans. In case you haven't heard she is marrying Lt. Dan S. Anthony at 7 p.m. March 10, I am going to try to go if I can possibly make it. I was glad to hear that she finally has solved her problems; she seems to be happy about her new job too. I want to thank you again for being so wonderful to Mary, mother. She was very happy about the little apron you gave her. I have to stop now, go out to the field, and take a Bubonic Plague shot, I'll write again before I leave.

Love, Ted

Mary and I had written almost every day during this time.

A letter dated February 29, 1944:
Dear Mother and Dad,

I should have gotten this letter off sooner than this, I'm sorry. I am going out again tomorrow morning. Things are pretty fast on the route. I imagine that perhaps you have heard a lot from Mary about my trip. I wrote every day while I was out and mailed the whole business to her when I got back. We fly pretty steadily from the time we leave until we return and don't have too much time to do anything else except sleep.

Pete Sanicola, who checked me out on the last trip, must have turned a rather good report because George Smith seemed quite well pleased. He has even learned that my first name is Ted, which is a step in the right direction. The only things that Pete said I needed brushing up on were my "Q" signals. I have spent several hours studying them since I returned. "Q" signals are an international system of abbreviations based on three letters starting with "Q." For instance, QRM means I am being interfered with by other stations; QRM? means, are you being interfered with by other stations? There are hundreds of these signals. I know all of the common ones; the RAF uses many that I have never used before.

It certainly was wonderful to get back to the C-54's again. They are luxurious compared to the ones we were flying in India. The legs of the trips on these routes are extremely long, twelve to thirteen hours. One time we flew twenty-one hours with only an hour's stop for fuel. We are going back to the old five man crews however, with more layover crews spotted along the way, so we will have more rest between legs.

We left New York about noon for Newfoundland, but were forced to stop in Maine for weather. The next day we went straight through to Scotland, after a short stop in Newfoundland. It was bitter cold in both Maine and Newfoundland. The temperature in both places being between twenty and thirty degrees below zero with snow drifts ten feet deep in some places.

Scotland was charming, very much as I expected it would be. People in the United Kingdom don't have very much these days. Everything is rationed, food, clothing etc. I saw some wool scotch plaid in store windows that made my mouth water, but of course, I couldn't buy any because I don't have ration points.

The weather there was much like our May. The grass was very green. I was lucky, I got two beautiful days. The sun doesn't shine very often in Scotland but it was out both days.

Our trip back was by way of island bases that I have told you not to mention under any circumstances. This is very important. I think you know where I mean. From there we went to Bermuda. I don't imagine that you would recognize the Bermuda that you knew when you were there. Things are completely changed; Army trucks and jeeps are everywhere. Airports have sprung up out of what was once water. The temperature was perfect there though. I have never seen water so blue. Perhaps the next time I get there I will have a little more time to see some of the island. We just stayed overnight on this trip. I spent the first three days after I got back catching up on my sleep. I was very tired. I am going to be flying with a Captain Ted Jonson (yes it's spelled that way.) I don't believe that I know him but the fellows who do, say that he is a nice guy.

I was very happy that Mary has decided on June [for our wedding], *I hated to think of waiting until fall.*

Pete and I are going to move into our apartment here on the fourth of March.

Our address will be:

Apartment B-7

4 Dartmouth Street

Forest Hills Gardens

Long Island, NY

I guess that's about all the news for now until I get back from the next trip.

Love, Ted

According to my logbook, I flew two long round trips with Captain Jonson in March, totaling 108 hours in the air. We didn't have much time to do anything but fly, eat, and sleep.

After a month flying with Captain Jonson, I was dismayed to learn that he had requested a more experienced radio officer. This was a severe blow to my self-confidence. I had thought the flights had gone well, and he had never criticized my work. Perhaps I was daydreaming about Mary too much. I know that I looked younger than my age; I didn't know whether this contributed to his request and I never will.

In early April I was assigned to a navigation class. I was pleased with this. Unfortunately, almost at the start of the course I came down with a severe sore throat and ran a fever for some days. The doctor prescribed sulfa drugs, one of the first antibiotics. I was forced to miss several classes. By the time I had recovered, the instructor felt that I had missed too many classes to continue.

Mary had settled on June 24 for our wedding, and the chief radio officer assured me that I could take my two weeks' vacation during that time unless something unforeseen happened. Our letters were filled with discussions about our future life together, where we wanted to live while I was flying. I dreamed of a summer cottage by the sea, a very ridiculous idea. Mary was much more practical, pointing out the transportation problem we would have and that she would be isolated while I was gone. She asked what kind of silver pattern I preferred and sent me a brochure. I really didn't care and felt that I could be extremely happy eating with a tin spoon if she was the cook. Not having a sister, I was unprepared for the myriad things that a bride and her mother were undertaking as they planned for the wedding.

> An excerpt from a letter to my parents dated April 3, 1944:
> *This last trip was very interesting; we went from here to Newfoundland, then to Iceland and on to Scotland. We had enough time to go into Glasgow, an interesting city. I had my first experience with a blackout in a big city. It is really quite an experience. It's practically impossible to find your way around. The noise certainly isn't blacked out; that goes on just the same for some reason or other, this was quite a surprise to me. British cities close up very early. The liquor is extremely scarce so there isn't much of anything to do but go to bed early.*
>
> *From Scotland, we went to Casablanca, Morocco, a most fascinating place. The buildings are simply beautiful. Almost*

> *all of them are white and practically all of the big buildings are of a modernistic design. It certainly is soldier's town; I have never seen quite so many of them in a foreign town in my life.*
>
> *I ran into a Lt. John Vilas, a fellow I went through school with at both US and Shaker high school. He is a P-38 pilot and flying out of Foggia, Italy. He married a Shaker Heights girl and I have asked Mary to call her and tell her that her husband is well.*

Mary did call Nancy. They found a lot in common and visited with each other several times before our wedding.

At the end of the second week in April, I once again headed for the southern route. Our crew flew along, as passengers, in an aircraft that had been partly converted for passengers. Half of the seats were hard aluminum, curved bottom bucket seats. The other seats would have compared well with today's first class seats. There was a mad scramble for the good seats each time we boarded. I think I succeeded about half of the time. My logbook shows that, after we arrived in Natal, Brazil, our crew made only two round trips across the South Atlantic before returning to New York. I believe that, on our trip home, we were delivering a C-87 back to the U.S. for service.

In late May I was able to fly home for a visit with Mary. While I was there, we purchased our marriage license and had a visit with the Methodist minister, Rev. Paul C. Meyers, who was going to marry us. Most of my time at home is a rosy blur in my memory; I do know we took a walk in the woods together, something Mary had always wanted to do with me.

I made only one North Atlantic round trip in June. I arrived in Scotland only two days after "D Day," when the Allied troops landed on the Normandy Coast of France. I knew the invasion was imminent because, for several flights, the only cargo we carried was a load of Paravanes, underwater gliders designed to be towed behind Navy minesweepers to carry their cables down and away from the ship to trigger underwater mines. The fact that they were being shipped as high priority cargo, by air, told us that they were urgently needed to clear approaches to the shore.

An excerpt from a letter to my parents on June 16, 1944, only eight days before our wedding:

> *I was very pleased to see the invasion finally get under way. There seems to be considerably less excitement in the British Isles than there is here. After what the British have gone through in this war, I think this is understandable. Then too, the British are naturally reserved and don't show their feelings as much as we do. I am very lucky to be getting my vacation as we had planned.* [I was referring to our wedding and honeymoon.]
>
> *Naturally, with things as they are, our operations are really going great guns. The round trip to Scotland and back is only taking four or five days. We are going to have just about the same amount of time off between trips, which is fine.*
>
> *The apartment which I found is just as nice as it can be. I'm sure Mary will love it. I was very lucky to find just what I wanted in Forest Hills. The people we are subletting from are grand folks and left the apartment in simply immaculate condition.*

I'll be home either Friday morning or Thursday afternoon. I'll wire Mary as soon as I know for sure. I'm not going out on any more trips. I am going to radio equipment school every morning through next Tuesday. I have an examination on equipment to take Wednesday morning and then I'll be through.

The Chief Radio Officer was certainly wonderful in setting my schedule to make our wedding and honeymoon possible, as planned.

CHAPTER 7

The Wedding

We were married at 7:30 p.m. on June 24, 1944, under a beautifully flower-trimmed marquee erected over the side garden of Mary's home. A canopy extended from the marquee across the front of the house to the door. The reception was held in the back yard. Several neighborhood children congregated on the sidewalk in front of the house because they thought we were going to have a circus.

Mary's father, Judge Orr, was a prominent person in Cleveland. He headed up the Cleveland chapter of the Red Cross all through the war. He was on the board of directors of the Cleveland Metropolitan Park System and many other civic organizations. As a result, we had many prominent people at our wedding. Mary was an only daughter, and her parents went all out to make her wedding memorable. A quick thunderstorm blew through the night before the wedding, and the Judge and others had to struggle to keep the marquee in place, but the next day was perfect for an outdoor wedding.

Barbara Fisher was Mary's maid of honor and Renee Irwin her other attendant. My brother Bob, who was at home on leave from the Navy, was my best man. My friend Dana, who I had hoped would attend, was out on a flight. Mary was breathtakingly beautiful in her wedding gown.

Tables and chairs had been set up in the back yard, and a string quartet played during the reception. We had the traditional cake-cutting ceremony. The cake was topped by an unusual little pair of French dolls dressed in colonial costumes. We still have the dolls. Much later, our two daughters used them on their wedding cakes.

The daylight was fading when we left the house; rice was thrown and Mary tossed a well-directed bouquet to her cousin. Our car was waiting for us, but when I tried to leave, I found that our brothers had blocked up the car so that the rear wheels didn't touch the ground. We have a picture of them pushing us off the blocks.

We only went as far as the Hotel Cleveland for the night.

This letter was dated June 28, 1944, written from the Beach House Hotel in Siasconset, Nantucket Island:

Dear Mother and Dad,

I don't imagine you expected to hear from us while we were on our honeymoon, but Mary is industriously writing thank you notes so I have taken her good example to heart.

The hotel room (in Cleveland) was waiting for us when we arrived with some nice flowers from Mr. Perce. We got a big kick out of the doorman at the hotel. He opened the door of our car, took one look at the rice and said, "Yes Suh, you want a room and right away!"

Our plane was about four hours late leaving Cleveland but we didn't mind that at all, because they called us at the hotel. We would have been rushed if it had left on time. The ride was beautiful, not at all rough. We didn't get into New York until almost nine.

At this point, we were almost dead on our feet. A big wedding is fun and beautiful, but we were both dead tired by the time we left. On the way to our apartment in the taxi, we decided to stay over an extra day in New York. Neither of us felt like spending the next day traveling.

We arrived here last night and we both feel we couldn't have picked a better spot. I haven't seen a more picturesque place anywhere in the States. I'll have pictures to show you eventually. The houses are simply beautiful, ranging from large ship captain's houses to quaint fisherman's cottages covered with roses.

We rented bicycles this morning and had a wonderful time exploring the local countryside. We met another couple of newlyweds on the boat, a corporal and his wife. They turned up as Mary and I were getting ready for a swim. Fortunately, we both had an extra suit so they joined us. The beach is fine but the water is very cold.

The hotel is just what we expected, a venerable old building, but in very good repair. We have a nice room overlooking the ocean. The season really isn't in full swing yet which really makes it more fun for us than if the place were filled. Mary and I have finally caught up with our sleep and are feeling wonderful tonight. We actually slept eight hours last night, although we didn't think it was possible! I think Mary and I are falling more in love every day.

Love, Ted

My Bride

The Beach House Hotel at Nantucket

Honeymoon Hug

Cutting the Cake

Happy Couple

On the Beach

CHAPTER 8

At Home in New York

I believe Mary and I had only two days together in our new apartment before I left on a flight. With the war raging on the European continent, my logbook was filled in July. My flights were averaging six days. Often I had about the same number of free days at home. When I was home, the only restrictions were that flight scheduling could always reach me. Their notice of a flight was usually far enough in advance that we were not tied to the telephone. Our time together was wonderful, and we were very aware of how lucky we were compared to most others in the service.

Our cargo varied a lot, and occasionally we would have a celebrity on board. One of our crews transported Bob Hope and his company. The only person of some import that we carried was Samuel Goldwyn, founder of Metro-Goldwyn-Mayer. He was a sorry-looking passenger because he had received several immunization shots and slept much of the trip. I did to get to talk with him briefly. I had just seen a Gary Cooper movie and told him that Cooper seemed like a quiet, deep-thinking man. Mr. Goldwyn replied that he found him just quiet. I remember a young-seeming Air Corps lieutenant general whom we carried both ways across the Atlantic more than once.

I am not certain when we started Medical Air Evacuation flights, but they were certainly the most emotional flights I flew. We would fly cargo and personnel to Europe, then the cargo bay would be converted with temporary rows of four-tiered litters, with nurses and sometimes doctors in attendance. The wounded soldiers who had been airlifted from the battlefield to central medical facilities were transferred to our planes for transportation to the States. All of them were critically wounded and were in desperate need of more advanced treatment. The heartbreaking thing was that, in spite of their terrible wounds, many were smiling and happy because they were "going home."

> This is an excerpt from a letter dated September 12, 1944:
> *Dear Mother and Dad,*
>
> *By now, no doubt you have heard our most important news. Of course we can't be certain yet, but all indications point to the fact that you will be grandparents sometime next spring. Mary and I are both delighted; it's just what we both wanted very much. Naturally, we hope that, for the present at least, you will keep this more or less a family secret. I wish that we could have told you and Orrs together at the same time but of course Mary wanted to tell her mother while she was here.* [Mary's mother had been visiting us.]
>
> *I'm back flying with Ray Mix the captain I flew with on 7-A. We had a good trip although it was a little longer than I like to have them. I caught a nice cold in Iceland and still had it when I got home. I hoped that I was far enough along with it so that Mary wouldn't get it, but I'm afraid she has it this morning.*
>
> *Love, Ted*

P.S. If it's a girl, she will probably be Barbara Orr Boynton, we want to use Orr for a middle name but we have to be careful of the initials. If it is a boy, he will probably be David Holmes Boynton or David Merrill Boynton.

Excerpts from a letter to my parents, dated October 18, 1944:

The day before I was supposed to go out on my next trip I came down with a nice case of intestinal flu. I stayed in bed three days. Fortunately, Mary has completely avoided catching it.

Our trips are growing longer now that winter is coming on. It's really quite cold up north now. We are going eastbound by way of Labrador, when we go to Prestwick which I like much better. It's a little longer trip but the base is much nicer. I went to Prestwick this time. My regular crew went to Casablanca. Even though I left four days after they did, we arrived back in New York on the same day, so I'll be going out with them on the next trip.

Mary is just about through with her morning sickness, in fact I would say she is through with it, she hasn't been sick in over a week. She still has to be careful not to eat overly rich foods. Undoubtedly, you have heard that we have a good doctor and he says everything is going just as it should.

Sunday after church we started our apartment hunt which isn't going to be any joke. The apartment situation here in New York is very critical. Optimist that I am, I think we will find something right here in Forest Hills. Naturally, we are anxious to stay in the neighborhood if we can. Mary has made a good many friends, among them is our butcher who treats us royally. With only two of us rationing is really a problem. Mary is getting very good at cooking odd un-rationed cuts of meat.

Dana and his current girl friend—I think he's serious this time—spent the evening with us. We took pictures of the girls and he took some of Mary and me so perhaps I'll be able to send you one. I saw the negatives and they look fine. I am going to develop those I took tonight.

Dana did marry Emily, a pretty little second-generation Spanish girl who had been born and raised in Greenwich Village. Before she married Dana, she had never been north of 34th Street in New York City. Mary and I took Dana and Emily on a memorable Circle Line boat trip circumnavigating Manhattan. Mary and Emily saw quite a lot of each other.

I could help out some with food, because on my trips I could usually buy butter at a base commissary and bring it home with me. On one layover in Stevensville, Newfoundland, when bad weather caused a couple of days' delay, I was able to go salmon fishing with a local guide and caught a very nice large salmon. I talked the GI in charge of the base freezer into keeping my catch for me until I was able to bring it home. It was a wonderful treat and large enough so we could share it with friends and neighbors.

A letter dated December 1, 1944:

Dear Mother and Dad,

We have some surprising news for you. Mary and I went out to the apartment in Flushing yesterday afternoon. I had previously seen the one immediately below the one I had reserved and it looked OK. When we were able to see our actual apartment, it was awful. The paint was in terrible shape and the furniture was lousy. Mary and I decided on the way home that we wouldn't take it. Seventy-five dollars a month was just too much.

So last night, we canvassed the local papers and saw one apartment advertised in Forest Hills that looked OK. We hopped in the car and went over to look at it. It had already been rented when we got there. On the way back, I spotted a real estate agent's office [in Rego Park] and dropped in to see him. I imagine that I have been turned down by twenty-five agents, but I thought I would try once more. Boy were we lucky!

To make a long story short we have a beautiful little junior-four apartment—living room—kitchen dinette—one large bedroom—one small bedroom and a bath. Two local subway stops, closer to town, is a very nice shopping center. But that isn't all! It isn't in an apartment house. It is upstairs in a nice terrace house, one of a group of connected houses; you probably know what I mean. The Dutch couple downstairs own the house and are really grand people. The apartment is simply spotless. But that isn't all, it's an unfurnished apartment and our rent will only be fifty-eight dollars a month.

We had fun furnishing our new apartment. Furniture was scarce, but we managed to find a bedroom set and a kitchen table and chairs. Later we located a sofa. At street level, the building had a short driveway leading to what had been a basement garage but had been closed off to make another room. I used the driveway as a workshop to build two plywood end tables. Our bookcase consisted of two plywood planks separated by bricks. One great way to meet your neighbors is to work in a driveway close to the sidewalk; many people stopped by to see how I was progressing.

> An excerpt from a letter dated Monday, January 2, 1945:
> *Dear Mother and Dad,*
>
> *I arrived back in New York very early this morning after a singularly uneventful trip. I almost got a Paris trip, in fact, we were set up for one, but a last minute change prevented our going. I'm just as glad though, because it has been very cold in Paris and the coal shortage is quite severe. I'll wait and see Paris in the spring.*
>
> *Mary had a much more pleasant time while I was out than she did over the holidays. I have been working hard on my navigation. I think that I will be ready to take my examinations by the middle of next month. Navigation comes very easy for me; in fact, I really enjoy it.*
>
> *I have certainly been tickled to hear the* [war] *news during the last week. We had a Time-Life correspondent on board our plane on the last lap of the trip. He has been attached to the paratroops and jumped with them on D-day and again on the ill-fated Holland jump. He has just returned from the front and said the news of the Russian breakthrough had really done a lot to boost morale among the American troops.*

Even the usually conservative British press is extremely enthusiastic over the latest Russian push.

Mary and I are going into town tomorrow to start furnishing our little room. We are going to buy a rug, bed and dresser first so that we can use it for a guest room until we actually need it for a nursery.

Love, Ted

CHAPTER 9

We Are a Family

Of course, I had to fly when my flights were scheduled, so unfortunately, I missed every holiday and anniversary during our first year, including the birth of our son. When I arrived home in the evening of April 2, 1945, I found a note on the stairs leading to our apartment. It was from Dana. I don't have it, but it said "Congratulations. You have a new son." This was a great surprise because we hadn't expected our child for almost a month.

Mary's mother flew in from Cleveland the next day and wrote this letter to my mother dated April 3, 1945:

Dear Eleanor,

This has certainly been a big day in my life and I only wish that you might have been here to share the pleasure of seeing your very young and adorable grandson. He is the dearest baby. Although he is very tiny he is not at all thin or weak looking and his head is beautifully shaped and his ears are close to his head. We all think that his forehead is like Ted's and his hands. His hair is surely going to be a very light gold. Having seen the baby once, no one else can see him again until he gets home. Ted may be able to before he leaves the country because he is in uniform. It is amazing how well Mary looks and feels. She has some stitches which aren't too comfortable but she doesn't complain at all. Dr. Watson said she had a very easy time and that the baby was fine and no problem even though he was premature. Ted found out today that he will probably have to go out again on Saturday. Mary would like to have me stay with her all of next week if possible.

Ted has been walking on air all day and it wasn't until he saw the baby that he could believe he was really a father.

With lots of love to you, Katherine

Mary's mother did stay the entire following week and I had a quick five-day turnaround. There is a funny story about when Judge Orr was notified of David's arrival. He had been working on a particularly complex charge to the jury in a complicated corporate case. He had closeted himself in his chambers and told his bailiff not to disturb him. When the bailiff got the news, he decided that this would be an exception and knocked on the door and said, "Your honor, I thought you would like to know that you have a new grandson." The judge looked up from his work and said, "Thank you," then looked back down at his work for a moment when the news penetrated his concentration and said, "My God, have they been married that long!" David was born nine months and nine days after our wedding; he was almost four weeks premature. In the following months, we were happy young parents. We purchased a very fancy English pram for David. We had no air conditioning so Mary, joining several other young mothers, used to put him out in his pram across the street, which was next to a schoolyard. I can't imagine doing this today. We took David with us everywhere. I particularly remember a wonderful trip to Jones Beach.

Our lives had settled into the routine of being away on flights and being home for the wonderful time off between flights. On one memorable trip, we landed in Paris awhile after it had been liberated from the Germans. We had enough time to visit the city. One look at our American uniform and people couldn't do enough for us. I brought home a bottle of French Champagne. On May 8, 1945 our crew was flying somewhere over the Atlantic when we received the news that the Germans had surrendered and the war in Europe was over. The war in the Pacific was still raging, and our flying continued. We had no indication at that time that we would be sent to the Pacific.

Once again, we were flying when I received information that the atomic bomb had been dropped on Japan. We had no idea what an atomic bomb was. With the end of World War II, on August 15, 1945, demobilization began to affect us.

CHAPTER 10

The War Is Over

Excerpts from a letter to my parents dated September 27, 1945:

When I returned from the last trip, all was confusion. The army had ordered crews cut back to 98. This meant about 20 crews. There have been no Flight Radio Officers let go to date, because we were short in the first place and the remainder have been absorbed to allow for vacations; schools etc. The way things look at present I will have a job as an FRO until some time after the first of the year, possibly my release will come in February.

The most important consideration at the present time is the draft. Until I can talk to the draft board, I can make absolutely no plans.

As Mary told you, we are planning to come home after the next trip. I hope that the Oil Strike doesn't change our plans. If gasoline is scarce, we might come by plane on American.

I will try to see Mr. Lewis in the next couple of days, if the activity caused by the cutback has subsided sufficiently. I think I know what I am saying when I say the last few weeks would have been a very bad time to bother him.

I did talk to Bob Hall, the assistant CFRO, who is much more apt to give us straight answers than George Smith.

> *I told him that I would not want to go on a ground station job and asked him what possibilities in other departments would be available. He said that he was sure present employees would have first choice on available jobs.* [He was referring to returning servicemen.] *Just what jobs would be available he didn't seem to know, but said that a bulletin covering this subject should be issued soon. Until that comes out, I hate to bother anyone. But enough on that subject, I will be able to tell you a lot more by the time I get to Cleveland.*
>
> *David had his first shots yesterday, "Dip and Tet," and a result he has a very sore bottom and a slight fever today. He has been remarkably good in spite of his condition.*
>
> *He certainly is progressing. He crawls after a fashion now. The best way to describe it is to say that he looks like he is swimming; arms and legs go in all directions but he moves forward and that's what counts.*

It's hard to remember my concerns about the draft. Release from American Airlines would have meant I would lose my 2-B classification and my draft board could classify me 1-A. Looking at it from my present perspective it is hard to believe that, with the war over, they would have drafted a young father with a child, and of course they didn't.

In the months before and after we returned to Cleveland, my father was using his business connections to find me a job which would keep me out of the draft. He arranged for me to meet with an executive at the B.F. Goodrich tire company at their New York office.

This letter from my father was dated November 6, 1945:

Dear Ted,

Guy Gundaker was away last week, but I talked to him on the phone just a few minutes ago. I told him that you had talked with Mr. Smith in New York but apparently had beaten his letter. Guy laughed and said you certainly were right on the job and gotten there quicker than he thought you would, but said he had since covered the situation and was sure that the next time you went in they would know more about you.

I asked him to tell me very frankly what his impressions of you were, and he said that he was very favorably impressed, as were all the others, that they felt you were aggressive, alert and on your toes and the kind of man they would like to see in their organization.

He again repeated that he wasn't concerned about your draft situation and I told him we had reason to believe that the right kind of letter from his organization would handle the situation. He said he would be in touch with the New York people the latter part of this week and perhaps by that time you would have been there, so apparently he is going to work on the situation, which should be a big help.

Bill Trout [a former salesman in Dad's office who was now a magazine publisher in New York] *told me again that he didn't think it was necessary for me to take this preliminary step if you were interested in getting into space selling. He could set things up with Dave Laux to get a job on the outdoor publication he is handling. However, I still feel quite strongly that the Goodrich move is the right one and will give you a sounder selling and business foundation for the future than almost anything else I know of.*

Also, Judge Orr feels very definitely that the Draft Board would not look with favor at a request for deferment on employment with an outdoor magazine as against a sound and stable proposition such as Goodrich.

We naturally are very interested to know how things work out, and I suggest that you give me a collect call on the phone after you have looked into these propositions.

Love, Dad

My last flight as a Flight Radio Officer, scheduled for seven days, left LaGuardia on October 8, 1945 and returned on October 21. It was memorable for one fact. The captain was Ernest K. Gann, who later wrote several best-selling books about his flying experiences. Perhaps the most noteworthy was *The High and the Mighty,* which was later made into a very popular movie.

Ernie and his crew were a very closely knit group. Ernie had a concertina which he sometimes played before takeoff while waiting for clearance. Just before every takeoff, the crew chanted in unison, "I said it to Wilbur and I said it to Orville, this thing will never get off the ground!" Then the throttles were pushed forward and we started down the runway.

CHAPTER 11

Civilian Life

A letter dated December 15, 1945:

Dear Mother and Dad,

Mary and I were tickled to get your grand long letter today, Dad. For the first time in quite a while, everything is definite and settled yesterday afternoon, and all the various pieces have dropped into place, one by one since then.

Mary is going to fly to Cleveland on United Airlines Flight 9 leaving New York at 5:15 p.m. on December 26. I found out that the company will pay both Mary's transportation by plane and my mileage by automobile. We both felt that it would be much easier for Mary and David to come by air, I will drive to Cleveland on either the 27th or 28th, probably the 27th.

Aero-Mayflower is moving our belongings. They will pack and move our things out of here on the 26th. They will be held in storage in New York for a few days then moved to Cleveland where they will be stored by Neal Storage for one month after which I hope we will have an apartment. Then they will be moved into our new home. All this including the month's storage is paid for by American Airlines. We were simply tickled when we heard this because it was one of our main worries. At the most, all we should have to pay for will be a few days storage.

The housing project doesn't sound bad at all. Of course, we realize that it will be quite different from our present apartment but it certainly will be all right as a temporary place to live and since we don't know what I am going to be doing after the draft situation eases up, perhaps it would be just as well if we didn't take anything too permanent. I hope we won't be too hectic boarders while we stay with you. David isn't nearly as peaceful as he was when we last visited you.

Mary wondered if you could get her mother's high chair, we would also like to have you arrange for diaper service if possible. I would call immediately because sometimes it isn't too easy to get. Oh, yes, if you know anyone who has a play pen which we could borrow for about a week, until ours gets to Cleveland that would help a lot. David is much easier to care for when we have one.

Thanks again for all the work you are doing for us we really appreciate it. I could almost see Mary relax when we got your letter today describing the housing project. I will keep you posted on any change and we will drop you a few lines every few days even if there isn't anything new to report.

Love, Ted

Housing was very difficult to find, but Mary's father had been working hard for us. He knew the head of the Cleveland Metropolitan Housing Authority. A project on the west side of Cleveland had been converted from low-income housing in order to house scientists working at the NASA facility at

Cleveland Hopkins Airport. With the war over, some of the scientists were moving on to new jobs. New residents had to meet two requirements; they had to be married returning servicemen, and have at least one child. Even though I hadn't technically been in the service, with the urging of the Judge, it was determined that we were eligible.

It was ironic that, many years later, there would have been no question about my eligibility as a discharged veteran. At least 40 years after I left American Airlines, I received a telephone call from a man who had also flown with AAL in World War II. He told me that if I applied for it, I could get an Honorable Discharge from the United States Air Force. The same man sent me the information about how to proceed. Upon request, American Airlines sent me a letter stating that I had served with them overseas during the war. I mailed this, along with my flight logs, to a sergeant in Texas. Several months later, I received an Honorable Discharge from the United States Air Force, which did not exist when I was flying! One month later, I received a package in the mail which contained my World War II Victory medal, an Asiatic–Pacific Campaign Medal, an American Campaign Medal, and a World War II honorable service lapel button.

We lived with my parents for about a month before an apartment became available. The housing project was perfect for us at this time. The buildings were two-story structures containing four apartments. Each apartment had a living room and kitchen on the first floor. There was a coat closet near the entrance and a small alcove that could hold a clothes washer, plus a large closet on the first floor which housed the water heater and small hand-stoked furnace, with a small coal bin that connected to a larger exterior bin. Two bedrooms and a bath were located on the second floor. We had an end apartment with its entrance on the driveway. Our living room window looked out over a green field, part of which was mowed to make a lawn.

Our quarters were really spartan; most of our closets had no doors so we hung drapes to hide the contents. We were living very close to our neighbors. I recall one time, while I was taking a bath, having a conversation with the woman next door who was doing the same. Our doorless bathroom cabinets backed on each other, separated only by a thin sheet of plywood.

Our fellow residents couldn't have been more compatible. Many of the NASA employees still lived there. One of our neighbors was a mathematician; several were engineers. All of us had at least one child, and most of us had two by the time we left. The atmosphere was somewhat like college married students' housing. We had a very social time. Our children played together, and so the wives had gotten to know each other as a result.

I have absolutely no recollection of how my Draft problems vanished. I did go to work at *Sports Afield* magazine as a junior salesman, selling advertising. My office was in Detroit, but with the understanding that I would continue to live in Cleveland. I was often on the road, calling on small sporting goods manufacturers.

Another part of my job was to sell small ads to fishermen who had created new fishing lures. Many serious fishermen, at one time or another, have had the experience of concocting a lure which was, on a particular day, was very successful in catching loads of fish. They would have a picture taken with a huge string of fish and then go into business trying to sell this new lure. I would find them at sportsmen's shows in towns and cities in my territory. It was fun. I got to know several professional baitcasters who had been hired by the show promoters to entertain the customers. With their help, I became quite proficient at using a casting reel (this was a time before spin-casting reels). I could cast a hook less lure about 30 feet into a large bucket most of the time. Obviously, however, I wasn't making enough sales to justify my job, because it was eliminated and no one was hired to take my place.

I just can't piece together the timeline for some of the several jobs that I held next. At one time I had a resume listing this information, but it is no longer in my files. I sold displays for a Cleveland company which created and manufactured display booths for trade shows. I know that I sold one beautiful little brochure holder, for department store table displays, of Fostoria glass. I had this opportunity because, by this time, my Uncle Frank was working for a Cleveland advertising agency which had the Fostoria account.

I worked with two different men who were manufacturers' representatives. One sold large "24-sheet" full color billboard posters which could be customized to fit many different retailers' businesses. The other representative sold manufacturers' "retail point of sale" signs. Neon beer signs are one example; large illuminated street signs provided by manufacturers were another. I temporarily joined Homer Lowe as a commissioned salesman. I went through all of our war bond savings before I was forced to find a real wage-earning job. Homer was a very honest man; shortly after I left him, he received an order from Westinghouse Appliance Division for all of their "point of sale" signs. My Uncle Frank, who worked on the Westinghouse account, had again paved the way for me. Homer paid me, in full, for my share of the commission. It was a little larger than the amount of money I had spent out of our savings.

Our daughter Constance Jane, whom we called Connie from the start, arrived about six weeks early, on December 19, 1946. She was a tiny little thing and taken from her mother immediately and kept in the hospital for about a month. In those days, we could not have any physical contact with our daughter until we brought her home. Today such treatment would be unthinkable. Mary came home alone the day before Christmas. I set up a small Christmas tree in our bedroom, and David, Mary and I celebrated our Christmas there together.

Mary and David

With David and Friend
In The Housing Project

Our First House in Maple Heights

The House we built in Chagrin Falls

The House we lived In for 41 Years

Our First Camping Trip to Nova Scotia

CHAPTER 12

Radio Days

The first job that I obtained entirely on my own with no outside help was with Radio Station WGAR in Cleveland. I saw an ad in the *Cleveland Plain Dealer* newspaper saying they were looking for someone to be the station's promotion manager. I applied, and the station's sales manager interviewed me first and then presented me to John Patt, the station's general manager. I am certain that mentioning both my father and the Judge helped. Looking back on the interview, I am quite certain John Patt probably knew my father because both were prominent in Cleveland advertising circles.

Radio was in its ascendancy. WGAR was the CBS Cleveland station, and CBS was the number one network at the time. My job was multifaceted. I designed contests for listeners, after which we were able to analyze the source of their entries and then determine where the responses came from, to show the broad reach of the station. I produced sales presentations and I photographed special events for station archives.

One funny incident took place during the 1948 presidential race when Thomas E. Dewey, the Republican candidate for president, gave a speech in Cleveland before a WGAR microphone which I photographed for the station. The station owned a 4x5 graphic camera which used flat film in holders inserted into the back of the camera. That year, the Cleveland

Indians had won the World Series and received a tickertape parade down Euclid Avenue, which I also photographed. That was the year that Dewey lost to Truman. When I developed my ticker tape pictures, I discovered that I had double exposed one of the parade pictures over a Dewey picture. The result is Dewey speaking to a tickertape celebration which was as illusory as his "sure thing" presidential victory. I think I still have the negative.

After two years, I was promoted to the sales department. I discovered that all the important customers were being covered by salesmen who were more senior than I. When hired, I was assured that I would have a regular review of my work and an increase in pay. This was not happening, and when I approached the sales manager and reminded him of his promise, he somewhat ambiguously replied, "I can't do that." I immediately began looking for another job. I had already determined that selling magazine advertising was better paid than selling radio ads.

I landed a job selling advertising out of the Cleveland office of *Motor* magazine. This was, and still is, a trade publication edited for automotive repair facilities. The northern Ohio area was the home of many businesses manufacturing parts used by automobile manufacturers and for what I learned was called "the aftermarket." Now I was calling on advertising agencies and their clients involved in this market. It was great training.

CHAPTER 13

Major Turning Points

While I was working for *Motor* magazine, all of the Riverside Park residents received a notice from the Cleveland Metropolitan Housing Authority informing us that our housing would soon return to its original purpose, to provide low-income families with housing. This meant that practically all of us were earning too much and couldn't stay. Two enterprising residents realized that there were enough families to do something as a group and started an organization called Cleveland Cooperative Homes. A large percentage of residents signed up by contributing $100.

In a very short time our group had optioned a beautiful tract of land west of Cleveland and hired an architect and land planner on a contingency basis. Within a few months they submitted to us a comprehensive plan. Roads would be laid out to minimize through traffic. Individual houses would be on similar floor plans, but their orientation on their lots and exteriors would be changed so that they would have individuality. Green spaces were included in the plot plan. It was a dream project which was scuttled by a period of double-digit inflation which priced the houses out of our reach. Mary and I felt the education we received from the effort was certainly worth our investment.

Cleveland is a divided city, East and West, separated by the Cuyahoga River. We were "East Siders," not "West Siders," so when we found a house that we could afford, it was located in Maple Heights, an eastern suburb. It was on Hanson Road, in a post-war development of small cottage style houses. Our new house was an exception. It was a two-story brick and solid masonry house, located on a corner lot. It was only four years old, but the first owner was being transferred to the West Coast. The living room ran across the front of the house with a large picture window opening on the street. We had a dining room and a kitchen. On the second floor were three bedrooms and a bath. The house had a large, clean, and dry basement with a tub and connections for a washing machine. We moved into our first house in 1948. We were happy in our new home and our children soon had new friends.

On May 21, 1950 James Stanley Boynton, our second son, was born. He was a healthy full-term baby who had to be induced by the doctor. On May 5, 1952 Mary, while she was pregnant with our fourth child, suddenly experienced severe internal bleeding. By the time we reached the hospital she was in critical condition. The doctor saved Mary, but an almost full-term daughter was stillborn. I don't think any of us really understood Mary's sorrow. The doctors and nurses treated the episode as just another unfortunate event and assured her that she could have another child. I was so grateful that the doctor had saved Mary's life that I gave little thought to the child we had lost. Neither of us saw the baby. It took Mary a long time to recover from her loss.

On August 4, 1953, ten days before Mary's 31st birthday, a major life-changing event took place. At suppertime I called home from my hotel room in Pittsburgh. Mary said, after a pause, "Charlie is going to take me to an AA meeting tonight." This came as a complete surprise to me, but I could tell from her voice that it was very important to her. So I replied, "Good, I'll call you later this evening." I just didn't realize that she was having trouble with alcohol. I did know that she drank more than I did at parties.

Years before, when I worked for the radio station where Charlie was an announcer, we had shared rides to and from work. One day, as we were driving, Charlie told me about the problems he was having with alcohol and asked me what I thought. All I said was that if I had his problems with drinking, I probably would feel that I needed to do something about them. Several months later he said, "I have joined AA." I don't recall our talking about it after that. I told Mary about our conversations.

When I called that night, Mary sounded excited and relieved. There were no alcoholic women at that meeting, but the men's wives welcomed her and reassured her that if she had a problem with alcohol, she was in the right place. She met several other alcoholic women at a subsequent meeting.

In the early days of the program, when Mary joined, a program for families was very new with mostly wives involved. I was anxious to share Mary's experience and learn about the program, so when possible, I attended meetings with her. The program changed our lives. Alcoholism is recognized today as a progressive and incurable disease which, if allowed to progress to its end, results in death or institutionalization. Most alcoholics are unable to stop drinking for any length of time by themselves, and need the help of fellow recovering alcoholics and God. There is a path to both. Today, I still go to an open meeting once a week with Mary. From the day that she joined the program until today, Mary has been an active participant. We have learned that we don't have to rely on just ourselves to make decisions. If we "let go and let God," He will help us and lead us in the right direction.

CHAPTER 14

Dobote

In 1953, my father was still working, but he and Mother were looking for a summer place in the north. They found what they were looking for on the shore of Georgian Bay. There are 30,000 islands along its shores. On the tip of McLaren's Island, located in the South Channel, about five miles from the town of Parry Sound in Ontario, they found an old cottage for sale. They fell in love with the location and bought the property and the cottage.

I describe the property, viewed from above, as looking like the thumb and forefinger of a hand. The old cottage was located close to the fingertip, and the thumb formed a cove where we located our dock. The shores very much resemble the Maine coast, without the tides or the fog. It has the same geological nature, with granite outcroppings covered with pine and birch trees. The old cottage had been built by the janitor of a local bank, who used whatever materials he could scavenge. It was located about 40 feet above the water and built directly on solid rock with no foundation. It had a kitchen, living room, utility room and three bedrooms. From the center of the house, the floors sloped toward the outer walls. A marble dropped in the middle of the living room rolled toward the nearest wall. A large screened porch, which covered one side of the house, was entered from the living room, as were all of the bedrooms.

The living room was heated by a free-standing, wood-fired Franklin stove. We had an outhouse located well away from the cottage. Because the cottage was built directly on the ground, it was almost impossible to keep the mice out, so eventually the cottage was named "Mouse Haven."

On Memorial Day weekend in 1953, my father, two brothers, and I took Friday off, giving us four days to upgrade the house. In that short time we completely remodeled the kitchen. We tore out the old shelves, put in a new sink, and built new open-faced cabinets made of knotty pine. We had no electricity; two large propane tanks supplied a Servel gas refrigerator and the kitchen stove. The water system consisted of a large tank, from an old hot water heater, mounted horizontally in the eaves. A connection led to a hand pump which then connected to a long intake hose in the bay water. Another hose led to a kitchen faucet which was supplied by gravity. The water in the bay was so pure that we could drink it without treatment.

One time, our daughter Connie, then a young sub-teen, was alone at the camp when two fishermen tied up to our dock. When she came down to the dock to see who they were, they apologized for intruding and said that they had run out of water. Connie told them that we just took our water out of the Bay. They said that if she wouldn't mind, they would prefer to have her fill their canteens at the cottage water tap. Connie complied with their request, but what they didn't know was that our water intake was only about ten feet from the bottom of their boat. Each year we sent a sample of our water to the Canadian government, which always sent back a report that it was pure.

No other habitation was visible from our cottage. A path led down the hill to our dock, which was built for us locally.

A small dock house was located next to the dock. We needed transportation to and from the city, so my father purchased an eighteen-foot Lyman Islander for the camp. It was a lapstrake inboard with great carrying capacity and was capable of handling any waves that it might encounter.

Until my father retired, my two brothers, my father and mother, and my family took turns vacationing in the cottage. Our children loved "Dobote," the camp name which my father concocted from his son's names, Doug, Bob and Ted. After my father's retirement, he built another cottage on the property, followed by another small building which housed a guest room and a laundry. Their new cottage was named "Headquarters."

Canadian Hydro, the electric power company, eventually ran an electric line down the center of the island ending at our property. With electricity, we were able to install a pressure water system. My parents' cottage and the guest house had hot and cold water, flush toilets, electricity, and a telephone! We were lucky to discover a large sandy area among the rocks for a septic system. One summer I was able to run an electric line and with Jim wiggling between the rocks and the house foundation, wired the old cottage. Eventually we built a small structure, just outside the old cottage back door, which we called the "Indoor Outhouse"; it had a flush toilet and running water.

We had the opportunity to acquire a 99-year lease on the property on the other side of the cove. This meant that we now owned all of the land surrounding the cove. To secure the lease we were obligated to build a structure on the new property. I designed a sleeping cottage. My brothers built the foundation and floor, and I erected the cottage itself with the help of our son David and a guest. The roof had wide overhangs which protected window-sized screened openings, which themselves had hinged battens that fastened to the ceiling when not in use. It had two built-in bunk beds. Because of the roof style, it was christened the "Tea House."

Gradually our boat fleet grew. First we added an aluminum rowboat fitted with a small outboard motor. One by one, our children were allowed to use this. To be qualified they had to be able to pull the starter cord hard enough to start the engine. Our next boat was a racy little runabout which had an outboard motor big enough to tow a water skier. Somewhere along the line we acquired a canoe, and finally a sailing surfboard called a "Sailfish." I had seen it advertised in a Cleveland paper. It had been built from a kit by a man who decided to sell it because his nephews were abusing it. He asked $100 for it. I couldn't afford that much at the time, so I convinced my father to purchase it for the camp. He never let me take it home.

We summer vacationed at Dobote for almost 20 years. Many times we asked other families to join us. Sometimes we had as many as seven or eight children at the camp. In 1954, on our first vacation at the cottage, Mary was pregnant. She found another woman who had started a meeting in Parry Sound. On many nights over the years, we attended the evening meeting and came back down the channel to the cottage in the dark. We left a light on the dock so we could find the cottage.

On November 9, 1954 our last child, Elizabeth Mary Boynton, was born (we called her Beth), and so we were blessed with two boys and two girls.

The View from our Point

Our Porch

Picnic on the rocks with the "Ellie B"

David Reading

My Father with Beth

We learned to sail on the "Sailfish"

Jim and friends in the Canoe

CHAPTER 15

Life at *Life*

In 1954 an amazing thing happened: another major turning point in my life. I found myself in the unbelievable position of being offered an advertising sales job by two major magazine publishing companies at the same time—McGraw-Hill, then the largest trade magazine publisher, and Time Inc., the most important and fastest-growing consumer magazine publisher. Both positions would be in their Cleveland office, and both jobs offered a substantial increase in salary. Selling for *Life* magazine, a Time Inc. publication, would mean that I would be in direct competition with my father, who was by then the Cleveland manager of the Curtis Publishing Company, publisher of the *Saturday Evening Post,* probably *Life*'s biggest competitor. I believe these opportunities happened because of my automotive magazine sales experience and perhaps because of my father's reputation.

Life offered the most glamorous possibilities, and I succumbed. Suddenly I found myself feeling like the bush league ball player who unexpectedly found himself playing for the Yankees. *Life* paid for me to join a prestigious golf club, and paid the membership dues. The same applied for a downtown club, where I could entertain customers at lunch. I discovered I would be eligible for a month's vacation. Time Inc. determined vacation time by the nature of the job instead of seniority.

What a time to join *Life* magazine, when it was at the peak of its popularity! My territory included Dayton and Columbus as well as several other smaller cities in the area. Many of my prospects were smaller companies, with small advertising budgets, but even they wanted to be able to display the "As advertised in *Life* magazine" symbol in their advertising and at the point of sale for their products.

Everything at *Life* was big, and photographing the news of the world for a weekly picture magazine required a large staff of photographers and reporters. At one time, it had 40 correspondents, which required a large support team of photographic technicians and editors in New York. Salesmen were supported by a department devoted only to producing individual flip-chart sales presentations for advertising prospects and to helping us create marketing plans using the *Life* logo for promotions.

We were expected to entertain customers, and our expense accounts were liberal. I never felt that I fit the *Life* salesman mold, as I really didn't like large parties. *Life* spent large amounts of money to help us to gain entrance to a customer's top management, where most important advertising decisions were made. While I worked for them, *Life* undertook a very large and sophisticated consumer marketing survey. It offered its salesmen the opportunity to be able to tell advertisers what their customers were thinking about their products.

One of my prospects was the Youngstown Steel Company, located in Youngstown, Ohio, which manufactured Youngstown Steel Kitchen Cabinets. They were the number one consumer brand name among cabinet manufacturers. Our marketing survey contained quite detailed information about women's preferences by age and income. I was able to get an appointment with the president and sales manager of the company to present our findings. On a blustery winter day another salesman, who was specializing in the housing market, flew in to join me. By the time he arrived, the weather had worsened and the roads to Youngstown were almost impassable. My associate solved our problem by hiring a helicopter to take us there. We landed in their parking lot.

Our presentation disclosed that a large selection of women were tired of the plain metal cabinets, so prevalent then. They wanted the warmth of wooden doors. When we had finished presenting our facts, the president thanked us for our interesting presentation and then said, "Of course you know we are in the steel fabricating business." He stood outside and waved to us as we took off for our return to Cleveland. His company eventually added wooden doors to their steel cabinets, but by that time, the wooden cabinet manufacturers had taken over most of the market. Only *Life* would have reimbursed a salesman for chartering a helicopter for a business call!

These were heady times for me. Salesmen spent a week in the editorial offices while an issue of the magazine was being created. As an amateur photographer, I was able to watch as the film arriving from correspondents around the world was processed and printed. I stood behind the editors as they selected the photos and laid out the pages.

There were problems with the job. When we received an order from our customer's advertising agency, we never really knew why we had succeeded. Perhaps the president of the company liked a picture or an article. When we didn't get the order or received a cancellation, we seldom knew why. The advertising agency would give us a reason, but often it was just a rationalization for a decision made by someone at the company itself. We never had the satisfaction of knowing for sure that we had been directly responsible for the sale.

We received a weekly report listing orders received and the name of the salesman involved. One time, a salesman handling the American Airlines account received a 52-week, full four-color page order. Each week this was listed in the report. He was listed as the salesman along with the name of the *Life* publisher. A short time after this, the editors ran a picture of an American Airlines crash which featured a picture of the tail with the AA logo. The next week the report listed each ad with a cancellation notice, and *only* the salesman's name was attached!

CHAPTER 16

A New House

With David in sixth grade and Connie only a year behind him, we thought that we would like to find a better school district. We began looking at possibilities in more affluent suburbs. Time Inc. in those days published a magazine called *House and Home,* a publication for builders. I found it very interesting because it featured all the new ideas for home builders. One of the advertisers in the magazine was Scholtz Homes, which was prefabricating beautiful homes for erection on site. We began looking for a lot on which to place one of our own.

We found a beautiful three-acre wooded lot, one-third of which was a ravine leading to a small creek. It was located on Ridgewood Road, right in the village of Chagrin Falls, 20 miles from downtown Cleveland. The Chagrin River runs through the village with, as the name implies, a small waterfall in the center of town. The schools were reported to be good. Mary's brother David at that time was a home building contractor, and agreed to erect it for us.

House styles change with the times. One can almost predict the decade in which a house was built by its style. Ranch-style houses were in vogue when we built. The house we selected was a four-bedroom, two-bath, one-floor design, with an attached two-and-a-half-car garage. It was built on a concrete slab. We really enjoyed watching our house being constructed and making all of the decisions that allowed us to customize it to our taste.

Building started early in the spring of 1956, one of the wettest on record. When the bulldozer arrived to start grading, it immediately sank almost two feet into the earth. Our education in home building started. David informed us that in order to have proper drainage, the ground level in front of the house would have to be raised several feet. This required many truckloads of fill dirt which could only arrive after he had built a plank road from the street to the site. Finally the concrete slab was finished with utility conduits sticking out at various locations.

It was an exciting day as we watched the prefabricated sections arrive on two large trucks. Once the trucks were unloaded, the erection of the exterior and interior walls and roof proceeded rapidly. Each section of the exterior was already finished, with windows and doors in place. Interior walls were not finished. The roof was erected and the entire house was under cover in little more than two days.

Our new home featured a high beamed ceiling living room, the back of which was almost all glass from the floor to the ceiling. The large windows looked out over a woodland back yard with beautiful large trees. Our dining room table was positioned in front of this window. On one side of the living room, a large window gave us a view of the wooded ravine. The other side had a stone-faced fireplace which backed on to the kitchen with a playroom which had an outside door and a corridor leading to the garage. The corridor also provided space for a washer and dryer. Four bedrooms and two bathrooms, on the front of the house, opened off a central hallway.

We only lived in the house for three years. We found that while we could afford it, with taxes and mortgage payments we couldn't afford to add landscaping. I had planned to use the half garage for my Shopsmith woodworking machine. We had the garage heated by a propane heater so that I could work there on winter days. What I hadn't considered was that ice and slush from our cars melted quickly and no one would choose to use electrical tools while standing on a water-covered floor. There was really nowhere that I could have a darkroom; we did process some photographic Christmas cards on top of the washer and dryer. Mary found that she had no place to put dirty clothes when she was doing the laundry. The children's playroom opened with a pass-through directly into the kitchen, which gave Mary no privacy from the loud children's programs on the TV when she was preparing meals. She said that *Howdy Doody* was going to drive her insane. We had hoped to attach a small building to the back of the house which would house a workshop and a screened porch, but we just couldn't afford it. The living room was impressive and would have been wonderful for large parties, but our idea of a party was to spend a quiet evening with another couple.

CHAPTER 17

Our Final Home

Chagrin Falls has an annual spring festival called "Blossom Time." It features a parade through town and carnival rides and booths on the high school grounds located on East Washington Street, which runs through the center of the village. The carnival was just a short walk from our house. In 1959, while walking to the fair with the children, we noticed a "For Sale" sign on an old two-story house just to the left of the entrance to the school grounds. We ended up buying it and lived in it for 41 years.

Mary describes our Washington Street house as one that a small child would draw. A peaked roof with symmetrically located windows and a front porch faced the street. It was located on one acre of ground with a large back yard. When we purchased it, the house was almost 100 years old. The exterior, which had been clapboard, had been covered with asbestos cement shingles. It had a large unfinished attic and a cellar, which I felt never deserved to be called a basement. When it was built, the house had no bathroom, electricity or central heat. Free-standing stoves had provided the heat. At one time there had been a water well, and undoubtedly an outhouse, on the property. Almost all of the interior walls had been moved at least once. For a period, it had been turned into an up-and-down duplex with an exterior staircase leading to the second floor. The front door led directly into the living room, which had built-in floor-to-ceiling bookcases on one side, facing a large clothes closet and built-in display shelves and drawers on the other. A small room with a lavatory, off the living room, served alternately as a bedroom and an office over the years. The back entrance to the house passed through a back porch which could be glassed in during the winter and screened in warmer weather. The back door opened directly into a large dining room with a bay window. The dining room became the center of family activities. Only strangers used the front door.

A U-shaped kitchen opened directly on the dining room. Before we moved in, while we were still living in our Ridgewood Road house, I completely remodeled the kitchen. A Sears Roebuck kitchen specialist designed the layout for me and provided the new cabinets. I assembled and installed them myself. I relocated a new modern kitchen sink and reduced the size of the arched kitchen entrance. I am particularly proud of the changed entrance because here I learned how to lath and plaster.

There were three bedrooms and a bathroom on the second floor. One bedroom faced the front of the house. A large bathroom, also on the front of the house, opened on the hallway. At the back of the house, doorways led from our master bedroom to what became the girls' bedroom, which ran all the way across the back of the house. The only way to get to the girls' room was through our bedroom. A staircase off the girls' room led to the attic. The house had been insulated and the attic walls were covered with soft particle board, which in time was covered with posters and magazine clippings of different teenage idols which were still there when we sold the house. I kept my woodworking tools and eventually built a very nice darkroom in the cellar.

I don't recall that we had any problem making the decision to move from our "dream house" to the less pretentious old house. The move cut our taxes and mortgage in half. We were never again "house poor."

CHAPTER 18

Our Church

Shortly after we moved to Chagrin Falls, Mary said she was going to find us a church in the village. That Sunday morning, I baby-sat while she went to a service at the Chagrin Falls Federated Church. When she returned, she said that she wasn't going to look any farther. This was the church for us. We were active members for 45 years. Typical of the church, the head minister called on us during the next week, before we had attended again.

The Federated had wonderful programs for children and youth. All four of our children attended Sunday school and, as teenagers, were active participants in the youth program. The church had an exceptional youth minister. Our kids attended UCC (United Church of Christ) summer camp, and one time Mary and I served as camp counselors. The church became a very important part of our family life.

It is amazing to me how God works in our life. The following is an excerpt from the web page of Wainwright House in Rye, New York.

Wainwright House is the oldest non-profit, non-sectarian holistic learning center in the United States. Our mission is to inspire greater understanding through body, mind, spirit and community. In this sacred space, we seek to inspire by offering initiatives in spiritual exploration, health and healing, cultural enrichment, and environmental awareness.

History of Wainwright House:

Col. and Mrs. Wainwright had one child, their daughter Fonrose. In the late 1940, Fonrose suffered the lost of both her parents and her husband in the space of just a few years. Whereupon, through a series of apparent coincidences, she met a then unknown young minister, Norman Vincent Peale. It is said that Peale walked through the door of Wainwright House, stopped suddenly and remarked with awe that even though it was empty and unused, the house was filled with love. Fonrose knew then she had found a compelling use for her parent's home. In 1951, she founded Wainwright House, Inc. With the belief that there should be a place under one roof where people from all backgrounds and all beliefs and even no beliefs at all- could aspire for a greater understanding of the creative force of life we call God. [errors in original]

Inspired by the programs offered at Wainwright House, a group of Cleveland men chose a 17-room turn-of-the-century mansion in Kirtland, Ohio to house their vision for an inter-denominational retreat center. In October 1957, Shadybrook House, once the summer home of a wealthy Cleveland family, had its dedication.

Two years later, Mary attended a retreat at Shadybrook House. Shortly after that, Mary and I signed up for a course called "The Group Search for Growth." It had a profound effect on our lives. The course was led by Don Boyce, a layman who had been hired as director of Shadybrook House. Don came from New York where he had been active with both Wainwright House and a group of businessmen called "Laymen's Movement for a Christian World." In 1960, twenty of us committed to the course, spending one weekend a month for six months. Mary's mother stayed with our children.

It is difficult to explain the course because it explored so many subjects and activities. We practiced meditation techniques, read books by spiritual leaders, and had long group discussions. We learned about receptive listening, how to listen without forming an immediate reply. We tried to understand what another person was really feeling instead of just what they were saying. We experimented with expressing our inner feelings through art. We talked about small group leadership. Our group became very close and many of us signed up for another year together.

We took much of what we learned there back home and to the church. Our older children became teenagers during the turbulent 1960's, but much of the time we were able to keep up close sharing relationships with them. We learned that sometimes we had to stay up well past our bedtime before they would bring up what was really on their minds. Our receptive listening training was very helpful.

With teenagers, how long they were allowed to stay out at night was often a point of family tension. We tried an experiment and told them they could pick their own time with the understanding that if for some unforeseen reason they couldn't meet the deadline, they were to call us. Also, if for any reason they wanted to come home but couldn't, they could call and we would pick them up. They felt empowered by being able to set their own time. It turned out that the time that they set often was earlier than what we probably would have allowed.

One day two teenagers from our church came to our house and asked if we would be willing to sponsor a prayer group for them. Of course we agreed. We had little to do with selecting the participants, although Connie and David joined us. They called the group "The Cell." We met in the church meditation room. A great deal of sharing took place at those meetings. Several kids had serious problems at home. Later, some of them talked with us individually. The group continued to meet until they graduated from high school.

During this same period, we were once again approached by some high school teenagers who were looking for a place where they could "hang out" after school. We were able to start a teen coffee shop on the third floor of a small old office building, rent free. One adult was always present during its open hours in the afternoon. We were able to enlist all of the churches in the village, who helped us provide non-judgmental adults to be present when the coffee shop was open. No one drank coffee, but the soft drink machine was very popular as was loud pop music in the smoke-filled room. Yes, in those days we permitted smoking, and I think it was one of the big attractions. The coffee shop lasted until the building owner decided to do a major renovation.

CHAPTER 19

A Life-Changing Event

Another major turning point occurred after I had been working ten years for *Life*. I lost my job. This was not surprising to me because I had never felt that I fit the Time Inc. mold. Also, I had made it known that I didn't want to be transferred to another location, knowing that *Life* often promoted by job transfer. Mary and I wanted to give our children the stability of living in one community. I was probably the "oldest junior salesman" when they fired me.

Time Inc. was certainly a great company from which to be fired. I received one month's pay for each of the ten years I had worked there. I was also invested in their retirement plan. In those days, one couldn't roll over the money into another plan, so I received a lump sum payment.

Another life-changing idea occurred to me. I said to Mary, "This may be the only chance we'll have when we will have the time and the money: Let's go to Europe for a month." She thought it was a great idea. We secured our passports, made plane reservations, and made arrangements with a local Volkswagen dealer to buy a VW Beetle in Germany. Beetles were so popular that we could buy a car in Europe, use it for our trip, ship it back by boat, and sell it in the United States for what we paid for it. We found a schoolteacher, single and teaching at the school next door, who was willing to stay with our kids.

Amazingly, I had another job before we left. The local manager at the *Saturday Evening Post* offered me a job. I accepted it but explained that we had completed our arrangements for a European trip and so I couldn't start until we got back. He agreed to this schedule.

Our children drove us to the Cleveland airport. We were so busy in the car giving last-minute instructions that we didn't have the car radio turned on.

We left on November 22, 1963, and as we taxied out for takeoff on our two o'clock flight to New York, we saw our children waving frantically to us from the airport observation deck.

After we were airborne, the captain came on the speakers and said, "I'll keep you informed about President Kennedy; of course you know he is dead." We left New York from Idlewild Airport and arrived back to Kennedy Airport, the same airport, a month later.

By the time we left for London, all of the flags at the airport were at half staff. When we arrived in London, every flag there was also at half staff. It was a strange time to be in Europe. We only saw brief glimpses of the funeral. Black-bordered pictures of the president were posted at churches announcing their own memorial services. People approached us on the street and asked if we were Americans and when we said yes, they would tell us how sorry they were about our president.

After a couple of days in London, we flew to Copenhagen for a day, then to Munich, where our VW was waiting for us. Because it was winter, we headed south through Germany. In Oberammergau, home of the famous Passion Play, we purchased beautiful hand-carved wooden nativity figures, which we still have. We drove south through the Brenner

Pass, which was not yet snow-covered, and continued south through Italy to the Mediterranean. Winter travel has its advantages; we never needed a hotel reservation. We used Frommer's travel guide, *Europe on Five Dollars a Day*. We did very well on ten dollars a day, staying in small unpretentious hotels not frequented by tourists and eating in restaurants suggested by "the book."

We found that there are few American tourists in Europe in early December, so we immediately introduced ourselves when we heard another couple speaking "American," not British English. We were in a little restaurant, on the waterfront, in the Italian naval port of La Spezia. Bob and Jean Lawrence, it turned out, had just reached the Mediterranean by way of the French canal system. They had started in Holland, where they purchased a small wooden center-cockpit sailboat. They were headed for the Greek Islands for the winter. They asked us back to the boat, where they regaled us with tales of their gypsy life. Bob was an engineer who moved from construction site to construction site. Over the years they had owned trailers and boats, not houses. Now that their son was active in the business, they were taking more time for cruising. Their stories and photographs that night, seen in the cozy cabin of their boat, made a profound impression on Mary and me and changed our lives. We thought that, if they could lead this exciting style of life, why couldn't we! We have never forgotten their kindness. We didn't realize then what an important turning point this visit would turn out to be in our lives.

We returned home by way of Paris, where a shipping service picked up our car. We arrived back in Cleveland on December 23, in time for Christmas.

After the holidays, I went to work for the *Saturday Evening Post*.

I worked for the *Post* for three turbulent years. Because of its declining advertising revenue, it could not survive as a weekly publication. While I was there, it had three different publishers, each of whom brought in a new management team. The only consistent thing was change.

Chagrin falls Federated Church

Shadybrook Retreat House

Kenedy Merorial Poster
in Europe

Bob and Jean Lawrence's Ketch
They Changed Our Lives

New Horizon Sloop "Chrisma"
Our First Sailboat

"Golconda" at the "Vermilion Yacht Club"

CHAPTER 20

World Publishing Company

One day, while working for the *Post*, I made a call on one of my customers, the World Publishing Company. This family-owned business published *Webster's New World Dictionary* and was the largest Bible publishing and manufacturing company in the country. Their advertising manager told me that the sales manager wanted to see me. I was very surprised when he offered me a job. The position which he offered was to be their premium sales manager. This would involve selling their various books for promotional purposes. An example would be Scotch Tape offering a small free back-to-school dictionary along with the purchase of a number of rolls of tape. My job would also include selling to the trading stamp companies which were so prevalent in those days. He offered me more money than I was making at the *Post*. This was a Cleveland company and the offer was for a home office job; we wouldn't have to worry about being moved again. I accepted the job.

I really enjoyed the job. I had a wonderful middle-aged secretary, Florence, who had worked in that department for a long time and knew so much about company procedures and existing customers that I quickly turned almost all of the details over to her and concentrated on selling. We were a great team and both of us enjoyed working together. However, storm clouds were looming over the World Publishing Company.

To explain what happened, I have to describe the structure of the company. World was privately owned. The president of the company, when I joined it, was married to the daughter of the founder and had successfully managed the company for many years. His wife and several other family members owned stock. World was unusual in that it was a fully integrated publishing company. They not only published books, but also manufactured them in their own factory. They were specialists in thin paper printing and binding. Many of the machines had been invented by early employees and were unique to the business. They also manufactured books for many other publishers. They had one salesman who just called on evangelists and religious denominations. He sold hundreds of thousands of custom-bound Bibles a year. World also published "trade books" from a small number of authors and had a sales force that called on bookstores. World had a staff of highly skilled lexicographers to maintain the *New World Dictionary*.

Len, the son-in-law of the president, was vice president in charge of production, but the plant manager actually ran the plant. His name was Oscar, and he was a feisty little man who ran everything. He scheduled the work and oversaw each step through printing, binding, and shipping. He knew every machine and activity in the factory. He was like a symphony conductor who was intimately familiar with every instrument. The president told Oscar that if Len ever gave him any trouble, "See me and I'll fix it." Len obviously resented this.

Shortly before I went to work, the company president and his heiress wife had a contentious divorce. The family resented this and pooled their holdings and sold the company out from under the president to the Times Mirror Company, publishers of the *Los Angeles Times* newspaper. They had been wisely advised by a management consulting company to diversify into the "knowledge business." From that point, things began to unravel at World. The president lost his job and was replaced with an ambitious man hired from the outside, who somehow thought that Times Mirror was more interested in expanding World than in immediate profit.

With the old president gone, Len was retained as VP of production and moved the plant manager, Oscar, to a position as manager of all "special sales." He therefore became my boss—but with absolutely no experience in sales and no idea of how my job worked.

From that moment on, plant production began to fall apart. The highly skilled journeymen workers resented what happened to Oscar and had never really respected Len, who they felt was a dilettante with no real understanding of production. Several of them left for more lucrative jobs. Productivity dropped and Times Mirror moved in engineers in an attempt to correct the problem. At one time, they had three men just to schedule production, a job which Oscar had handled by himself along with all the other details of production. Finally, the plant arrived at the point where many of its large contract jobs were losing money.

The new president hired some new high-priced editors, based in New York, who were expected to bring in profitable, experienced best-selling authors. As losses mounted, this president was replaced by another, who had no more success than had his predecessor. Times Mirror moved World's headquarters to New York City. The dictionary staff, my secretary Florence, and I were the only people remaining in the Cleveland office. The sales manager asked me to move to New York. Mary and I actually looked at houses in Connecticut, but when I learned that the VP of sales had left and a new sales manager had been appointed, we decided not to go.

The new sales manager had sold books for World. He was moved into the new position and paid more than he had ever made in his life, so he was really fearful of losing the job. He invited the "special sales" staff to a meeting in the Catskills. The night before the meeting, I woke up chuckling to myself in my hotel room. I had thought of a great way of solving my problems at World.

The next day I talked to the new manager privately and suggested that if he put me on straight commission instead of salary, he would be able to know exactly what new business would cost the company. He and his superiors bought the idea and I received a contract. My commissions would be two percent of the amount of the sale. They also agreed to pay for my secretary and the office in Cleveland. Shortly after that, I received an order from the Kroger Company for a supermarket continuity promotion. It consisted of a three-book preschool children's dictionary with Charlie Brown character illustrations. Eventually they bought almost two million books and I still received a commission on each book until the promotion was concluded.

Times Mirror finally gave up on World, closed the factory, and sold the dictionary and Bible business to other companies. My last checks came from Random House.

CHAPTER 21

Back to Magazines

By 1970, my brother Doug had started a quite successful publisher's representative company that handled advertising sales for a number of small publications. He needed help in the Ohio and Michigan area, so I became a publisher's representative. I was able to arrange to represent *Boating* magazine in the same territory. *Boating* was great because at that time it was the magazine with the largest circulation in its field. Circulation, of course, determines advertising rates. The higher the rates, the greater my commission. As it turned out, *Boating* took care of our necessities and the smaller trade publications provided the frills.

I loved working for *Boating;* they paid my expenses to go to several boat shows including the big trade show. I enjoyed being part of the boating industry. In the early fall of 1974, I received a call from the *Boating* sales manager, who gave me some bad news. The publisher had decided to combine two representatives' territories and hire a company salesman. My contract would not be renewed at the end of the year.

Fall is boat show time on the East Coast, so Mary and I drove to several of the shows. This is where I could talk to the publishers of marine publications. By the time we returned home, I had a good possibility of representing two of them. *Cruising World* magazine was just starting up, and a successful newsprint boat-listing publication was planning to start a Midwest edition.

The problem with both of these publications was that they were new. There would be no current advertisers in the territory I would cover. I had some income from the small trade publications, but they wouldn't cover our expenses.

Drawing on our Shadybrook experience, Mary and I made three lists. The first was headed "Things we must have": Beth was still in college and we had certain fixed living expenses. The second list was headed "Things we don't need to have." I didn't necessarily have to sell advertising. The third list was headed "Things we would like to have." At the top of this list, we wrote "Summers off for sailing." Then we turned our list over to God and prayed for guidance.

CHAPTER 22

The Answer

About a week after we returned from our trip, I was sitting in my home office when the phone rang. The voice said "Ted Boynton?" I answered "Yes," and he continued, "You don't know me but my name is Jack Schmidt. I live here in Chagrin Falls and I got your name from Standard Rate and Data. You are a publisher's representative, aren't you?" I said "Yes," and he went on to say, "I don't have anything to offer you but I just want to find out more about how publisher's representatives work." I invited him to come over to my office. There were two publisher's representatives listed in Chagrin Falls; he had called the other one first but he was out of town, so he called me. This meeting was certainly one of the most important turning points in our life.

Jack explained to me that he and his two sisters owned an annual directory listing funeral homes called *The National Directory of Morticians,* known to most customers as the "Red Book." He was looking for help in creating more sales in large cities. I explained that publisher's representatives would not be at all interested because they called on manufacturers and their advertising agencies. He told me that his representatives, all straight commission salesmen, made personal calls on their funeral home customers. He went on to tell me that they started their trips in the fall and finished in the spring when the next edition closed. I realized right away that this schedule allowed them to be free all summer and asked Jack to tell me more. It turned out that in addition to selling the directory, his reps also sold small ads to their customers. Often deaths occur in one location and the deceased are buried in another. Funeral directors therefore need a way to find other funeral homes to handle things at the other end. The sales were small, but the commissions were huge compared to what I had been receiving. I let him know that I might be interested in representing the book. Jack explained that his brother-law Harry, who was then in charge of publishing the directory, lived and worked in Youngstown, Ohio and that I would have to talk with him.

Harry and I sat down in his office on a Wednesday the following week. I was totally overqualified for the job. He soon said that they would like to have me represent the "Red Book" but that they didn't have any territories available. He went on to say that they did have two western states open, but that they were terrible states to work. Customers were often separated by a hundred or more miles. Also, there might be only one prospect in a town, one who hardly ever sent a body to another location and who therefore didn't see a reason for a directory.

I told Harry that I would be willing to sell in those two states as long as I would be guaranteed to get the first territory that became available. He agreed and told me he was going out the next week to make some sales calls on funeral homes in his vicinity and asked if I could go with him to see how the "Red Book" was presented. I said I would be happy to go with him.

I had decided that I could still service my small publications and the "Red Book" at the same time. Money was not a problem because I had received large commission payments from World

Publishing and had been able to save much of the money. The decision was still a leap of faith, but it was resolved when I arrived in Youngstown on Monday morning.

Harry greeted me and said, "You won't believe this, but over the weekend I had a salesman call me and resign a territory!" The territory included all of New England, New York State and eastern Pennsylvania. I never did go west.

After about a year, Jack Schmidt resigned from his important job to take over the full-time publishing of the directory and he opened an office in Chagrin Falls, walking distance from my house. I represented the "Red Book" for 24 years. I had only one business-related telephone call during my summers off, when Jack called, via marine operator, to offer me a better territory which included southern states for more pleasant winter travel.

CHAPTER 23

The "Red Book"

I had always thought that I would like to travel in a motorhome, so immediately after going to work for the "Red Book," I purchased a 24-foot Class B Travelcraft. It was November and I thought it wise to head north in a hurry, so I drove over one weekend to reach Fort Kent, Maine, close to the Canadian border. The winter season had begun and no campgrounds were open, but I found a gas station with a cement pad next to it where, for a modest payment, the owner let me spend the night and ran an electric cord to my vehicle.

Bright and early Monday morning, I knocked on the door of my first funeral home. A very nice lady came to the door and, when I inquired if I could see the funeral director, told me he was out hunting. The same thing happened at the other funeral home in town. In fact, it happened at every call I made that day until my last call of the day. When I rang the bell, a man answered the door. I asked if he was the funeral director; when he said "Yes," I almost without thinking said, "Why aren't you out hunting?" He burst out laughing and said, "I shot a very nice buck this morning in my back lot." I had picked the first day of the hunting season to make my first calls in northern Maine.

Just before the Thanksgiving weekend, I met Mary at the Portland airport and we drove to Five Islands, Maine to spend Thanksgiving weekend with Ann and Phil Hermann at their cottage, which was located on a small island. We left the motorhome parked at the dock and they took us to their island by boat. We had a lovely time in their newly insulated cottage with a warm wood fire burning in the free-standing stove. When we returned to our motorhome, we found the holding tanks frozen solid. As we traveled south they slowly thawed. When we returned home, I built an enclosure for the holding tanks with a heating element. I had a lot to learn about motorhomes.

My first years selling the directory were not easy. I discovered in a short time that the previous salesman in my territory had given up his job because he was starting a competitive directory, which he named the “Yellow Book.” All during the year, he had been selling it to our customers. In some cases, he said the “Red Book” was merging with his directory. He was saying just about anything to get an order and a check. He was financing his new directory with money from our customers.

When I called on my customers, they would tell me that they thought we were going out of business, or that their regular salesman had already renewed their subscription. When I called Harry about this, at first he just shrugged it off—until he had it happen with one of his good customers. I suggested that the very best solution would be to tell anyone who had bought the “Yellow Book” that we were so sorry that it had happened, but that we would not charge them anything for the next “Red Book” or for their ad. Harry went along with this solution. Needless to say, I lost a lot of commissions that year.

The following year when the "Yellow Book" was distributed, I quickly found out that many of our customers liked the book. The "Red Book" listed telephone numbers only for funeral directors who advertised in the directory; other funeral homes were only listed with an address. The new "Yellow Book" had telephone numbers for every funeral home in the directory.

Harry said that if we provided telephone numbers, funeral directors wouldn't need to buy ads. This kind of thinking was a great example of putting the company's interests ahead of the customers' needs! If a family was making an arrangement for burial in another location, and was requesting use of a funeral home that didn't have an ad in the "Red Book," the book was useless for the director making the arrangements because there was no phone number listed. When Jack took over the directory he started the process of modernizing the format to create a superior book.

I haven't mentioned that the *American Funeral Director* magazine was also publishing a directory, called the "Blue Book." It suffered from all the same faults as the old "Red Book." It had been published for many years, but the management of the company paid little attention to the directory because their focus was on magazine advertising. The "Red Book" had one great advantage over its two competitors because it was the only directory with a national sales force of salesmen who called on their customers once a year. This also enabled us to keep the directory up to date because when changes occurred in our territories, we learned about them first. Part of my job was to keep the information in my territory current.

When I took the job representing the "Red Book," I expected to take a cut in income. Amazingly, we lived comfortably on what I earned selling the "Red Book." The work really suited me because I was not an employee. As long as I completed my work by the deadline, I could schedule my work any way that suited me best. I had a great incentive to work because much of the time when I left the customer's office I had a check in my pocket and knew that more than half of it was mine.

CHAPTER 24

Charisma

Before all of these job changes, when I received another check from Time Inc. the next spring in spite of having been fired, I said to Mary that I would really like to buy a boat. Without our experience in Italy with the Lawrences on their cruising boat, I don't think I ever would have suggested it. Mary thought it was a good idea as well, so we started looking at ads. While I worked at *Life* and now at my new *Saturday Evening Post* job, I often traveled during several weekdays. When I returned home, I felt I should be with my family, not on a golf course. Our whole family could participate in boating.

We answered an ad for a 26-foot sailboat and drove to Vermilion, Ohio where it was docked. The boat was a New Horizon sloop built by Ray Green in Toledo, Ohio. Ray had worked for Owens Corning Fiberglass. He was one of the very earliest to build boats entirely of fiberglass. We bought the boat and named her *Charisma,* then only a theological term for the "gift of the spirit." Perhaps we should have called her "Life Savings," but we felt she was an inspired purchase. The man we bought her from asked us where we were going to keep her. We actually hadn't looked that far ahead. He suggested the Vermilion Yacht Club, where he was a member, so we took his advice and joined the club.

Even though the club was located about 40 miles west of our house, this turned out to be a very good decision. The Vermilion

Yacht Club was located at the mouth of the Vermilion River, where it flowed into Lake Erie, in an area of reclaimed land. The bottom had been dredged up and canals had been opened off the river. Small Cape Cod type houses lined the canals. The main club docks were located adjacent to the club property on two of the canals. The clubhouse faced the river, with a lawn leading to additional docks on the river itself. The building contained a large meeting space, two smaller lounges and a big double kitchen. The developer, when he deeded the land for the club, stipulated that no alcoholic beverages be consumed on club property. This prohibition was strictly enforced because violation could have resulted in the club losing the land. Because the club couldn't have a bar, it precluded having a restaurant which, in turn, discouraged social memberships. It was a family club and most members had boats at the docks. We did have some wonderful potluck parties, and members, if they wanted, could serve drinks on their boats.

Even though we had to drive 40 miles, when we reached the club, we were within easy sailing distance of the Lake Erie islands. On Friday afternoon, when I arrived from work, we would load the kids into the car along with provisions for the weekend and drive to the club. Put-in-Bay, the Bass Islands and Canadian Pelee Island were close enough for weekend cruises. From the start, going places was our preference.

We had taught ourselves to sail at our cottage, on a Sailfish, a small sailing surfboard. When we bought *Charisma,* we had never sailed a boat with a jib! The sailing book that I bought wasn't easy for us to follow because we didn't know any of the terminology. I didn't know the difference between a sheet and a halyard. For four years, we sailed on Lake Erie and studied boating. By now I was totally hooked on sailing and Mary was going along. We took the Power Squadron courses and read all of the sailing books we could find. Gradually we became more competent.

We made our first long cruise, from Cleveland through the Welland Canal and the St. Lawrence Seaway, to Montréal and "Expo," the 1967 World's Fair. We sailed an acquaintance's 32-foot sloop to the fair, and he brought it back. Three of our four children went with us. We had a wonderful time. This trip was the catalyst that brought about my attack of "South Sea Island Syndrome."

CHAPTER 25

Golconda

In my early fifties, I was exhibiting all of the symptoms of male midlife crisis. I was tired of my job. Early signs of aging made me aware that I was not immortal. I longed for a change. The lure of exotic places and adventure was becoming irresistible. The "South Sea Island Syndrome" was taking over my life. I needed to do something before it was too late. It could have happened any day; any little problem could have set the wheels in motion. It happened on a Sunday in May 1968. Mary was not feeling well, so I went to church alone. I should have been concentrating on the sermon, but my thoughts were spinning elsewhere. Suddenly the idea was there. We'll sell our boat, the house, and the cars, buy a larger boat, and spend a year and two summers sailing in the Caribbean. The children could go with us. It would be a great learning experience for all of us!

I broached the subject at Sunday dinner. As when I first suggested buying a boat, Mary, to my surprise, once again acquiesced. Perhaps if she had offered resistance to my scheme, the symptoms would have subsided and life would have continued on its normal course. She must have had tremendous faith in me, or a sense of adventure that I had not yet discovered. With her approval, we rushed headlong into a screwball adventure. We planned our departure for spring of the following year.

Our children, with one exception, fell into line. Only Beth, our 13-year-old daughter, who was bound for high school the next year, while outwardly agreeing to the plan, decided that no matter what, she wasn't going along. Jim, 18, would graduate from high school that spring and had no college plans. David and Connie, our older children, had finished their education. Both had been living away from home for two years but enthusiastically agreed to join us.

The boat search began. Mary felt that it was important, with four children, three of them adults, that we have many separate cabins. This meant a large boat. There was only one problem; we didn't have a large budget. This meant a large cheap boat. Using the listings in the back of *Yachting* magazine, I called brokers. Boat descriptions arrived in the mail. They were either too small or too expensive. One affluent owner actually flew son Jim and me, in his private plane, to the Palmer Johnson boatyard in Wisconsin to view an exquisitely restored wooden schooner. It turned out to be both too small and too expensive.

On the telephone, an East Coast broker was running though his listings: "Here's a nice-looking sloop; I don't suppose you could possibly spend a little more than the figure you quoted?"

"No," I said.

"Here is a funny-looking"... he quickly corrected himself ... "an interesting-looking boat in your price range," he said, and continued to describe her. "Please send pictures and information," I replied. The die was cast.

Illuminated by the soft early morning sunlight, *Golconda* lay at the end of a pier in the Brielle, New Jersey harbor. Dew glistened on her rigging. Her owner was already on deck with a mop swabbing the teak decks. I was transfixed. The boat ignited my dreams of faraway places. Here was a boat on which to build dreams, and she could be mine. I lusted for her. Reason was replaced by passion. We had an appointment with the broker later in the morning to inspect her. I had been too excited that morning to stay in bed, so I had left my sleeping family in the motel, to walk to the dock for a preliminary look at her.

We agreed to buy her later that morning. Perhaps if I had been more experienced or if I had commissioned a proper marine survey, reason would have prevailed, but I doubt it. Love is not easily dissuaded, and I had fallen hopelessly in love with *Golconda* at first sight that morning. Named for the fabled Indian city of vast riches, *Golconda* was a 50-foot-long Danish-built motorsailer. Completed in 1948, not long after World War II, she was built, as a yacht, by a yard that had previously specialized in North Sea fishing trawlers. Her construction was massive. Two-inch larch planking was laid on four-by-four-inch frames, spaced on eight-inch centers. She displaced 32 tons. She was rigged as a gaff ketch. Like most motorsailers, she carried a very moderate sail plan for her displacement.

Her lines were those of a North Sea trawler. She was double-ended with low freeboard aft and a very pronounced shear, ending in a high buff bow. Teak bulwarks surrounded her teak decks. An incongruously prominent aluminum deckhouse was located about two-thirds of the way aft. Her wheel and controls were located on the aft side of the deckhouse behind a windshield affixed to the top of the house. She drew six feet of water with a long straight keel. A massive variable pitch propeller was well protected by a skeg and rudder. Her bottom was sheathed with copper against ship worms.

Later that morning we were taken aboard by the yacht broker and introduced to the owner. *Golconda* had passed through a number of hands. She had been sailed as a charter boat in the West Indies until the present owner purchased her. He was a small, wiry man with a cultured English accent. His partner or wife (one often cannot be certain in the cruising world) was an attractive, shapely young French woman in a fetching bikini. Perhaps if I had looked at her less and the boat more, the outcome of our visit might have been different.

The deckhouse interior was impressive. It featured fluted mahogany paneling, a marble-faced fireplace, and a large mahogany table. An impressive rack of radio transmitters and receivers, a chart table, and a beautiful flag locker added to the nautical ambiance of the cabin.

The sleeping cabins were forward, down five steps. The toilet was located to starboard, just aft of the companionway. Forward of the head was a single cabin with a bunk and dresser. A cabin with double-decker bunks and a dresser was located on the port side. The owner's cabin stretched across the entire width of the boat. It featured luxurious twin bunks, port and starboard, flanked by two hanging lockers and a dressing table with a large mirror. By lifting the hinged dresser top and swinging the mirror, one gained access to the crew quarters in the forepeak with two more bunks. The crew cabin was also accessible through a hatch in the foredeck. A chain locker was located in the forepeak.

Two deck hatches were positioned just aft of the deckhouse. One led, down a steeply inclined ladder, to the captain's cabin with two bunks, dresser and head. The second hatch led down a similar seven-step ladder to the galley and engine room. Mary said later, "The galley must have been designed for a Chinese cook who stayed there for the duration of the voyage." All the food had to be passed up the companionway, where it was exposed to the weather, until it reached the deckhouse. A two-burner propane hot plate and small gas refrigerator were located opposite the companionway. Portside were cupboards and the sink. We quickly decided that we would move the galley into the deckhouse.

A lifting shelf and door led from the galley to the impressive engine room. A massive four-cycle, two-cylinder, 100-horsepower Burmeister & Waine ship's diesel dominated the center of the room. Textured steel plates covered the bilge below. There was standing headroom with space to walk around three sides of the engine, which was covered with a jungle of glycerin-filled tubes, pipes, and other mysterious levers, valves, and pumps. Two large compressed air cylinders were located on the forward bulkhead. Behind the engine was a rusty-looking small 24-volt diesel generator. Large iron 250-gallon diesel fuel tanks were located against the port and starboard bulkheads. Sensing my resistance to this monstrous engine, the broker said, "These low RPM diesels will run forever. The owner will show you all about it. It really isn't as complicated as it looks."

The whole scene terrified me. I had never before had to contend with anything except a small 25-horsepower gasoline engine. Nevertheless, that afternoon I agreed to buy the boat and gave the broker a check to bind the sale. He said he would hold all the funds until the final paperwork was completed. We had no idea how fortunate this was. We learned later that the owner had already taken deposits from two other people. We were fortunate that we had purchased *Golconda* through a broker because we got the bill of sale papers.

We took delivery of *Golconda* early in July. With us, as crew, were daughter Beth, 13; son Jim, 17; our nephew David, 16; and Dick, a friend the same age. Our daughter Connie joined us in New York City for the trip back to Lake Erie, where we planned to prepare the boat for our "great adventure."

Our introductory trip out of the harbor, with the previous owner, was a forerunner of things to come. He took me below to introduce me to the process of starting the engine. A process it was, taking about ten minutes to accomplish. First I opened the compression releases for the two cylinders. Then I inserted a crowbar into holes in the massive four-foot iron flywheel and rotated it until an arrow, inscribed on its rim, was on top. This positioned the piston in the starting cylinder at the top. I closed the compression releases. Next I disengaged the fuel injector for that cylinder. In a series of steps, I turned on the water pump and primer valve, and then opened the compressed air valve on the engine. Next I pumped up the engine oil pressure, with a hand pump, and opened the valve on top of one of the compressed air tanks. Finally I was ready to pull the starter valve. This released a blast of compressed air into the starting cylinder, forcing down the piston. With a wheeze and a groan, the engine gasped into life with a thump, thump, thump as it ran on one cylinder. When I engaged the second injector, the frequency of thumps doubled. Now all that remained was to reverse the procedure and use the number one cylinder to recharge the compressed air tank.

On the bridge, the previous owner then introduced me to the controls. *Golconda* had no reverse gear! A 12-inch wheel on the bridge changed the variable pitch propeller, in stages, from forward to reverse. We were to learn that when she was going slowly enough to stop, there was very little steerage. When she was going fast enough to steer, she was almost impossible to stop quickly. The throttle, another smaller wheel, changed the RPM from about 75 to 400. We cruised at 350 and maneuvered at 250 RPM.

On our demonstration cruise, we took *Golconda* through the narrow opening of the railroad swing bridge out into the open Atlantic Ocean where, several minutes later, the engine stopped. There was no warning when it quit; it went from thumping along to total silence in an instant. "There is nothing to worry about," the previous owner assured me. "We just replaced a fuel line which was crushed by a falling floor plate. It's just a little air in the fuel line; I'll show you how to bleed the engine." Today this would have set off mental alarm bells, but in my infatuation and ignorance, I didn't have enough knowledge to anticipate our future problems.

Two weeks later we arrived to take delivery on our boat, prepared to take her back to the Great Lakes. After unloading an automobile full of supplies aboard the boat, we set sail for New York City and the Hudson River. We passed through the swing bridge channel, which seemed much narrower now, with me, white-knuckled, at huge *Golconda*'s helm. Once again, only about 30 minutes after we entered the Atlantic, the engine quit. We hoisted the sails, which we discovered were a mismatched assortment of Dacron, obviously made for other boats. Even so, Mary managed to make about two knots toward our destination while I went below into the engine room, where I found the problem. A piston pump, powered by a cam on the engine, transferred fuel from the main tanks to a two-gallon day tank above the engine. This small tank, with a sight gauge on its side, fed the injectors by gravity. Every once in a while, the transfer pump would stop working and the sight gauge would show that the fuel had stopped being transferred. When the day tank ran dry, the engine would stop. To start the engine again involved not only the usual starting procedure, but also a completely new one.

First I would loosen a junction in the fuel line from the main tank and fill a small plastic pail with diesel oil. Next I transferred this fuel to a little watering can with a spout small enough to reach a small hole in the top of the day tank. Once the day tank was full, I could begin the usual starting procedure. The engine ran until the next time the fuel in the day tank ran dry. There was no way to anticipate this event. It could run for days, then suddenly quit several times in a row. The only way to prevent engine failure was to catch the declining level in the sight gauge and hand-fill the tank before it ran dry. When her engine was running, *Golconda* chugged along at about ten knots, so we planned a daylight trip to New York City and the 79th Street Marina on the Hudson River. The engine stopped again in the middle of New York Harbor, so Mary sailed slowly through the busy harbor for about 20 minutes while I got it going again.

We arrived at the marina in the early evening. I had made reservations, but the man who had taken them obviously hadn't bothered to tell the "night man." We talked by bullhorn. He assigned us a slip. The marina in those days had a narrow entrance that led to an almost circular harbor with large yachts docked, stern-to, around its parameter. The sharp bows of the yachts reminded me of the teeth in a shark's mouth. Our slip was just inside the entrance so that I had to enter, then quickly make a sharp turn to starboard. I didn't even think of backing in. I was so frightened that my knees felt weak. I had never docked *Golconda* before.

Somehow I managed to avoid the docked boats and put *Golconda*'s bow into the slip entrance. Immediately, it became apparent that there was no way we could use this slip; the opening was much too narrow for our boat. The dockhand said that this was his last slip.

"Why don't you pick up one of the moorings in the river?" he said.

"Which one?" I asked.

"Any of them will be OK," he replied.

Now all I had to do was to turn *Golconda* around in the basin, which seemed smaller than my boat. Somehow we managed to avoid the shark's teeth and headed out into the river, where we picked out a substantial-looking mooring and moored for the first time in my boating life. We shut down the engine and relaxed.

While all this had been going on, Mary had been preparing dinner. We settled down to eat, greatly relieved that we had survived the first leg of our journey. Suddenly a loud voice boomed into our cabin. "You're on our mooring." I jumped up and looked outside. Close to us was a very large yacht, which was the source of the voice.

I called out, "Could you possibly use another mooring for the night?"

"No," his voice boomed, "this is a special heavy-duty mooring."

"OK," I said, "it will take me about twenty minutes to start the engine," and headed below.

Our daughter Connie joined us in New York City. We learned later that she was greatly dismayed when she saw *Golconda* but hid her concern. The city and the boat were very hot, but by now we had become used to the peculiar odor aboard, created by a blend of rot, mold and diesel oil. From our mooring in the Hudson, we watched the same familiar garbage floating by our boat, on the rising and falling tide. We turned our teenagers loose in the city while we taxied from the marina to a marine supply store. We purchased a large Danforth anchor and line to use for emergency engine failures. Our heavy main anchor and chain were too cumbersome to deploy quickly.

By now we were noticing other peculiar things about the boat. There were two extra teak steering wheels aboard. None of the radios were functional and the loran had no power cord. The serial numbers had been ground off two scuba regulators. There were numerous other items and tools aboard that were often duplicated or didn't seem to make sense. It was puzzling—but we were learning!

Our trip up the beautiful Hudson River went well. The engine failed only once on our way to Catskill, where we had been told there was a boatyard that would pull our masts and secure them on deck for the trip though the Erie Barge Canal. Pulling the heavy masts out of the boat was not easy, but it should have been. *Golconda* had been designed to go under low bridges. The masts were stepped on deck in tabernacles, which would allow them to be folded down. The windshield also folded, to allow the mast to rest on the cabin top. Unfortunately, a previous owner had added a rigid top to the windshield, making it impossible to do any of these things. So the yard spent hours freeing the heavy masts. Years of paint and corrosion had to be removed before the masts were finally pulled from the tabernacles and secured horizontally, on temporary wooden supports, on deck.

The Erie Barge Canal winds its way from the Hudson River at Troy through northern New York State until it branches at Three Rivers, where it joins the Oswego Canal, which leads on to Lake Ontario. The Erie Canal continues to Lake Erie. Thirty-five locks lift traveling boats 300 feet. It was an exciting trip. Sometimes it was difficult to find a place to tie up our 50-foot-long, six-foot-draft boat. By now, I had practiced maneuvering enough so that every stop was no longer a nail-biting experience. We had learned to use spring lines to bring the boat into a dock. I no longer had to bellow at my inexperienced crew. Connie was greatly relieved. Earlier she had complained to Mary, "Mother, you just have to stop Daddy from yelling at the boys."

At one port, we had a mechanic work on our fuel pump. Although he totally disassembled and reassembled the pump, it didn't help a bit. No one suggested that a small electric pump in the fuel line would have solved our problem, and I wasn't experienced enough to think of it.

We had looked forward to visiting my brother Bob, who lived walking distance from the canal in suburban Rochester. We were only two locks from there when we went aground. At many of the locks we had to wait while the lockmaster emptied the lock to lower the water to our level. Usually this presented no problem, but this time I got the boat too close to the lock gates. A final, small surge of water, as the gates opened, caught the bow of our boat and very neatly turned us around so that we were facing down the canal. When I turned to bring us back to the right direction, I got too close to the canal bank and we became grounded. Sixty-four thousand pounds of *Golconda* was securely fastened to the bottom of the canal!

We tried everything to get loose. Full reverse just muddied the water. We launched our dinghy, took our Danforth anchor to the middle of the canal, and led our new nylon line to our large hydraulic windlass. Danforth anchors were invented to pull landing crafts off the beaches in World War II, so we were asking it only to do that for which it was designed. The anchor dug in and we pulled until the nylon had stretched to the danger point. If it had snapped, it would have acted like a huge whip. We gave up on that approach. When we eventually got free, the anchor had dug in so deeply that we couldn't get it up. We had to cut the line and leave our new anchor in the canal.

All this time, we had been communicating with the lock keeper by bullhorn. He said that he had two powerboats approaching in the canal whom he would ask to circle us and try to rock us free. Their wakes hit *Golconda* as if she was a stone wall; nothing moved. When none of our efforts had succeeded, the lock keeper called, "Well, I guess we will just have to raise the water level in the canal." Three hours later *Golconda* gently floated free. We were poor guests when we finally reached my brother's house in Rochester; all we were interested in was showers and food.

There was only one place to re-step masts, at Tonawanda, near Buffalo, where the canal joins Lake Erie. We were dismayed when we saw the equipment they were going to use. They had an ancient truck frame and motor with a tripod and windlass mounted on the truck's back. We need not have worried; they had lots of experience and quickly and efficiently put the heavy masts back in the boat.

Our arrival at the Vermilion Yacht Club dock was not met with great enthusiasm. One member, whose house was located on the lagoon where we tied up, complained that we were blocking his view. Other members' attitudes might have been colored by the fact that, shortly after we arrived, we had to hire a fumigator to kill five different varieties of cockroaches aboard our boat. He was impressed by the variety. We discovered what had been causing the nighttime scrapings and rustlings.

Shortly after we returned home, we received two telephone calls. The first call was from an FBI agent, who was looking for the previous owner who was being accused of stealing two boats on the Intracoastal Waterway. Also, it seemed that he had taken two other deposits on *Golconda* before ours. Our deposit, however, was held by the broker pending transfer of the papers, so we were lucky—we got the boat. However, by this time we were beginning to wonder if we were really the lucky ones.

The second caller had a cultured English accent.

"Are you the people who purchased *Golconda*?" he asked.

I said "Yes."

"Well, my name is Michael Pym, and you bought her right out from under me," he continued. "What are your plans for her?"

I told him about our proposed trip, and he asked if it would be all right if he kept in touch. I said that would be fine, we chatted for a while, and that was that.

I spent all of that summer and into the fall working on the boat. The jobs seemed endless. We found electric wires that contained nothing but insulation, with green dust in the center.

There were plumbing pipes that led nowhere. The decks leaked and I tried to caulk them. I learned later that if I had just kept them wet regularly they would have closed themselves. It was discouraging and tiring. We purchased new sails.

By fall, after we laid the boat up for the winter, I was having serious back problems. If it is possible to have psychosomatic disk erosion, that's what I had. Subconsciously I realized that we were in over our heads and were trying to find a way out of our "dream trip." In February I found myself in the hospital recuperating from surgery for a spinal fusion operation on my back. I was faced with one month flat on my back followed by many months in a back brace. The trip would be impossible!

Only two days after the operation, when I was still on pain medicine and somewhat groggy, the phone rang. A familiar voice said, "Mr. Boynton, this is Michael Pym. I'm so sorry to hear about your surgery. Does this mean that you won't be able to make your trip?"

I said "Yes."

"Does this mean that *Golconda* will be for sale?"

Again, I said "Yes."

"Fine, I'll buy her," he replied. I floated one foot off the bed! All my problems were solved, or so I thought. He asked if a deposit would hold her for him until spring. I agreed, and, two days later, a sizable deposit appeared in my bank account. He committed to purchase the boat without having seen her for a year.

When spring arrived, Michael called to apologize; he couldn't raise the balance of the payment for the boat. He had planned on money from sales commissions, which had not materialized. We were forced to find a buyer for a large ocean-going boat located on Lake Erie. It took us two more years to find that person.

We showed *Golconda* to an amazing number of dreamers ranging from the sad to the ridiculous. A young man who had had six heart attacks dreamed of a world trip. One Sunday morning a very inebriated elderly man arrived, accompanied by two very embarrassed sons, and insisted on seeing the boat. He had never owned any kind of boat but was certain he could take it to the islands. My only concern was getting him on and off the boat before he killed himself.

I advertised in newspapers all over the lakes and finally found a real buyer. A gentleman in his sixties, from Chicago and about to retire, arrived with his much younger wife, and we reached an agreement. He had been a Navy deck officer in World War II but had no small boat experience and never had sailed. He said he had experienced crew to help him get the boat to Chicago. When he arrived with only his wife, I offered to get him some free crew. He demurred and said that they would do it alone. They left the next morning, and *Golconda* vanished at last from our life. All that was left was a piece of rusted metal on the dock. I picked it up and kept it for several years as a reminder of past follies.

Our experience with *Golconda* was sometimes exciting, sometimes painful, and above all, expensive. By the time we were finished owning *Golconda* she had cost us, in those days, the equivalent of a year's tuition in college. But we certainly got an education in boat ownership! Ultimately we sold our next cruising boat for a profit which almost exactly matched what we had lost with *Golconda*.

Aboard "Golconda"

Flying Junior (FJ)

Hinkley Sou'Wester
"Cynosure"

Bristol 33 "Cynosure"

"Mary Constance Under Sail"

Kaiser Christina Ketch
"Mary Constance"

CHAPTER 26

Racing and Beyond

We still were hooked on sailing, so we purchased a 14-foot, one-design Flying Junior sailboat which we raced on LaDue Reservoir near our home. A new boat dealer, located near the reservoir, had sold enough Flying Juniors so that there were enough boats for weekly Sunday afternoon races. Everyone, with our exception, was a novice. Even though we were probably twice the age of any other crew, we never lost a race for two years. Others raced for second place. We found ourselves teaching as well as participating. We owned our FJ until about a year ago. Our son sailed it for years in the Chesapeake Bay area.

In 1972, I saw an ad in the newspaper advertising a Hinckley sailboat. When I called to inquire about the boat, the first thing the man who answered said was "Of course you know it's an old wooden boat." Wow! He didn't mention Hinckley who, even today, is a premier boat builder. I was able to buy it for a small amount of money. It was owned by two brothers with very wealthy parents. They had used it as a playpen until they married. It no longer interested them.

We named the boat *Cynosure,* an archaic name for the North Star. It is also described in the dictionary as "a center of attraction." My wife and I sailed her for five summers, from Cleveland up the Detroit River into Lake Huron and Georgian Bay and back. She was a 34-foot Hinckley Sou'wester sloop and sailed well. She had a 25-horsepower Universal Atomic Four gasoline engine. The boat had one major problem: it leaked. An earlier owner had raced the boat. One spring, when the boat had dried out over the winter, he caulked the open seams in the hull with hard caulking compound to make a smooth racing bottom. When the boat was launched, as wooden boats do, the wood swelled. The hard caulking compound compressed the wood, which as a result never regained its natural elasticity. After sitting at the dock for a few days the boat hardly leaked at all; however, when we were sailing upwind, with the boat heeled over, the stressed hull took on a lot of water. We had two high-capacity pumps aboard, and at times one would run constantly while the other cycled. There was another problem which we were unable to fix. The engine cooling system discharged its water through the muffler along with the engine exhaust. This problem occurred when we were tacking with the boat heeled over and the exhaust pipe would scoop up a small amount of water. Then when we tacked and heeled in the other direction, the water entered through the exhaust and into the engine. We were never able to prevent this but solved the problem by starting the engine, which then blew out the offending water before we tacked.

In spite of her problems, we loved *Cynosure,* and she gave us many wonderful experiences. We joined the Great Lakes Cruising Club, a large organization, which publishes complete information about many of the best places to explore. Using their guides, we discovered many of the wonderful uncharted anchoring places in the Georgian Bay. One time we cautiously entered the narrow entrance to a one-acre cove, where the

Cruising Guide said there was ample depth except for one very small spot with a submerged rock. We found the rock when *Cynosure* ran into it. We were moving very slowly, and the only things damaged were our egos. Later we tried to find the spot again with our dinghy, with no success.

We attended three Cruising Club rallies in Georgian Bay harbors with dozens of other boats. The last rally was held in Parry Sound. There we met George and Margaret Vilas, who were guests on a friend's boat. They kept their own boat in the Bras d'Or Lakes in Cape Breton, Nova Scotia. We tucked this bit of information away in our memories.

We met Ken and Jean Moore when our boats were anchored in the Pool at Bay Finn, a very small anchorage. They were on a small sailboat and visited us aboard our boat. They were so impressed by our boat that they purchased one just like ours and joined our yacht club. We made one of our trips in tandem from Vermilion all the way to our cottage near Parry Sound. They were unsure of their abilities. We enjoyed their company but found it difficult to be the "mother duck." Sailing with other boats obligated a "leader" to stay with them in case of a mechanical failure or any hesitancy to depart. This could be for various reasons, or sometimes simply because they overslept and couldn't leave at what we had determined was the best time. Therefore, if at all possible, we never sailed in company with another boat. We would simply say that we could meet them at a certain destination as long as we were able to arrive while they were there.

While sailing in the heavily trafficked Detroit River to Lake Huron, we learned a lot and had what I still believe was our most frightening boating experience. It was imperative to stay clear of the large freighters plying the water. Often they were in dredged channels and had no room to maneuver; also it took them a very long time to stop. We were crossing the river from one side to the other, under power, when our engine stopped. A huge freighter traveling with the current was headed toward us. Fortunately, we also had one sail up and managed to clear the channel just minutes before she passed us with her whistle blowing. We learned that the speed of a large vessel is difficult to judge.

All of the water from Lake Huron, Lake Michigan, and Lake Superior flows under the Blue Water Bridge. Often headwinds make it necessary to go under the bridge under power. The first time we tried to pass under the bridge, we could make no headway. The current was stronger than our small engine. While we were struggling to move forward in the center of the river, we saw a small sailboat near the shore happily moving in the direction we wanted to go. We realized that sailor knew something that we didn't, so we headed close to the shore, where we found an eddy in the current which carried us under the bridge. With our new knowledge, we passed under the bridge several more times, in future trips, with no problem.

In 1976, the year of our country's Bicentennial celebration, we had hoped to sail our Hinckley to New York Harbor, by way of the Erie Canal, to watch the Tall Ship Sail-in celebration. I was now selling the "Red Book," so we could take all summer for the trip. Our plan didn't work only because we couldn't find anyone to fix our exhaust problem in time for us to go. So we once more headed up to our cottage, which by this time was up for sale.

Our joint decision to sell Dobote was a sad one. By this time, my mother's health and my father's advancing age made it no longer possible for them to go to the cottage. My brother Bob had moved to California, and my other brother Doug had married a very nice lady who had five children. She felt vacations should be spent somewhere where she could be waited on, not roughing it in a cottage. Mary and I were more interested in sailing to interesting places than in staying at the cottage. None of the next generation of our families had either the time or the money to maintain the property. We quickly found a buyer and were really delighted to be able to sell the property to a Canadian family. After all, it was their lovely views and waters that we had enjoyed all those years.

In the fall of 1974 my mother began showing the early symptoms of Alzheimer's Disease. Sensing the inevitable, my father moved them from Naples, Florida to Shell Point Village, a total care retirement community. I am writing this from an apartment in the same community.

In the fall, we left *Cynosure* on shore for the winter, in a marina close to downtown Cleveland. Mary said that she would like to sail all the way down the St. Lawrence Seaway to the ocean and then to the Bras d'Or Lakes in Nova Scotia. However, we felt uncomfortable about making the trip in *Cynosure* with her continuing problems.

At the same boatyard where we left our boat, we found our next boat. She was a fiberglass 1969 Bristol 33 sloop. Although she was a foot smaller than *Cynosure,* she had a longer waterline and actually had larger accommodations. She had a table which could be lowered to make a berth; there were V berths in the bow, and a settee berth opposite the table. It also had an Atomic

Four gasoline engine which was located in the bilge, in the center of the boat under the raised table. We hired a marine surveyor who found her in good condition with no serious flaws. The yard which had brokered the sale agreed to keep her stored inside until spring at no cost. We kept the same name and received a Coast Guard Certificate for *Cynosure* in May 1977. I told the boatyard that they could broker our old boat.

That same fall, my mother died in the memory care unit of the Shell Point nursing pavilion. My father insisted that before she began to fail, she had said that she wanted no memorial service.

CHAPTER 27

Down to the Sea

After we returned to Cleveland from our business travel, we immediately went to see our new boat. We had expected to find her in the shed and were surprised to discover her outdoors in the yard. But we secured a ladder and climbed aboard. When we opened the hatch, we discovered the entire cabin sole (floor) covered with iridescent gray water. It took us a short time to realize that the engine in the bilge must be submerged as well. We learned that the yard manager had moved the boat out of the shed early in the spring. What he didn't realize was that one of the cockpit drains had not been connected. They had the usual spring snow fall and rain, and all of the collected water had flowed into the boat.

Even a distressing situation such as this can sometimes work out well. The boatyard paid to have our engine overhauled, and we got new brown carpet to replace the gaudy bright orange one that had been ruined. They did a great job of laying the new carpet because they had previously been carpet layers. We felt they knew more about installing carpet than about running a boat yard.

Once we had our new boat at the dock in the Vermilion Yacht Club, we worked feverishly to get her ready for our long-awaited St. Lawrence Seaway trip. My brother Bob, after reading one of our trip stories, said "It seems to me that sailboat cruising consists mainly of fixing things." This was certainly true of

Cynosure B. (We referred to our new boat as *Cynosure B* for Bristol and the previous boat as *Cynosure H* for Hinckley.) Mary kept a journal on most of our trips and in 1977 kept a list of all the things we did to make the boat ready and comfortable for cruising. There are 46 entries. Some of the changes were made before we left; others were accomplished during the trip. I am going to list them here. For any non-sailor who might be reading this someday, you can skip this.

Installed a cockpit dodger (a collapsible cover over the companionway)

Rebuilt the sunshade (a large awning used at anchor to cover much of the boat from sun and rain)

Removed five cushions (there were far too many cushions in the cabin)

Added four sleeping pillows

Sewed new curtains and mounted them on a track above the ports

Built a shelf over the wet locker

Built a cupboard for bedding and linen over the hanging locker

Moved the clutch and throttle controls to the steering wheel pedestal

Reworked our "First Mate" (autopilot for wheel steering)

Chocked a large anchor on the foredeck

Installed a mahogany ceiling in the cabin

Mounted a fan and our clocks and pictures

Added a depth sounder

Added two radios

Installed a CB radio and stereo tape player

Installed a Sumlog (this measured distance through the water)

Remade the lampshade for the oil lamp

Covered the ceiling above the Aladdin lamp with aluminum-covered asbestos

Added a new hand bilge pump

Added controls for the automatic bilge pump

Added a 20-gallon gasoline tank and gauges

Fixed a burner on the cooking stove

Varnished bulkheads

Varnished cockpit coamings

Had vinyl cockpit cushions made

Reset lifeline stanchions

Built a helm seat

Built a footrest attached to the steering wheel pedestal

Installed a Velcro screen for the main hatch

Purchased and installed screens for the opening portholes

Made a ventilated hatch for the companionway entrance

Added a dinghy and outboard engine

Added an inflatable life raft

Added a silver rack and paper towel holder

Mounted a prayer plaque

Installed a radio direction finder

Installed netting on the foredeck lifelines (to keep sails from falling overboard)

Installed fairleads on the mast (to prevent losing halyard bitter ends)

Added a handheld "Whistler" radar

Installed a cockpit power source for the radar

Moved the key starter and ignition switch close to the helm

Added a paper napkin rack

Hung a shoe bag in the hanging locker

Lined the galley shelves with contact plastic

Rewired the installed baseboard heaters to make them safe

Had the compass compensated

We left our yacht club dock at 11:00 a.m. on Tuesday, June 28, 1977. We only sailed as far as Cleveland. We stopped at Sailing Inc., the boatyard, to drop off some things that belonged to *Cynosure H,* and then motored around the breakwall to the Forest City Yacht Club where we met a man who compensated our compass. We spent the night at the club.

CHAPTER 28

The St. Lawrence Seaway

I'm not going to describe our trip in detail. I will try only to write about some of our more notable experiences. The St. Lawrence Seaway is the greatest inland waterway in the world. Stretching 2300 miles, it connects the Great Lakes to the Atlantic Ocean. Its locks lift large ocean-going vessels to the height of a 60-story building.

The Seaway links not only the cities of the Great Lakes, but also historic Canadian cities along the St. Lawrence River. We visited Kingston, Montréal, and Québec City on our way to the Gulf of St. Lawrence.

Our summer's trip took us from Vermilion, Ohio, down Lake Erie, and through the Welland Canal, bypassing Niagara Falls. Then we traveled the length of Lake Ontario into the St. Lawrence River, which flows through the Thousand Islands and the St. Lawrence Seaway locks, past Montréal and Québec City. We followed the shore of the Gaspé Peninsula into the Northumberland Strait, which separates Prince Edward Island from New Brunswick. Finally, we passed through the Strait of Canso and into the Bras d'Or Lakes in Cape Breton, Nova Scotia, where we left our boat for the winter.

Transiting the Welland Canal usually takes a full day; it is 28 miles long with eight locks which lower boats 326 feet. Even though we got in line at 6:00 a.m., we didn't enter the first lock until 2:00 p.m. Our engine broke down shortly after we left the first lock. I called Canal Control, and eventually a mechanic arrived and cleaned our carburetor. We resumed our passage several hours later. We finally exited the last lock at 3:30 a.m.

We had better luck passing through the six huge locks in the St. Lawrence River. The last lock is close to Montreal, and we motored to the Expo marina which was now a private yacht club. We managed to go aground inside the marina; "Le Barge" got us floating again, and we finally were tied up at a dock. The club members were very solicitous and concerned by our grounding. I should mention that an extremely important part of our cruising experience is the connections we make with fellow cruisers, and people ashore, with whom we have been privileged to spend time. Many of the pages in Mary's journal have names and addresses.

We spent three days in Montreal, sightseeing and shopping for boat equipment. Several repair parts, which we had arranged to be shipped to a local marine store, were waiting for us. We purchased the 20 Canadian charts which we had previously ordered by telephone. We shopped at a large supermarket, in the center of the city, located in the basement of the Hudson's Bay store. We always bought block ice for our ice box wherever we could find it. I owned a pair of ice tongs to move the heavy blocks. All was not work, however; we had several delicious meals in French restaurants.

Tidal water extends up the St. Lawrence River to halfway between Montreal and Quebec City, and it creates very high tides and strong currents. We found it important to time departures just before high tide, so that we could ride the ebb tide, which flows toward the sea.

It was hot in Montreal, so we started down the river at 4:15 p.m. We had no cruising guides below Montreal, or for the rest of the summer. On the navigation chart we found Lavaltrie, a town behind an island, with a small, high municipal dock. When we reached the dock, a young man caught our dock lines and helped us to tie up. At that time, there was considerable agitation in French-speaking Quebec Province about its separation from English-speaking Canada. The young man who took our lines spoke some English, and we invited him aboard our boat. In his broken English he explained that it might be noisy this evening on the dock, located at the end of the main street, because the teenagers "hung out" there. We assured him that we liked young people and their noise would not bother us. Sure enough, after we had finished our supper, they arrived and opened up their car doors, playing their radios as loud as possible. We waved to some of them to come aboard. We had dozens of young people aboard that evening. They were uniformly polite and very interested in the equipment we had on board. It was a wonderful experience, and after they left we had a quiet night.

Early the next morning, before we left, the young man who had helped us with our dock lines came down to the boat. He said to us, in his broken English, "You know we don't usually like people who speak English very much, but you won't have any trouble here." From that time on, whenever we docked, we always asked people on the dock if they would like to see our boat. They were usually boat owners, or people who would like to own a boat. We met some wonderful people this way. To ourselves we called this "the Lavaltrie System."

Below Montreal the scenery along the river was beautiful, with high cliffs along one side of the river. We were sailing with the current helping us and making wonderful time when we heard "The Star-Spangled Banner" booming out from the cliff top. Then we could see the United States Ensign hoisted along with the Canadian flag. We later learned that a retired naval officer watched the boats going by and, no matter what nationality was recognized, he was able to play their anthem through a loudspeaker and raise their flag.

We had a very enjoyable stay in Quebec City and didn't leave the Yacht Club until about 2:30 p.m. We had rain right from the start, but we had a great sail with the current until it turned, before arriving at our destination. However, the last miles, fighting the current, seemed to take forever. We finally got behind L'Isle-aux-Coudres and spotted the lighted government dock just before it began to pour and the fog closed in. We thought that they had turned off the lights! However, with the handheld radar and the depth sounder, we were able to find the harbor and to drop our anchor in 30 feet of water. This was the first time that we had used the radar for a blind approach.

The tides were huge now, 20 feet or more in this section of the St. Lawrence, and where we could, we tied alongside a larger boat and let them worry about the necessary long dock lines. In one harbor, we tied to a 50-foot Canadian Coast Guard boat. We also looked for large fishing boats and got quite good at locating ones that didn't seem to be active. If they were, we had to leave early in the morning so that they could depart on schedule. Another time we had no choice but to tie to a dock with 30-foot tides. At low tide I climbed a ladder, carrying long dock lines, securing the boat before we went to bed. I awoke very early the next morning to find our boat floating, at high tide, about 20 feet from the dock.

Anchoring in big tides is also tricky. With *Cynosure,* at high tide, we needed an anchor line six or seven times the depth of the water, part of it on chain. Usually this was sufficient to set the anchor. As the tide goes down, the boat has more line and the circle expands in which the boat can wander with the shifting wind and currents. At low tides, we had to take into consideration, in our calculations, the increase in the water depth as the boat rose. When picking a spot to anchor, these factors needed to be carefully calculated in order to stay clear of shallow water or other anchored boats. We always hoped that the other boats had also made these same calculations.

We sailed down the west coast of the St. Lawrence River, which became wider and wider as we proceeded downstream. I used a hand bearing compass to take bearings on the shore to determine our speed in the current. We plotted our position from identifiable locations on the chart. One of the things indicated on the chart were tall church steeples, but this wasn't much help in determining which town we were seeing because every town along the river had a tall church steeple.

We stopped at a small marina in Tadoussac, at the mouth of the Saguenay River. The next day we motored about 15 miles up the very spectacular Saguenay shore where we found a small cove, anchored, and spent a relaxed afternoon and a peaceful night. The next morning, as we returned down river, a young couple in an inflatable Zodiac dinghy pulled alongside our boat and asked if we had seen any whales. We replied that we hadn't, but as we left the river mouth, we were able to watch several all-white beluga whales and a very large humpback whale.

We saw many different pelagic seabirds on our journey, two being our favorites. We watched as one large streamlined bird dove, from about 50 feet above, straight down into the water. We learned that this was a gannet, a pelagic bird that lives at sea and only comes ashore to nest. The other bird was the puffin, a small swimming bird which disappears underwater only to reappear some distance away. They also are adept at taking off from the water. We found their antics very amusing whenever we approached them under sail. They were perfectly able to dive and swim out of our way or to take off and fly away. Instead they preferred to put on a total panic act with great fluttering of their wings. They would bounce from wave top to wave top moving away from our boat.

On August 3, 1968 we rounded the tip of the Gaspé Peninsula and sailed up the Bay of Gaspé to the Town of Gaspé, a beautiful spot at the end of a small sound, where we found a small yacht club and tied up at their dock. Opposite us on the same dock was a French boat, *Gallad,* which had just arrived after sailing nonstop from France with a crew of two young women, two young men, and the older captain. We spent a day in Gaspé visiting with the crew and the town police chief, who spoke excellent English and acted as our translator. Nearby, the crew of a training ship was using divers to bring up a large, very old wrought iron chain.

We left the next morning, and everyone was on the dock to wave goodbye. We motored and sailed down the 20-mile bay. At about 11:00 a.m. the fog rolled in and we suddenly had very limited visibility. We decided, however, to continue on. We had planned to go only a short distance to a harbor just around the point at the bay entrance. I had been plotting our position on the chart, so I knew our location and speed when the fog closed in. I felt confident that I could locate the point and the next harbor entrance buoys with my hand-held Whistler radar. This worked by pointing the radar using a compass. The radar sent out a signal which was returned as sound into earphones. The farther away the objects, the lower-pitched the sound; conversely, the closer the objects the higher-pitched the sound. Traveling along a shore, the signal was a rumbling sound; a buoy offshore stood out against this background as high-pitched chirping.

We continued on and in about 45 minutes, Mary checked the chart and said that we had come about ten miles, halfway to the entrance. Sometime later, when I scanned the shore with the radar, the shore signal stopped and I determined that this was the point at the bay entrance. I told Mary to turn in to round the point. I made two major mistakes! I relied on my new electronic "toy," radar, to set our course, instead of plotting our dead reckoning position on the chart, to account for the time traveled to confirm our position. The second bad mistake was that we had been in very deep water and so didn't have our depth sounder turned on.

In about five minutes, we had run up on the submerged rocks along the shore. It took us about ten minutes to extricate ourselves from the rocks and, in the disorientating fog, to plot a course which would take us away from the shore. It was a frightening learning experience. The pounding on the rocks had stirred up sediment from the bottom of our fuel tank, and our engine was running very roughly.

I checked the bilge and we didn't seem to be taking on any water, but I felt that we had to have the bottom checked, so we headed back to Gaspé. The fog lifted before we reached the town. I was able to get one of the divers who had been working on the chain to check the bottom of our boat. He found one small gouge that he repaired with two-part underwater putty that I had aboard our boat. When we had the boat hauled at the end of the summer, the patch was still smooth and hard.

I was a very mortified captain when we arrived back at the yacht club. We spent the next day at the dock while I disassembled and cleaned the carburetor and fuel line. That same day the second French boat, *Lomilot,* arrived. We learned that the captain planned to base a sailing training school in Gaspé.

We later stopped at the fishing town of Lamèque. A man on the dock, who took our lines, asked us if we needed a car for anything. We thanked him, said no, and asked him aboard. He returned later and asked us to have dinner at his home. Roger and Rejeamaine Noel and their four children served us cold lobster and crab and potato salad with blueberry pie for dessert. This was a taste of the hospitality which we experienced repeatedly from the people in the Maritimes.

We sailed for 28 hours down the Northumberland Channel to Prince Edward Island, where we stopped at Sunnyside and found a small yacht club. We were overwhelmed with friendly visitors on our boat and met Dick Wedge, who invited us to a lobster boil at a cottage on the other side of the island. It was a wonderful party and we both ate all the lobster we could manage. We discovered that it was the first day of the lobster season and many of the men at the party were lobstermen. We were allowed to pay our share of the feast; it was $11 for the two of us. I calculated that we had consumed $90 worth of lobster at Stateside prices.

Dick Wedge told us a funny story about one of their yacht club cruises. They anchored one night in a harbor with a fish processing factory. These factories supply crushed ice for the fishing boats. Dick volunteered to get ice for their fleet. The man at the dock said he would have to charge for ice. When Dick asked how much it would cost, the man quoted a price by the ton. Dick did some quick calculations and said he would like 50 cents' worth. With that, they lowered the ice chute and filled his cockpit to the top. Dick said that he had enough ice for the fleet and still left several floating patches of ice in the harbor. I could just imagine the factory man telling his buddies about this at the local pub. Most of the time we found that fish factories were happy to give us ice at little or no charge.

On August 15, the day after Mary's birthday, we sailed across the Northumberland Strait and anchored in Ballantynes Cove on Cape George, Nova Scotia. Almost seven weeks to the day after setting out, we had reached our goal.

The Strait of Canso separates Cape Breton from the rest of Nova Scotia. A few days later we passed through a tidal control lock into the strait. A very large supertanker and a Russian freighter passed us going the other way. After leaving the strait, we anchored in lovely calm Janvrin's Harbour. We had rain, fog and wind the next day and stayed on the anchor. While there I received a call through the marine operator from Jack Schmidt at the "Red Book." He was offering a chance to cover some southern territory instead of New England. This would give us a warm place to work in the midwinter months. I accepted, and it turned out that I was able to make more money as a result of this switch.

When we left the anchorage, we soon encountered large ocean swells for the first time. When we entered the tidal lock in St. Peter's Canal, which leads to the saltwater Bras d'Or Lakes, we were greeted by the lockmaster who gave us refuse bags for our rubbish. The lakes offer wonderful scenery and many anchorages, and are largely protected from ocean winds and fog.

We arrived at Baddeck, our final destination, on Friday, August 19 and tied up to the government dock. According to our log, since we left the Vermilion Yacht Club, we had traveled 1476 nautical miles or about 1700 statute miles. That same day we arranged with Henry Fuller, owner of the Cape Breton Boatyard, to leave our boat there, on land, for the winter. He had purchased the old Pinot Boatyard the year before from the last of the Pinots.

The boatyard was already serving the area in 1885 when Alexander Graham Bell discovered Baddeck. Bell fell in love with the Bras d'Or Lakes and purchased a large tract of land there, on which he built two houses. Bell, a Scotsman who could speak Gaelic, named the property Beinn Bhreagh, meaning Beautiful Mountain. He built a laboratory on the property and did a lot of experimenting with very large kites, trying to understand aerodynamics. He also built high-speed hydrofoil boats, and for many years his boat held the record for the fastest speed over water. Henry Fuller found one of the hydrofoil engines in the rubble of the boatyard.

We found Carl and Margaret Vilas, who had told us about Baddeck, aboard their famous boat *Direction* on their mooring in the Washabuck River. *Direction*'s voyage to Greenland was described by artist Rockwell Kent in his book *N by E*.

We had thought that we would return home in a rental car but found it would be much too expensive, so we flew home from the Sydney airport. Many of the things that we were using on the boat we also needed in the motorhome, so when we reached the check-in counter at the airport, we had with us one suitcase and seven assorted cardboard boxes filled with dishes, pots and pans, utensils, and assorted hoses and electrical cords. The agent at the counter asked us where we had come from and how we had liked Nova Scotia. We answered "Very much" and explained that we had arrived by boat. All during this conversation, he was attaching baggage labels to our weird luggage. When he finished, he handed us our boarding passes and luggage receipt and hoped we'd have a nice trip without any mention of excess baggage. We transferred flights and cleared United States Customs in Toronto. The customs agent asked us what we had in our luggage, and when we explained the contents, she waved us on through without checking anything. Imagine the same trip today!

That fall we resumed our business-related motorhome travel. The introduction to our new state, Alabama, occurred at the first rest stop in the state. Mary went in to get an Alabama road map and was greeted by a life-size cardboard figure of the militant segregationist governor, George Wallace. A lady who stood looking at the picture said to Mary, "Isn't he wonderful!" Actually, in spite of this introduction, Alabama turned out to be our favorite state. Southern hospitality made my calls very pleasant. It also has some of the most beautiful state parks of any state we traveled.

At "Expo in "Montreal

"Saint Lawrence Seaway" Lock

St.Lawrence Artificial Harbor

Tied beside Fishing Boats
waiting out a Storrm

Mary on "Cynosure B"

Thomas on Ladder
at Low Tide

Entrance Lighthouse
at Saguenay River

CHAPTER 29

The South Coast

On June 24, 1978 we arrived, in our motorhome, back at our boat in Baddeck and found her on a boatyard mooring looking immaculate. We didn't leave the Bras d'Or Lakes until July 12. We spent the first days working on the boat.

On June 27 we had dinner with Harry and Mary Harper at their cottage. We had met them in the boatyard. That evening they asked us if we were going to sail the "south coast." We asked the south coast of what, and they told us Newfoundland. Their enthusiasm about Newfoundland changed our plans. We had planned to sail south, down the United States coast and back up through the Barge Canal to Lake Erie. That evening we decided to sail the south coast of Newfoundland instead. This was an important turning point in our lives. We didn't get back to fresh water for years.

On June 30, my father joined us for four days. We housed him in the motorhome and we slept on *Cynosure*. We watched a Canada Day celebration parade the next day before going sailing. We sailed to an interesting harbor in the morning, anchored for lunch, and then Dad took a nap. Later we sailed back to Baddeck, where one night the three of us were invited to dinner with new friends at their home. This visit with us was the last time that we had my father aboard our boat.

Sometimes people ask us if we don't get lonely on our trips to more remote places. Actually, our days were often very social. In just the year 1978, Mary had almost 40 names and addresses of people we had visited with on our boat, on their boats, or ashore. These were all people whom we had asked to give us their names and addresses. We had talked to probably as many more people in more casual conversations.

On July 12 we set out for Newfoundland. We sailed out of the Bras d'Or Lakes by the north entrance and then headed north to Ingonish harbor. The next evening we left our anchorage to cross the 90-mile Cabot Strait. We wanted to arrive at our destination, Port aux Basques, in the morning light, so we sailed overnight. The strait had a reputation for being very rough. We actually had a calm trip, with so little wind that we motored most of the way. We were about halfway across when we heard a voice on our VHF radio saying, "This is Seaway Control. Please to identify yourselves and your destination." We complied, and he told us he had us on his radar and would contact us on the hour. He did this and, close to Port aux Basques, told us to wait for a large ferry which was leaving the harbor. Then Control led us by voice to a dock where we could tie up. This was our introduction to the wild south coast of Newfoundland.

The next day we walked to the Seaway Control Station, where we were warmly welcomed by the radar operator. We spent almost two hours conversing with Jim Deveraux. He told us that this was a very new operation and that we had been one of their first contacts, made while they were calibrating their equipment.

Our trip the next day was very different! We worked our way in the fog, hugging the coast, toward an anchorage in Dublin Cove.

Once, we heard Seaway Control warning the *Marine Runner,* one of the high-speed motorboats serving the small outports along the south coast, that there was a small craft inshore of him. That was us! The fog lifted as we entered Dublin Cove, and we had a breathtaking view of the high sides of the cove and of a small waterfall cascading into the anchorage. Suddenly four small fishing boats appeared and ran circles around our boat as we anchored. It frightened us for a few moments until we realized that they were waving to us and smiling. After we had finished anchoring, a very young man asked us if he could hold onto our boat. I immediately said "Yes" and asked if he and his friends would like to come aboard. They were particularly interested in my handheld Whistler radar, which I demonstrated for them. They were from Les Petites, a small nearby village, and asked if we would like to visit there. We said "Yes" again, and one of the group said that he would guide us into their harbor. After we had finished our dinner, another boat arrived carrying a very young captain and his wife, who looked as if she was still in her teens. With them were their two children, her ten-year-old brother, a friend of his, and his friend's mother who all arrived for a visit on our boat. The captain told us that he had heard that an American boat had arrived with a very interesting radar aboard. We invited the whole gang aboard! The children had a great time, over and over, dropping down our forward hatch, passing through the cabin and out the aft companionway, then around the deck back to the forward hatch. They were boat-savvy, sure-footed youngsters. Shortly after they left, the fog came rolling into the cove. First it curled over the tops of the cliff, then it rolled down to the water.

The next morning the young men arrived to lead us into their harbor. The entrance channel was deep, but at one point it was very narrow; we couldn't have had more than two feet on either side of our boat. Les Petites was a charming sight. We tied up at the fish house dock. I think there probably were no more than two dozen houses that circled the tiny harbor. Other houses were perched on the rocky hills behind the harbor. Many of the houses were painted in bright colors. Fish house stages, covered with equipment, perched over the water. Small fishing boats were tied to docks around the harbor. There was a freshly painted white church, with a steeple, overlooking the harbor. The main street in town was a footpath. The village was supplied by a government-run electric plant, and the coastal boats arrived almost daily with passengers and supplies. That was a very social time at the dock.

Soon we had visitors aboard and met Norman Strickland, who invited us to use his telephone that evening to call home. Many of the residents of Les Petites were named Strickland. We learned that when young men were of marriageable age, they went "over the mountain" to find their brides at other outports. Most of the South Coast residents were of Scotch-Irish decent. They spoke with a distinctive brogue. They also used words which we had to learn. Take for instance this: "I tell ye, me lad, it was thick out that night and we had several strong puffs off the cliff, but then it were so smooth that we couldn't hear the groaner because it only works when there's a lop out." It roughly translates as "There was heavy fog that night and we experienced several strong gusts of catabolic winds from the cliffs, but the water calmed and we couldn't hear the whistle buoy because the water wasn't choppy enough to activate it." These were uniformly warm, friendly people! Norman Strickland and I had several good conversations. At one, he said to me, "You know none of us has much money, but none of us owes any money, and every boat in the harbor, with one exception, was built right here." They had been there since their ancestors had settled in these small outports when the French lost their fishing rights. They were proud, self-sufficient people.

They were inshore cod fishermen; some "jigged" for cod and caught the fish with a weighted jig with a hook, which interested the fish enough to allow them to be caught with a quick jerk of the hand line. In the various harbors we visited, we saw large dories row into the dock loaded with so many large cod that their gunnels were only a few inches above the water. Other men, with engine-powered boats, set out buoyed long lines of hooks which were baited with squid. These were set one day and picked up the next. Their livelihood was fishing, and they fished all year in all kinds of weather. They led rugged lives.

The inshore fishermen's competition was the large number of offshore draggers (trawlers) which scraped the bottom with huge trawls that scooped up everything in their path. When their catch was dumped on deck, the desirable fish were selected and the remaining fish, many of which were dead by this time, were thrown back in the sea. Everyone believed that the cod could be caught in unlimited quantities because plentiful catches had always been there.

The draggers were being subsidized by both the Canadian and American governments. An international agreement had been recently signed which gave both countries control of fishing 200 miles off their shores. I asked Norman Strickland if this would help protect the fish, and he replied, "No, it will just force the draggers onto the spawning grounds." He knew what none of the people regulating fishing yet understood.

We left Les Petites and harbor-hopped from village to village, many of which were located in spectacularly beautiful fjords. The Village of Francois, pronounced by the residents "Frenchways," was located in what looked like a huge amphitheater. There we received the same warm welcome we had learned to expect.

For many years, French fishermen were given the right to land and cure fish on the "French Shore" on the coast, but were prohibited by treaty from establishing permanent settlements. They had a permanent base on nearby St. Pierre and Miquelon islands. American fishermen had similar rights along the coast. When British settlers moved into the temporary French fishing camps, they kept the French names. This was why so many English-speaking outports have French names.

We were on the dock at "Frenchways" when we met a young couple, Mary and Garry Hiscock, and their two children, who had arrived on the coastal boat. They had visited several outports using this transportation. We thought it was courageous of them since many of these villages had no lodging facilities. If they couldn't find a family to take them in for the night, they pitched a tent. They were anxious to visit the nearby deserted village of Rencontre, where the coastal boat didn't stop, so we offered to take them.

In 1949 the government of Premier Joey Smallwood pursued a policy of forced/"encouraged" resettlement of residents from small outports to larger communities where schools, health care, and other government services could be provided more cheaply. They subsidized the move and resettlement. In some cases they actually moved their houses. Rencontre was one of these villages.

As we entered Rencontre Bay, the village looked like many other outports except that it wasn't quite as brightly painted. It was located in a very beautiful bay. We found the village dock and tied up against a pier which was completely detached from the shore. Our passengers were going to camp ashore for the night, and the next morning we would return them to "Frenchways" in time to catch the coastal boat. We took the dinghy to shore.

The village was completely deserted; we were the only people there! Many of the structures looked ready to use. The church pews and windows had been removed, but the pulpit stood waiting for a preacher. In the one-room schoolhouse, we actually found the pupil attendance records for several years in papers scattered on the floor. It was sad to see the number of children decline from year to year. The next day we delivered the Hiscocks back to "Frenchways."

We found piloting along the coast easy because almost every fjord that contained a village had an offshore buoy clear of any obstructions. These were either whistle buoys or, in a few instances, lighted ones. All had radar reflectors which I could locate with my handheld radar. The harbor entrances were also buoyed. Some of the largest fjord entrances had a lighthouse. We had good coastal charts which told us where these navigational aids were located.

On August 3 we sailed 50 miles to the French island of St. Pierre, where we anchored in the harbor and cleared customs.

That night we had dinner at a restaurant with genuine delicious French food. We stayed four days at St. Pierre. We bought real French bread, croissants and pastry. A great treat! The third day we moved to the government dock. There we met Jean Paul Andrieux and his wife Andree, who took us to their home for coffee and a visit, before taking us on a trip around the island. St. Pierre was celebrating the Fête of Jacques Cartier, so that night there were fireworks over the anchorage.

Having cleared customs, we left St. Pierre in the fog for the 40-mile trip back to St. Lawrence Harbor in Newfoundland. We continued following the east coast, and on August 11 we rounded Cape Spear, with its lighthouse on the easternmost point in North America. I had only one picture left in my camera. As I snapped the shutter, two pilot whales broke the surface of the water!

The entrance to St. John's, Newfoundland's largest city, is hidden until suddenly an opening in the cliffs appears along the shore. The channel is between World War II gun emplacements to port, and a small fishing village to starboard. It leads into the large harbor of this modern city.

After a very enjoyable visit, we left St. John's and sailed south, then west to Nova Scotia, visiting several small villages along the way. We left *Cynosure* at the boatyard in Baddeck for the winter. By now we had decided that we wanted to see more of Newfoundland and planned to circumnavigate the island the next summer.

Mary's 70th Birthday
in Baddeck

Les Petites Newfoundland

Norman Strickland
Newfoundland Fisherman

Newfoundland Coastal Boat

Village of Grand Brit

Iceberg
in the Strait of Belle Isle

Fjorid Entrance and the Lighthouse

Codfish Catch in 1978

CHAPTER 30

The Mary Constance

In order to tell about our next turning point, I have to step back in time. I was still representing *Boating* magazine. I spent some time walking the docks at the New England Boat Show, where I discovered an exhibitor with an absolutely gorgeous 34-foot cruising sailboat which he called the *Gale Force*. I asked the builder, Henry ("Rex") Kaiser, if he had literature about the boat that I could take home to show my wife. He said he would be glad to mail some to me. When the literature arrived, Mary said it was much too expensive and, after all, we already had a 34-foot boat. But now, of course, we were on Kaiser's mailing list.

Several times during the following years, we received rambling newsletters from him. While home at Christmas time in 1978, we received one of his letters telling his readers of his plans for the spring boat shows. At the end of the letter was a description of his 48-foot Kristina ketch *Claire*, which was for sale or for winter charter. At my request, he sent me a sheet describing it. Mary and I agreed that in March, when we were traveling for business in the Chesapeake area, we would like to look at the boat. When we got to the Annapolis area, we called Rex Kaiser and made arrangements to look at the boat, which was moored at a private dock near Oxford, Maryland.

March is a poor time to look at a boat that has been laid up for the winter. My first impression, when we went below, was not favorable. There were empty liquor bottles on the counter and much disarray in the cabin. Mary liked the boat. In the main cabin there were single berths on either side with quarter berths above. There was a beautiful teak drop-leaf table which, when open, could seat six. There was the usual "V berth" forward. A passageway, with another quarter berth, led to a very nice aft cabin. The boat slept nine people!

When I called Rex Kaiser, he was planning to pick up some cushions, near Annapolis, for a new boat. I said that Mary and I wanted to discuss the boat and asked if we could meet him later in the day. He suggested that we could meet for cocktails in Annapolis at Middleton Tavern, located on the city dock. On the way to meet Rex that evening, Mary and I decided that we would like to buy the boat and figured out how much money we could afford to spend. We had money saved from the sale of the cottage and figured we could borrow the balance as a second mortgage on our home.

Rex was waiting for us when we reached the tavern. I think he had already had a couple of drinks. I had suspected, from his winter charter offer, that he really wanted the boat for the summer. I told him that we would be willing to buy the boat now, and then charter it back to him for two years. I pointed out that he had advertised a charter fee and I thought the fee should apply to him. This arrangement would suit us because we really wanted to circumnavigate Newfoundland the next year and would need another summer to bring *Cynosure* from Newfoundland to the Chesapeake, where we would put her up for sale. He agreed to our offer, which brought the price down to an amount we could afford. He also agreed that before he delivered *Claire* to us he would remove the two salon quarter berths and substitute storage lockers.

For two years, we owned two boats. Rex said he would like to keep the name *Claire* for the new boat which he was going to build. I decided that since it had been named for Rex's wife, I would rename it after mine. So she became the *Mary Constance*.

CHAPTER 31

Circumnavigation of Newfoundland

On June 24, 1997, our wedding anniversary, we once again drove to Baddeck in our motorhome. We crossed into Canada across the Peace Bridge near Buffalo, New York. There we cleared Canadian Customs and found that our motorhome was selected for a thorough inspection. We had many things for the boat stored in the side lockers of the motorhome. We had to declare our used boat radios and other electronic equipment, but they missed a new RVG steering vane.

It took us ten days to prepare our boat for our trip. Installing the wind steering was time-consuming but very much worth the effort. One again we crossed the Cabot Strait to Newfoundland. This time we had great sailing winds.

Anchorages on Newfoundland's west coast are farther apart and required longer sailing days, but the rugged mountainous coast was beautiful, and once again we experienced great hospitality everywhere we went. We sailed 50 miles out of our way to visit Stevensville, where I had flown so many times during World War II. The airbase was actually six miles from the dock. A local man, whom we met on the dock, volunteered to drive us on a tour of the base. The Americans had turned the base over to Canada, and it had been converted for several projects. The runway was now a private air strip. The base infirmary was now a small hospital; the airport fire station was being used by the village. Several hangars and buildings were being used by small businesses. I still recognized the Officers' Club and the barracks where we had been housed.

At Woods Island Harbour, which was near Corner Brook, Newfoundland's second largest city, we met people aboard two local sailboats. They welcomed us and took us on a walking tour of the island and served us a "real Newfie dinner": corned codfish, potatoes, turnips, and carrots with home-baked bread, molasses cake, and tea. We tied up at the dock in Corner Brook, provisioned at a supermarket, bought ice, and hauled three five-gallon jerry cans of gasoline back to the boat.

We started out from Neddys Cove, in Bonne Bay near the Gros Morne National Park, northwest along the coast early in the morning on July 18. We had cold, wet fog and soon discovered that neither our Sumlog nor Whistler radar was working, so we retraced our course back to Neddys Cove, where we spent the day.

I discovered the flexible cable to the Sumlog underwater propeller had broken. The Whistler radar was equally discouraging. I traced the power as far as the circuit board, so determined that the problem had to be there. We would have to do without them for the rest of the summer! Our copy of "Bowditch" provided the answer to our log problem. Under "Life Boat Procedures," we found instructions for the use of a chip log. I built one using a 1"x4"x6" piece of scrap mahogany weighted on one end with a spare toggle. To this I secured a triangular bridle, which caused the board to tow upright with considerable water resistance. We fastened 33 feet of light nylon line to the bridle and fixed the other end to the stern of the boat. Using a stopwatch, we measured the time that it took for the line to go taut after we dropped the chip off the stern. Four seconds worked out to five knots. Using the formula from Bowditch, I charted a table of times and speeds. Of course, it wouldn't average varying speeds like the Sumlog, but I think it had less error. We would have to navigate with a compass, depth sounder and chip log for the rest of the summer.

Early the following morning, as the skies lightened, we were delighted to discover that the fog had broken up into patches. As we motored down Bonne Bay, the sun rose over the eastern hills to illuminate the towering butte-like bulk of Gros Morne Mountain. By the time we rounded Rocky Point into the Gulf of St. Lawrence, the sunlight had descended the side of Gros Morne, painting the roofs of the village at its base a brilliant gold. Wisps of white fog clung to the hollows, contrasting with the gold-brown of the mountains. The wind freshened from the southwest, and we set our mainsail and poled out our small genny to run before it, northeast, along the coast. Soon the wind settled to a steady 15 knots and we turned the steering over to our RVG steering vane. The rising sun burned away the last of the fog patches. Points along the coast provided numerous checkpoints with which to check our chip log table. We were averaging more than six knots, now sailing wing on wing.

I practiced taking sun lines with the sextant, plotting them along with our hourly dead reckoning position on the chart.

They indicated a northerly current was adding about one-half knot to our measured speed. This was cruising at its best!

Midsummer days are long at latitude 51 degrees north. The sun was still well above the horizon at 5:00 p.m. when gathering clouds obscured it. The winds had risen to 20 knots. We dropped the jib and sailed under main alone, speed undiminished. As was often the case, it was Mary who first noticed that the shore was becoming less distinct. I said it was just afternoon mist; Mary attributed it to fog. She was right. Then we had what was probably the most trying piloting experience in all of the years of our sailing.

By 6:00 p.m. the fog had closed around us and our visibility had been reduced to about 100 feet. By now we were sailing with only a reefed main. The winds were gusting to 25 knots. With the fog and wind, temperatures dropped. It might as well have been raining; water dripped from the sails and the rigging, pooling on the cockpit cushions. The steering vane was still holding the course well, so we huddled under the cockpit dodger, taking turns checking the compass. Somehow, the dead reckoning positions I plotted on the chart seemed more real than the gray-white fog which cloaked the world around us.

Our original destination had been Port Saunders. The pilot book, however, indicated that this harbor, with its unobstructed approach, offered poor protection from the southwesterly winds which were driving us. So, in the late afternoon, we changed our course to head for Port au Choix harbor, located on the north side of Point Riche. It was seven miles farther, around the point, but would offer better protection from the wind. Unfortunately, our coastal chart didn't give much detail for either harbor.

Mary says that for her, the essence of cruising is making choices, right or wrong, and then living with the consequences. No one else makes them for you. Pilot books and cruising guides give you information but, quite literally, you are the captain of your own fate. Perhaps we would have been wiser to choose Port Saunders, with its wide-open approach. Maybe we would have found shelter in that harbor behind a pier or larger boat. We had to round Point Riche, and the waters off the point were shoal. We would have to rely on dead reckoning and our depth sounder to round the point and to find the Port au Choix outer bell buoy.

Now we were grateful for our careful records, which we had kept all day in the sunshine. The hourly positions, plotted on the chart, gave us an accurate dead reckoning position from which to lay our course. Having calculated our speed, I had a good idea of the velocity and set of the current. Relying on our chart, the compass, and the depth sounder, we could use a series of soundings to round the point. When our depth sounder indicated 25 fathoms, we changed our heading to northwest, sailing on a beam reach under just a double-reefed main, on a course parallel to the coastline of the point. Mary took the wheel while I remained below with the chart, stopwatch, and depth sounder, calling up the course in degrees for her to steer. It was not an easy task as salt spray lashed her face and glasses. Now that we were no longer running before it, the howling wind added sheets of spray to the fog.

We had only seven miles to go, less than two hours, but in retrospect, it seemed to last forever. To avoid the shoal water off Point Riche, we continued our northwest heading past the point until the depth sounder went off scale (over 40 fathoms). We then turned on a northerly course, aiming for a small six-fathom shoal lying in deep water northwest of the point. Mary concentrated on maintaining an accurate course. Forty minutes later, almost exactly at our estimated time, the depth sounder rose and steadied at six fathoms. We turned northeast, on a starboard tack, to find an even smaller four-fathom shoal. The boat passed several large bright orange fishing floats. Meaningless to navigation, they were somehow reassuring evidence that we were not alone in our fog-proscribed world. Four minutes later the sounder showed four fathoms, and we turned once again for the outer bell buoy. "It should take only two minutes," I shouted over the noise of the wind. "Listen for it." We saw the buoy before we heard it. Miraculously, it appeared out of the fog dead ahead. For the first time in hours, we knew exactly where we were and our spirits soared. The abstractions of the chart became the reality of that beautiful black and white striped buoy with "Port au Choix" painted on its side. But our trial by fog was not finished.

The winds, funneling out of the still invisible fjord-like harbor, had reached thirty knots. The harbor entrance, marked by a light on a small island, lay directly upwind. We started the Atomic Four engine, but even at full throttle, the boat could make no headway against the wind and waves. There was no choice; we were forced to tack toward the harbor entrance. With the fully reefed main strapped down, aided by the engine, we motor-sailed into the wind; three minutes on a starboard tack, six minutes on a port tack, then six again to starboard. I was at the wheel now, Mary with the stopwatch, watching the depth sounder. Suddenly, ahead, we saw surf breaking. We had found the tiny island with its skeletal white tower and light, marking the harbor entrance. Still there was no relief from the tension.

We did not know whether the harbor entrance channel lay to port or starboard of the white light. While I held the boat stationary against the wind with the engine, Mary consulted the pilot book. It gave us no answer. The chart was inconclusive; its scale was too small for us to be certain. We gambled. With our eyes glued to the depth sounder, we left the island to port. With the engine at full power, we inched by the island on the course indicated on the chart for the invisible harbor leading lights. The water shoaled to less than ten feet; then the depth sounder steadied and slowly moved downward to a reassuring 20 feet. We were in the harbor at last. But the little island had vanished into the fog behind us as quickly as it had appeared. Once again, we saw nothing.

The boat made agonizingly slow time against the wind. All we could do was maintain our course toward the unseen shore. Ten minutes passed; then twenty. The strong wind persisted, but the waves were smaller. Slowly land materialized, followed by the outline of first one, then two small fishing boats tied against a dock. There was space ahead of them. We would be able to approach directly upwind. I wrestled down the sail while Mary held us stationary against the wind. With dock lines and fenders in place, we inched, crab-like, toward the dock. Three fishermen appeared and took our lines. The same fishermen warned us of an impending wind shift which would have made the dock too exposed. Again we motored for 20 minutes more in the fog to the head of the harbor where we tied up alongside a fishing boat for the night. The captain of the fishing boat was aboard. We asked him aboard and told him about our experience. He was not very impressed; after all, he ventured out, winter and summer, in all kinds of weather.

We left Port au Choix in bright sunlight and had great sailing for two days. We arrived at the village of St. Barbe, at the entrance to the Strait of Belle Isle which separates Newfoundland from Labrador. We tied up with some other boats at the ferry dock. The next day, while we waited for the foggy weather to clear in the strait, we decided to take a round-trip ride on the ferry to Blanc Sablon, Quebec. On the ferry, I saw a pretty young woman with a beautiful big Labrador dog. I introduced myself and discovered that she was going to be the new Grenfell Mission doctor for that part of the Quebec and the Newfoundland coast. She was accompanied by a third-year medical student who would be with her for the summer. Her name was Dr. Ann Roberts, her student was Lynne Watson, and the dog's name was Saxon. She had a car on the ferry, and while we were waiting for the return ferry, she drove us around the bleak town. I bought us all Eskimo Pies.

The next day, the weather finally cleared and we had a perfect sail across the Strait of Belle Isle to the village of Red Bay on the south coast of Labrador. On the way, we saw our first iceberg. Only a few years before, the strait had not been clear of pack ice until late August. That year our passage would have been impossible.

When we arrived at Red Bay, we found that the only satisfactory anchorage was a long dinghy ride to the small dock. When we got there, we were greeted by Ann and Lynne, our new friends from the ferry. They had driven the six miles from Blanc Sablon to visit a nearby clinic. Six miles was the entire road system for this area. They had to make their visits by water or, in the winter, by dogsled.

The village of Red Bay, located half way through the strait, has been occupied since Basque fishermen established summer fishing camps there in the 16th century. There was a frontier feeling about the village. The houses were perched on the rocks with no sense of order. Great tepee-shaped piles of firewood, which had been hauled out over the snow from inland forests in the winter, dotted the village. There was practically no vegetation in evidence. We did discover one small garden. Killing frosts can occur any month of the year. The air was brisk; we saw one small child in a snowsuit. We were presented with a large cod, which Mary baked in our oven.

The only garden in Red Bay, Labrador

The Park Guide, Mary and, Roy Decker at Lanse Aux Meadows

Battle Harbor Labrador

Abandoned Homestead in Labrador

The Crew- Mary, Ted, Stan, Jean and, Ken

The Nantucket Lighship
Appeared Out of The Fog

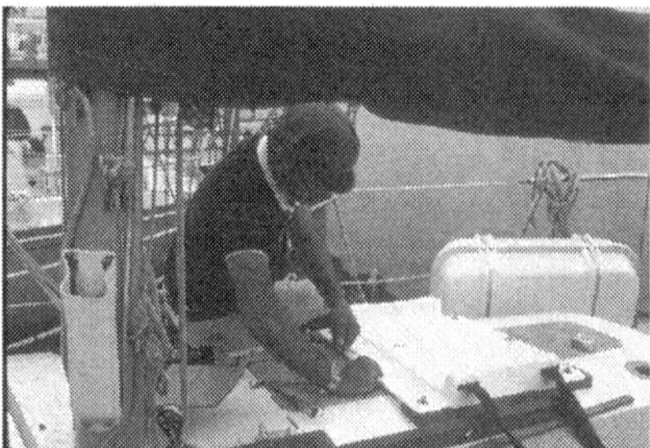

Stan Installing the Inflatable Life Raft

Leaving Annapolis for Ireland

CHAPTER 32

L'Anse au Meadows

The next day we left at six in the morning, had another great sail across the strait, and arrived at the small village of Ship Cove. There were bales of salt cod on the village dock, awaiting shipment. We had picked this location because it was the closest we could find to the Viking Settlement at L'Anse au Meadows. We had a great stroke of luck when we met Roy Decker on the dock. He was a retired university professor from St. John's. We thought he was just one of the local fishermen. He was wearing rough work clothes; one side of his glasses was cracked and taped together. I asked him if he knew anyone who could take us across the bay to the Viking archeological site. He said that he thought he could and he would ask his partner. It turned out that Roy was a native of the village and was the first resident to matriculate and graduate from college. He spent his summers in Ship Cove, and he and his partner, a retired fisherman, were proud of the fact that they had brought in the largest catch of the summer.

Roy and his partner took us, in their large outboard boat, to the Viking settlement which had been just recently declared a Canadian Park. It turned out that Roy knew more about the settlement than the park guide.

In 1960 the remains of a Norse village were discovered in Newfoundland by the Norwegian explorer Helge Ingstad. Archaeologists determined the site is of Norse origin because of definitive similarities between the characteristics of structures and artifacts found at the site, when compared to sites in Greenland and Iceland, which dated from around 1000 A.D.

Helge Ingstad and Anne Stine Ingstad carried out seven archaeological excavations between 1961 and 1968, investigating eight complete house sites as well as the remains of a ninth. L'Anse aux Meadows is the first authenticated settlement in North America. It existed almost 500 years before the voyages of Christopher Columbus. One of the items excavated by archeologists was a spindle, only used by women. The presence of women proved the site was a true settlement. When we visited, work was in the planning stages to build a reconstruction of one of the buildings.

Roy visited us that evening on our boat. It turned out that he and his brother had been the local contacts with Helge Ingstad after he arrived at the site. That night in the flickering light of our oil lamp, Roy told us a fascinating ghost story.

Years ago, long before the discovery of L'Anse aux Meadows, Roy's father was hunting in the area of the site when he saw two figures on a hill silhouetted against the sky. One of them seemed to have horns growing out of his head. When Roy's father climbed the hill, all he found was a lightning-damaged tree. Roy, who was then a little boy, said that his father told him about the experience that night. Roy's father was illiterate so had no way of knowing about Vikings. Roy had forgotten the conversation until years later when the settlement was discovered.

When we left Ship Cove, we sailed through the Quirpon Tickle ("tickle" being a wonderful Newfie term for a narrow passage between islands) and stopped at St. Anthony, where we visited the Grenfell Mission. Then we went from harbor to harbor, south along the Newfoundland coast toward St. John's. When we sailed across the mouth of Bonavista Bay, there were humpback whales everywhere. We also passed a number of icebergs along the shore. When we reached St. John's again, I rented a car for two days so we could do some shopping and visit the Royal Newfoundland Yacht Club in Conception Bay some distance from the city. One of the members told me that in early summer the club had been closed when a large iceberg drifted in and blocked the club entrance. They had to wait several days until the wind shifted and the iceberg departed.

It was now mid-August and the weather was becoming more problematical, so we decided to sail offshore directly to Sydney, Nova Scotia. We left St. John's in the morning, rounded Cape Race at about 10 p.m., and found that we would have to tack to maintain our course to Sydney. Wet, cold fog rolled in and it was bitter cold in the cockpit. Our wind steering vane broke at about 6:00 a.m., and we discovered that our engine wouldn't start. I determined that the problem was our fuel pump. I didn't dare use our autopilot because with no engine, we would have no way to recharge our batteries. I felt that we needed to turn back to a town with land connections to St. John's, so we turned back north and set a course for the village of Trepassey. After a sleepless night, we reached the harbor at 10:00 a.m. and with my urging, Mary sailed the boat to the dock. We pulled *Cynosure* around to the protected side of the dock. I left Mary to get some sleep and had walked only a short distance from the road when I met a young man. I told him we had a broken engine and needed a mechanic. He told me that we had to talk to his father. On the way to his house, I learned that the village had had a big wedding the night before and everyone was there. His father told me where there was a mechanic and said, "Take my car, but George may not be up yet because we had a big wedding last night."

When I arrived at the shop behind his house, it was closed, so I knocked on the door of his house. It took a little while before a disheveled, obviously hung-over man answered the door. When I told him my problem he said, "Well, me boy, let me have a cup of coffee and I'll come down to your boat." In about half an hour, he appeared on the dock, climbed aboard and into the bilge, and removed our fuel pump. I could tell that every move he made was painful. He said he would telephone a St. John's part store and thought we would have a new fuel pump the next morning. When I described the problem with our RVG steering vane, he told me that I could probably get it welded at the fish plant. Once again the young boy's father, who had come down to the dock, said, "You'll need to use my car to get there."

At the fish plant, it took me a while before someone directed me to the machine shop, which was dark. A mechanic there told me that the power had gone out and that they didn't expect to get it back that day. Then he said, "Let me see your part." He continued, "We have some power in another part of the plant. Maybe I can fix it there." While I watched, he groped his way into the tool bins and came back with the needed welding equipment. He led me to a lighted bench in another location where he welded the part. He would not take any money for what he had done. I was able to get the vane working that afternoon.

The next morning, a refreshed George arrived with the new fuel pump and got our engine running. Then we discovered that even though the engine was running well, every time I put it in gear it stalled. I obviously had something in my propeller. He said, "A diver works at the fish plant. Let me see if I can get him." About an hour later, he returned with the diver, who had left his job to help us. He removed a large greasy ball of netting from our propeller.

Once again, we sailed nonstop to Sydney, Nova Scotia. This time we had no problems, and after an overnight stay in Sydney, we were back in Baddeck the next day. After preparing our boat for winter storage in the boatyard, we left in our motorhome on August 25.

CHAPTER 33

South to Chesapeake Bay

On June 23, 1980 we arrived back in Baddeck to find our friends Jean and Ken Moore in town on their boat. Mary and I celebrated our wedding anniversary at the AA Club, which was having a lobster boil. What great timing! Our plan was to sail *Cynosure* from Nova Scotia to Maine and then south along the east coast of the United States to Chesapeake Bay, where we would put the boat up for sale in Annapolis. We always tell any new cruising people to set plans but never set schedules because, if you really *have* to get somewhere, you will find yourself leaving a safe harbor when you should wait for better weather.

We finally left Baddeck on July 1 for our trip southwest along the Nova Scotia coast. We had a good cruising guide which told us about many small anchorages. We experienced a lot of rain, blowy weather, and fog, so we spent many quiet days waiting for favorable weather. But the places were interesting. Anchored in remote Yankee Cove, we waited for 36 hours and saw no people, but were not alone. We saw a porcupine, seals, cormorants, loons, gulls, terns, and a merganser duck with three ducklings.

At Halifax we rented a car for two days and were able to find some needed parts for the boat. At Gabriel's Marine Supply we learned that they had just purchased a very large order of Loran C navigation receivers and they were selling them to fishermen at a very low price. We purchased one and they installed it on our boat the next day; however, we discovered that they didn't have any Loran Marine Charts for the area where we were headed. Loran was useless without them, but they promised they would get some to us along the way and they did.

We stopped in Lunenburg, a famous old fishing city, for a day. We did some shopping and visited the Fisheries Museum of the Atlantic.

On July 19 we left Nova Scotia from Port Moulton on our offshore sail to Maine. Using our new Loran C, I plotted so many fixes on the chart that it looked like someone's cross stitching. We were able to sail most of the trip. Thirty-eight hours later, at 10:00 p.m., the unlighted buoy near Mt. Desert Island appeared out of the fog, directly in front of our boat.

We anchored that night off Little Cranberry Island and the next morning took our dinghy to the Ilseford dock, where we called U.S. Customs in Portland and checked into American waters by phone. The last time *Cynosure* entered U.S. waters was the 5th of July 1977.

We were now sailing in "Vacationland" waters. On our way south we visited several harbors including Bar Harbor. We stopped at Five Islands, Maine on the Sheepscot River to visit for several days with our old friends Ann and Phil Hermann in a cottage on one of the islands.

On August 27 we left Five Islands bound for Cape Cod. We had a comfortable sail overnight and made our "landfall" at the Cape Cod buoy at eleven in the morning. It took us another three hours to reach Provincetown Harbor. It was a beautiful, gentle sail along with all kinds of other boats: tour boats, ferryboats, fishing boats and large charter schooners. We spent a day in Provincetown.

The heavy pleasure boat traffic that we experienced during the next days was amazing to us. In Nova Scotia and Newfoundland we might have seen one other sailboat all day. We passed through the Cape Cod Canal to Marion Harbor, which we entered as part of a traffic jam of sailboats returning from a day's sail.

The next day we had an interesting trip motoring through the Woods Hole passage into Vineyard Sound, and then sailed on to Edgartown, Martha's Vineyard. We knew that our new boat, *Claire,* was moored somewhere in the large harbor but we didn't see her. Just after picking up a mooring, we heard the Edgerton Yacht Club calling *Claire* on our VHF radio and heard Rex Kaiser talking to his son. We called Rex and said that we were in the harbor. Rex told us that they were going sailing for a few hours and asked us to come by later for a drink. We left our dinghy on the mooring and beat them out of the harbor. I was able to take pictures of our new boat on all points of sail.

Later, when we were asked aboard *Claire,* Rex greeted us in the cockpit and gave us a drink, but his wife Claire never left the cabin or invited us below. It was a very frosty reception on her part. Rex had sold the boat to us. Claire had used it like a summer cottage and expected a new boat right away. The yard had gotten busy and the new *Claire* was just a hollow shell in the boatyard. After we took delivery of the *Mary Constance* the next spring, her replacement still was not under construction. Rex had to rent a cottage for two years. That winter he offered to buy it back from us with interest, but we declined; we wanted the boat.

On August 14, Mary's 58th birthday, we sailed into Nantucket Harbor. We had two wonderful days in Nantucket, on what Mary called "our holiday." We had her birthday dinner in a nice restaurant ashore. The next day we rented mopeds and drove to Siasconset, where we had honeymooned 36 years before. The old Beach House Hotel was gone, replaced by three large gray cottages, one of which was named Beach House. We had luncheon sandwiches at the same place that we had eaten years ago. We went out to the Sankety Head Lighthouse, the first we had seen together. Mary prepared a pressure cooker beef stew, to use on our projected 300-nautical-mile offshore trip to Cape May, New Jersey.

On August 17 we purchased fuel and ice at the Nantucket Wharf and left the dock at 8:30 a.m. We had to sail close to the wind around Nantucket, then a fast reach (with the wind on our side) resulted in a rough fast passage through the water. Mary got seasick at about 4:00 and was sick all night and the next day until about 4:00 p.m. when she was finally able to eat some food. She remained below most of this time, so I had to sail the boat alone. During the night we had several rainsqualls but we were making good time and our wind vane handled much of the steering, so I catnapped, sitting up, under the dodger for short periods.

We continued to have good sailing the next day, and Mary was able to relieve me at the helm in the afternoon. The second night was warm and clear as we motor-sailed offshore, along the coast. The glow of the lights of New York was apparent in the sky one hundred miles away! The wind came up at about 8:00 a.m. and we sailed with our wind vane steering until we got close to Cape May. Mary made popcorn in the afternoon and biscuits with our beef stew for dinner. We tied up at the Cape Island Marina at about midnight.

We have learned that the only way to sail up Delaware Bay to the Chesapeake and Delaware Canal is to start out from Cape May at the early start of the flood tide and with the wind blowing with the tide. Delaware Bay can be a mean body of water if you don't do it that way. We had a lovely day with good wind and a strong current, and reached the canal entrance at 6:00 p.m. We were able to stop at the Chesapeake city anchorage in the canal before dark.

On August 21 we sailed 65 miles and reached our summer's destination, Annapolis, Maryland, after another great sailing day. Once more, with a helpful current, we dropped anchor at the city anchorage at about 6:30 p.m. We arranged with the Bristol boat dealer, Atlantic Sailing Yachts, to list our boat for sale and moved to Horn Point Marina where we planned to haul the boat for the winter.

We spent four days preparing *Cynosure* for inspection. We removed some of our personal things and the equipment which we intended to keep. We added a few things to make the cabin look more attractive.

Sometimes the logistics involved in our way of living were complicated. Jean and Ken Moore, whom we had seen in Baddeck before we left, had decided to sail the south coast of Newfoundland the next summer and then to leave their boat in Baddeck for the winter. We suggested that they could drive our motorhome back to Chagrin Falls, which was close to Oberlin, where they lived, and thus save airfare. They did this and our son Jim brought the motorhome down to Annapolis to take us home.

We spent a final day moving all of our personal equipment and belongings to the motorhome. We left at 4:00 the next morning and arrived home that evening on August 28, 1980.

CHAPTER 34

Business Travel in a Motorhome

Every year, Jack Schmidt had a "Red Book" sales meeting on Labor Day. The new edition was ready, and many of us delivered these directories to our customers on our early fall calls. I did this in Pennsylvania and New York. Mary usually didn't go with me on this trip.

During the 24 years that we traveled for business, we had experiences that remain indelible in our memories. One early afternoon, when I was driving alone in the motorhome on an elevated highway in Brooklyn, I discovered to my dismay that the oil pressure gauge reading had dropped to almost nothing. I left the highway at the first exit and found a gas station where they changed my oil filter and oil. When I started the engine, the gauge still showed no pressure. The station attendant directed me to a nearby Dodge dealer, where I talked to the service manager, who said that they could work on the engine in the morning. I explained that I was living in the motorhome and asked if I could spend the night there. He was sorry, but they had nowhere for me to park. I realized this was true. This was a small dealership in the city. Every inch of space was in use. He said, "You must have some oil pressure or you wouldn't have gotten here; just drive slowly and find a place for the night and we will see you at eight o'clock."

The place I found was next to a gas station adjacent to a small market parking lot. I paid for an electrical connection. I found myself in a black ghetto close to where the old Ebbets Field had been located. Shortly after I was settled, I saw a little boy, probably about ten years old, standing beside the motorhome looking amazed. I opened the window and asked him if he had ever seen a motorhome, and he shook his head no. I asked if he would like to see inside and he nodded his head yes. We spent quite a long time while I explained what everything was and did. Then he asked if he could bring his brother and I agreed. A short time later he arrived with his teenaged brother, who in turn brought his friends. They were all uniformly polite, and at dinnertime I had to ask them to leave so I could make supper. The little boy asked if he could come tomorrow and I explained that I would be leaving early in the morning. He was there to wave goodbye when I left. I think that, had I shooed him away when he first showed up, I would have been lucky to find my tires still inflated in that tough neighborhood.

The Dodge mechanic worked hard on the motorhome all day; it was a big job because the oil pump was located in the oil pan and in order to get at the pan, they had to drop the transmission. At about 4:30 he had enough of the engine back together that he could start the engine. We still had no oil pressure. I asked the service manager if I could spend the night in the motorhome, which definitely wasn't ready to be driven anywhere. He thought about it and finally agreed, but I would have to stay in the motorhome. If I left, it would set off their sonic alarm system. I assured him I would only leave in case of fire. That night I spent the night five feet off the ground, with the motorhome, on the lift. I had electricity, the TV worked fine, and I slept well.

The next day they started work early, and in mid-afternoon they had the problem solved. A small adjustment screw, which was set at the factory to create optimum oil pressure, had worked almost closed. I asked him how I could be sure it wouldn't happen again, and he handed me the screw. He said it wasn't really necessary. I was surprised at the bill; they had charged me for only the second day's work.

Another time, Mary and I were traveling in Alabama when we discovered we had a flat tire in one of our rear wheels. With dual rear wheels, often we were unaware of our problem until the driver of another vehicle waved a warning to us. We drove carefully to the next town, where I planned to make calls on several of my customers, and found a repair garage which replaced the tire with our spare. I told him I had some calls to make in town and would pick up the repaired tire later. When I arrived, he put the spare tire in the storage area under the vehicle.

About three days later, we finished our calls for the day at a new, not quite finished funeral home that was located in a cemetery. I was lucky. I found the funeral director there and secured the necessary information for the next directory. As I recall, I gave him a current "Red Book" and told him I would try to sign him up as a subscriber next year. Then I asked him if we could spend the night there. He told us that we certainly could, so we spent that night parked in a cemetery.

It was a very quiet night there, and both of us were sound asleep when a large explosion rocked the vehicle. My first thought was of a propane explosion, but we didn't smell anything or see any signs of smoke or fire. Outside, with a flashlight, I discovered that all the cargo compartment doors on the passenger side had been blown out. Shortly after that, my investigations found the cause; our spare tire had exploded. Apparently, the man who had repaired our tire several days earlier had been distracted. When truck tires are mounted, they are filled at a very high pressure to seat the tire on the rim. Then the pressure is reduced to normal inflation. Somehow the repairman had neglected this last deflation. We had been traveling for several days before the stressed tire exploded. We were grateful that it hadn't happened while we were driving. We were able to find a motorhome repair shop in the next town. They reattached our cargo doors and we were back on the road before noon.

CHAPTER 35

Big Plans

During the winter of 1980–81 we decided that we wanted to sail to Europe after we had gotten our new boat ready. When we talked about this, Jean and Ken Moore said they would like to crew for us. Later, Mary's brother, Stan Orr, said he also would like to join us.

Nineteen eighty-one was an eventful year for us. On Monday, June 22, we arrived at the Kaiser Boatyard in Wilmington, Delaware to pick up the *Mary Constance*. We learned that Rex Kaiser was away for a couple days, but his wife Claire had come to the boat to remove their personal belongings from the boat. We discovered that some of the things she removed should have been considered part of the boat equipment. I don't think we ever mentioned this to Rex. We felt that he had enough problems with his wife without our further inflaming their relationship.

Rex had certainly lived up to his part of our agreement; the boat was in true "yacht condition." All of the exterior brightwork was newly finished, and the new cupboards below were in place. However, I found that the battery, anchor windlass, and main halyard needed to be replaced. When Rex returned, he agreed to do this, and we were able to finish our paperwork together.

We spent most of the summer in Annapolis, Maryland, which was convenient to the facilities we would need in order to outfit the *Mary Constance* for an Atlantic crossing.

We kept the motorhome close to the boat all summer. It gave us an air-conditioned refuge from the sultry hot Chesapeake weather, and Mary was able to sew curtains and lee cloths in comfort.

We spent much of the summer, with a couple of exceptions, working on the *Mary Constance*. We detoured to the Chester River Campground and made reservations for a family reunion on August 24.

Our first trip on the *Mary Constance*, from Wilmington to Annapolis, was wonderful. We left the boatyard at 10:30 and had a fast sail down the Delaware River to the C&D Canal. We discovered, as we motored through the canal, that we not only had a great sailboat but also a fine motorboat. Using our 75-horsepower Westerbeke diesel engine, we averaged seven knots through the canal, and then sailed to the Sassafras River where we anchored for the night.

On our sail from the Sassafras to Annapolis, we tried out every sail on our new boat except the mizzen staysail. At 5:30 p.m. we anchored in Back Creek, across from the Port Annapolis Marina. We spent much of our time that summer anchored there, and when necessary we rented a dock for a day to fill our water tanks and do laundry. It was in the laundry room that Mary met Audrey Uhthoff, and later we met her husband Steve, who had a ship's carpenter shop on the marina grounds. They lived aboard an old Friendship sloop in the marina. Audrey worked for the marina, cleaning various buildings.

It was obvious that the Bristol boat dealer with whom we listed *Cynosure* was much more interested in selling new boats and had not produced one prospect for our boat. One day when we were visiting with Audrey, she said, "I'll sell your boat for you." I told her that if she did, I would pay her a normal brokerage fee. Amazingly, she came up with a buyer late that summer. She bought her first car with the commission.

Mary kept a list of the things we added to the boat that summer in preparation for an ocean crossing, and I'll list them, not necessarily in order of importance.

Aries wind steering vane and blades
Masthead five-way light
New main battery
Two auxiliary batteries
Loran antenna on the mizzenmast
New sheets for the jib
Separate track on mast for a storm jib
Automatic battery charger
Amateur radio and aerial
Curtain tracks for all ports
Five new interior lights
Two relocated lights in heads
Twelve-volt outlets in cockpit
Storm port tracks for large opening ports
Kenyon three-burner propane stove with oven
Aft storage for two propane bottles and tubing to stove
Soap dishes
Man overboard pole and light
Mary sewed 22 panels of curtains and six lee cloths

Four white cockpit seat cushions

A reaching pole and deck brackets

Two floor mats

Two pillows and two double sheets

Two wastebaskets

Mary's brother Stan flew in to spend ten days with us. I couldn't have accomplished all of the projects without his help. Before he left to go home, we were able to have a wonderful four-day mini-cruise in the Chesapeake. We sailed from Annapolis to the Chester River, on to St. Michaels and Oxford, where Stan had kept his Grand Banks trawler at one time.

Mary and I felt that we needed to have at least one offshore practice trip, with our crew, before we left the next year to cross the Atlantic. We planned to sail to Bermuda and back, about 650 miles each way. Our plans changed when Jean and Ken called to say that they had talked to Hal and Margaret Roth, very experienced round-the-world sailors, who said that early August was much too late to sail to Bermuda. So we changed our plans and decided to make an offshore passage to Five Islands, Maine, which would be the same distance.

Our crew arrived on August 1. Jean and Ken shopped for groceries while Stan and I spent part of the day trying to get our Loran C working, to no avail. That summer an Annapolis Furuno dealer had sent it back to the factory, which returned it to us with a note saying it worked perfectly in their tests. We left the marina at 11:30 a.m. on August 2 and had a slow sail up the Chesapeake to the C&D Canal. When we were about 20 miles from Annapolis, our loran started working. We discovered later that a very powerful low-frequency Navy transmitter near

Annapolis interfered with loran reception in the area. We were amazed that a dealer selling electronic equipment hadn't known about this. He could have saved us a lot of work.

We motored a lot on our offshore practice trip because of the very light winds. We did have a brief but heavy thunderstorm, with wind gusts of 45 knots, which gave us some experience in reducing sail under these conditions. For me, another memorable moment was when, in a light fog, we heard the foghorn of the Nantucket Lightship, one of the last still on station. When it appeared out of the fog, its crew turned off the foghorn. We talked to them on our VHF radio, and they confirmed that they had seen us on their radar and activated the foghorn for us.

We reached Five Islands before noon, almost exactly five days after our departure. We spent three nights on a Five Islands Yacht Club mooring. Jean and Ken caught a ride to Portland to return to their boat.

Stan, Mary and I left on a leisurely trip back to Annapolis. Along the way we stopped at a number of harbors. In Boothbay, we picked up a mooring at the Down East Yacht Club, which Stan had joined several years before. All the club had was moorings, no dock or clubhouse, but it gave us a free mooring for the night. We spent a night at the Isle of Shoals, in Smuttynose Harbor. (I just loved that name!) We motor-sailed in Massachusetts, to Marblehead, then Provincetown and Cuttyhunk Island, before finally arriving at the Great Salt Pond on Block Island. This was mid-August and the harbors were filled with boats.

After we had finally set the anchor to our satisfaction, I started a fire in our charcoal grill which extended over the water, off the transom. Mary put three little steaks on the grill and went below. Stan and I had been down below fixing a water pump. When we finished, I went up to check the steaks; two of the three were gone and a flock of gulls were getting ready to make off with the third. Mary heated some leftover chicken while I stood guard.

We sailed, offshore, for two days and one night, from Block Island to Cape May, New Jersey. Two days later, on August 20, we were back in Annapolis. On August 25, Stan flew home.

CHAPTER 36

Our Reunion

For some time we had been planning a family reunion at a campground some way up the Chester River. We had purchased a chart indicating that we would be able to sail the *Mary Constance* to the campground. All of our four children and the grandchildren would be there, camping on shore. Connie and her kids had already pitched their tents. Our son David drove our motorhome to the campground, and his wife Charlotte arrived towing our 14-foot Flying Junior. Beth and Jim drove in with David's two canoes on their car. We had a wonderful time!

One day we drove the motorhome and a station wagon to Cape Henlopen State Park. It had a beautiful unspoiled beach. There was just enough surf to be fun. We all swam, and the kids spent a lot of time digging for little crabs in the sand.

The last day, we loaded everyone into the *Mary Constance* and motored to Chestertown, but not without difficulty. The channel down the river, which we had scouted with our dinghy, was hard to find, and we had to plow through several shallow spots. When we reached Chestertown, everyone was able to do some shopping ashore and then we had lunch on the boat. By now we realized that with a falling tide, there was no way that we were going to get the boat back up the river to the campground. We had a great break: an outboard speedboat that I recognized from the campground approached us. I waved them in, and they were willing to take Dave and Jim with them. Dave and Jim drove the motorhome and a car to back to Chestertown and then drove all of the gang back to the campground. Mary and I said our goodbyes and set sail for Annapolis. We learned later that for years, no large sailboat had managed to get as far up the river as we had.

CHAPTER 37

The Atlantic Crossing

Nineteen eighty-two was an eventful year. We sailed the *Mary Constance* across the Atlantic, our destination being Cork, Ireland. We selected Ireland because Stan's wife Joey was planning a sightseeing trip there and could meet Stan when we arrived. During the winter we studied *Ocean Passages of the World,* a large book of suggested passages for sailboats, collected over the centuries from the reports of ship's captains. Expected wind direction and wind velocity were indicated along each route. There were several routes we could take, all of which took advantage of the prevailing westerly winds. The shortest passage involves sailing to St. John's, Newfoundland and then to Ireland, a short but miserable trip. This route took one north through the Grand Banks, at that time the world's fishing grounds, which were shrouded in fog 60 percent of the time. These waters were not only plied by hundreds of large offshore fishing trawlers, but also were on the main shipping routes to Europe. The south-flowing Labrador Current brings not only 40-degree water temperatures but also icebergs, which were common in early summer. We had sailed in these waters and knew how uncomfortable they could be.

The southern route, via Bermuda and the Azores, would be warm and had the advantage of breaking up the crossing into three shorter passages. It takes longer, however, because it is almost impossible for anyone to leave these lovely islands without sightseeing. In addition, winds are more likely to be light because of the Bermuda and Azores highs. The probability of headwinds from the Azores to Europe is much more likely than on a more northerly route. We chose a central route, due east for 1500 miles, then northeast for another 1500 miles. We set our departure for June 1 because this month provides a window between the winter's storms and the hurricane season. *Ocean Passages,* pilot charts, and books by experienced transatlantic sailors all said this was the best month and, on average, we could experience one gale.

We arrived in Annapolis on May 16, and during the next ten days before our crew arrived, we worked feverishly on the boat. I discovered that the inflatable four-man life raft, which we left with the dealer to be inspected, had somehow disappeared. He claimed it had been stolen. He finally replaced it with a new six-man raft, and we paid only the difference in cost. We purchased a small portable Honda generator. We felt that we needed some way to recharge the batteries in case the engine generator failed. We took delivery of a new club jib. I installed a gold-plated ground plate on the bottom of the boat and connected the ground circuits in the boat to it. This would give us better amateur radio performance. While the boat was out of the water, I sanded and painted the bottom with two coats of anti-fouling paint. I lowered and painted the centerboard. We emptied and cleaned our water tanks, then filled them and measured their capacity. The two 67-gallon tanks held 134 allons of water; we also would carry two ten-gallon jerry cans of water, lashed on deck. We stored our inflatable dinghy in the chain locker. We would not need either the anchor or the dinghy on our trip.

There are hundreds of details to be considered when preparing for an ocean crossing. You cannot run down to the local yacht supply store in the middle of the ocean. If something breaks, you fix it or it stays broken, so you carry as many spare parts as you can. If you run out of something, you just do without it. We checked the boat supplies as carefully as if our lives depended on them—and actually, they did.

Jean, Ken and Stan arrived on May 25. Now we had more hands to help complete the remaining things to be done. We fastened our new life raft on top of the aft cabin. I went aloft, to the top of the mainmast, in the bosun's chair to make some last-minute changes to the masthead light. Mary and Jean started provisioning the boat. They stored cartload after cartload of groceries aboard. Our daughter Beth, who had a large pressure cooker, home-canned seven quarts of beef, six of turkey, and five of chicken for our trip. We moved all of our things from the motorhome and left it for the summer in the boatyard parking lot.

Finally, at 5:15 p.m., we waved goodbye to our friends on the dock. David and Charlotte, in our small sailboat, followed us and took pictures as we left the Port Annapolis Marina. We had all worked hard on last-minute preparations and were tired, so we anchored in the Chester River for the night. I don't think any of us slept very much because we left the anchorage at 5:45 the next morning. We had motored most of the way, so we stopped at Schaffer's dock in the C&D Canal to top off our diesel and water tanks. We wouldn't touch land again until Ireland! We had planned to stop at Cape May, but were all so excited that we decided just to keep on going.

This was another "what if" point. If we had known what the next two weeks would bring us, I wonder if we would have turned around and headed back to the Chesapeake and missed all our wonderful experiences in Europe. I'm not going to describe our trip, day by day, but we had seven gales on the crossing, four of which were headwinds. Of the 33 days at sea, we had 21 days during which, at some time during the 24-hour period, we had gale force winds.

For the first 16 days, we had headwinds out of the eastern quadrant, which meant that we had to make long tacks into the wind against large waves. We averaged only 60 nautical miles a day for the first 16 days and only made 972 nautical miles toward our destination before the wind finally began to blow from the west. We had three more gales with the wind behind us, but we were headed directly toward our destination and made 1936 nautical miles in the next 17 days.

Each point of sail offered different difficulties in the strong winds. When the boat was heeled and pounding into the waves, moving about the boat was difficult and the old sailors' saying, "one hand for the boat and one hand for yourself," was true. If you let go of the boat, a quick jerk could throw you across the cabin or the cockpit. We were all grateful for the lee cloths we had installed, which kept us from falling out of our berths. For the entire trip no one was allowed above decks without a safety harness attached securely to the boat. We had a line running down the center of the boat from the stern pulpit to the bow pulpit and attached to both masts, to which we could clip our harness. This allowed us to move forward on deck for sail handling.

Beating into head seas, which several times reached 20 feet, was wet work. Spray blew back to the cockpit as the bow would plow into a wave. We all had foul weather gear and boots, but even so, the spray managed somehow to penetrate. Whenever possible, the person on watch sat hunched up under the cockpit dodger or stayed below, coming up regularly to check the course, to adjust the steering vane if necessary, and look out for large ships. This was possible because our Aries wind steering vane steered most of the time.

The Aries was a critical device, and it broke down twice. The first time, early in the crossing, a pulley wheel dropped out of its bracket on the vane, apparently because a cotter pin had not been spread properly. We were able to replace it when we discovered that the wheel on a spare block (pulley) aboard was exactly the right diameter. Stan and I sawed it out of the block and were able to replace the missing one on the vane. It worked so well that I never felt the need to replace it. Stan achieved the title of Chief Engineer.

The second problem was the flexible steel cable that went from the vane to a drum attached to the wheel and then back to the vane. It couldn't stand the strain of constant flexing around the drum. We used cable clamps to form loops in the cable before it reached the drum. We then tied a line to the loop and let it do the flexing on the drum. We were very fortunate to have those cable clamps on board. I had added them to the ship stores for possible rigging failure. Making these repairs on a plunging boat, without dropping anything overboard, was wet and difficult work. While we worked, Ken steered the boat on course, faced into the wind and spray.

It took all of us about four days to adjust ourselves to the motion. Early in the trip Mary suffered a serious bout of seasickness. She was in her bunk for 27 hours until I discovered that the Transderm Scopolamine patch, which she had been wearing behind her ear, was mostly in her hair with only one small corner touching her skin. A few hours after I replaced it, she began feeling better.

Jean cooked during Mary's sickness, and the two women decided that it would be better if Jean did all the cooking and stood no watches. Mary cleaned up after meals and stood regular watches with the men. We kept a rotating watch system; day watches were four hours long and night watches two. It worked out well and provided us all one daily eight-hour period of sleep. It always has taken me at least two days before I get tired enough to sleep. By day four, most of us had acclimated to the motion of the boat.

Amazingly, Jean prepared a sit-down meal each day of the trip. We were all able to sit down together for dinner almost every day. Jean baked bread every few days. Food is critical and she did a wonderful job. Most of the trip we ate out of large bowls. Our yachting tableware had rubber rings on the bottom to keep it from sliding. Even though our plates would stay on the table, they weren't much use if the food wouldn't stay on the plate.

With our amateur radio we were able to maintain a daily schedule with Ralph Turner, a retired psychology professor in Oberlin, Ohio. We missed only a few days, when Ralph was away for the weekend. He was a 50-year veteran of amateur radio who was also a boatman. He knew exactly what to tell our families without frightening them. In addition, several times on the trip, we were able to achieve an amateur radio phone patch and talk directly to our families by telephone.

We were not alone all of the time. A large Coast Guard cutter circled us on the sixth day, and the skipper called us on the VHF radio. He asked us our identity and where we were headed, then thanked us and sped away. One night, when Mary was on watch, she saw a vessel's lights heading directly for us. Mary got on the radio and said, "This is the *Mary Constance*. Do you see me?" The vessel changed course and then a voice answered on the radio, "No, I didn't see you." By this time I was in the cockpit, and the captain and I had quite a conversation. He was bound for Italy. Later, a freighter bound for the Great Lakes, with passengers, called us. He asked us many questions and kept saying, "My passengers will be interested in this." I assumed that he had to create a ship's bulletin for his passengers and that we were providing something new for him to report.

Several times we had to deal with headwinds into which we just couldn't make any headway. In one strong gale, we hove to and drifted in a circle for two days. "Heaving to" is achieved by turning the steering one way and backing a small jib the other way. The helm wants to make the boat go one way and the jib tries to go the other way. Motion diminishes as the boat moves very slowly forward. It makes a great improvement in the comfort below! We actually did this procedure several times just to allow comfort while preparing and eating a meal.

On June 16, our 17th day, still facing headwinds, we had a crew meeting and decided to give the weather two more days. At the pace we were making, it would take us seven weeks to complete a passage that we had expected to take four. If we were still having headwinds, we would seriously consider turning back.

Only one day later, the winds shifted into the West and we were able to make our course downwind toward our destination. We still had three more gales, but going downwind with the gale force winds behind us was much easier. We were now making much more progress each day. Our runs were all over 120 nautical miles, and one day we made 160 miles.

Sailing downwind in heavy seas presented a different problem. We had to be very careful not to be overtaken by a large breaking wave, slewed over and knocked down. Mary and I had just such an experience, riding down the face of a large wave when we were overtaken by the next wave. Both of us were thrown across the cockpit and thankfully caught by our harnesses. Our wind vane did a great job of bringing the boat back before the wind.

Between gales we had some wonderful days when everyone was able to be on deck. We also had clothes drying in the rigging. Sometimes we were able to watch the porpoises circling our boat over and over again. One day we had a wonderful soft rain and were able to fill our water tanks. I let each of us take a quick fresh-water shower. Normally our pressure water system was turned off, and we could only get water from the hand pump in the galley.

We were about 300 nautical miles from Ireland when a large white vessel approached us. We had talked to several other vessels on our trip, but this one was headed directly toward us. She was flying a Russian flag, and as she neared us, the

Captain called us on our VHF radio. The captain spoke perfect English and asked us where we had come from and where we were headed. I asked him the same question. He said, "We work these waters and will be in Dublin in a few days." Then I recognized that she was a Russian electronics surveillance ship; I counted 20 antennas and a large radar dome. The encounter was very friendly; her decks were lined with people all waving to us, many with cameras. The crew dipped their flag, circled us once and left.

We were alone again, but by now I had determined an estimated time of arrival to be July 2. That night we had our "Captain's Dinner." Before dinner we had sparkling white grape juice and bubbling white wine, with peanuts, which someone had been hiding. Jean fixed home-canned turkey with dressing, peas and onions, hot biscuits, artichoke hearts, and bean salad. For dessert Mary baked our last "stir and frost" cake. Not bad after 32 days at sea.

At 2:30 a.m. on July 1, Mary was on watch when she spotted the glow of the Fastnet light as it swept just above the horizon. The actual light was not visible. Nights were short at that latitude. By 4:00 a.m. on July 2, I could see land, faint on the horizon. I was on watch alone at 5:00 a.m. when I made this entry in the log "Land ho, captain spots Mizzen head, no gold doubloon for the crew." To which someone added later, "Cheap bastard," signed "crew."

At 5:00 p.m. we passed the Cork entrance buoy and tied up at the Royal Cork Yacht Club at Crosshaven. After 35 days, 33 of them at sea, we were in Ireland. Our crew all slept on shore that night! Stan's wife Joey, who had been touring Ireland, was at the dock to greet us when we arrived. Jean and Ken stayed in a hotel.

I went ashore to the club, which was closed, but I found the bar was open. When I asked about clearing customs, a bartender said, “You just give them a call and they’ll come down to the boat, probably tomorrow evening. They like to come then.” At which a customer at the bar said “You’ll need a fiver for the phone,” and handed me a coin, which I immediately lost in the payphone. The bartender called customs for me. The customs man arrived as predicted, in the late afternoon, and spent ten minutes on paperwork and an hour just visiting with us.

Our First Storm

Jean Making Bread

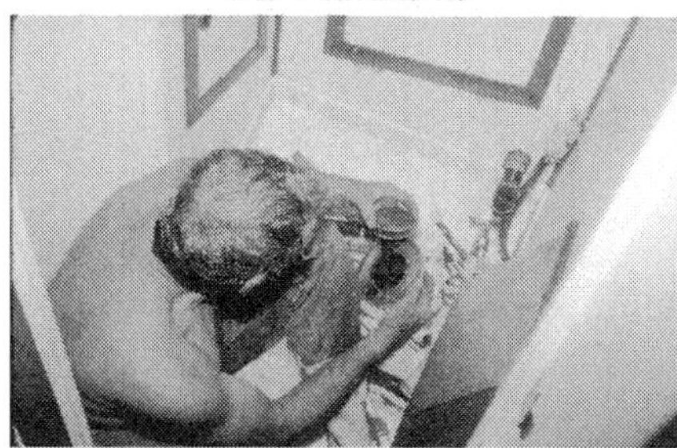
Stan Repairing Head

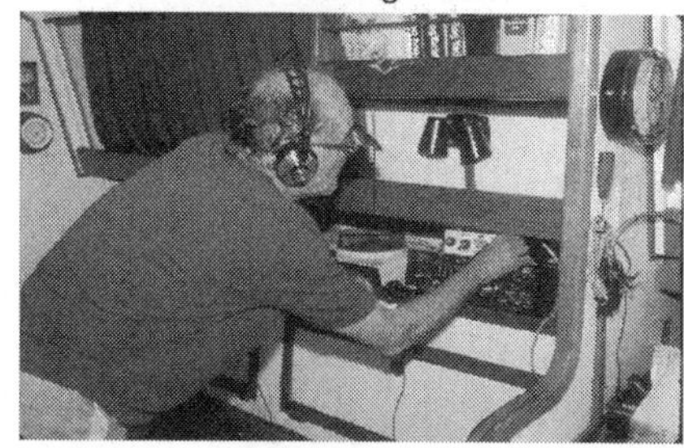
Ken at Radio

Twenty-Foot Waves

The Captain's Dinner

Up The Mast at Sea

The Light at the Head
of Old Kinsale

CHAPTER 38

Ireland and England

We spent ten days in Crosshaven while repairs were made to the boat, which was suffering from the rigors of the crossing. We met several wonderful Irish people on the dock. I was at the masthead when a club member, Ken Dixon, called to me and asked if I was an amateur radio operator. He and his wife Claire were also amateurs, and they visited us on our boat several times. We would be spending much more time with them later.

Finally we left for our cruise west along the Irish coast. The harbors were close together, so our sailing days were short. Most nights found us in a different location. We explored and shopped in many of the small coastal villages. The coast of Ireland is dotted with reminders of history. Almost every promontory had its castle ruins. Celts, Romans, Vikings, and English have all left their marks.

Ireland really is green; long northern latitude summer days, with the moderating Gulf Stream and frequent showers, result in a verdant countryside. Wildflowers abound. Much of Ireland has been deforested, but where the trees grow, leprechauns live.

The high point of our trip along the Irish coast was our visit to the Skellig Islands, which we had seen featured in a *National Geographic* magazine article years before. They lie off the coast of Ireland and have been described as the "outposts of Europe." On a misty day, as we sailed toward them, Small Skellig appeared first, white-sided, in contrast to the dark Skellig Michael. We circled the island; every ledge was covered with gannets and the air was filled with their cries. Their droppings had painted the island white. We later learned that this is the second largest gannet rookery in the world, with 20,000 nesting pairs.

Atop Skellig Michael are perched the remains of a sixth-century monastic settlement. We circled Skellig Michael, too. However, deep water precluded anchoring and the only dock was too small and too exposed for our boat, so we sailed on to Valencia Harbor. We anchored for the night and contracted with a local fisherman to take us to the Skelligs the next day. We were fortunate to be able to visit the island, because, many days, rough seas make it impossible to use the small stone dock. Passengers were discharged and the boats put out to sea to wait.

At first, the climb to the top was easy, up the graded lighthouse road, but not for long. Over 500 years after the birth of Christ, monks had carved steps into the steep face of the rock and set stones to mark the Stations of the Cross. The climb was breathtaking! Often, on one side of the path, there was a sheer drop to the sea hundreds of feet below. There were no guardrails!

The small beehive-shaped buildings have stood intact, largely unchanged, through the centuries. It seemed inconceivable that people could have lived here for a thousand years. This is one of the places where Christianity survived the Dark Ages. The Bible was preserved in settlements such as this. There was a thousand-year-old Celtic cross marking the very small common grave. The climb to the summit was physically difficult and frightening at times. Nevertheless, we left feeling awe for the faith of these early Christians.

When we arrived back at Valencia harbor, we found our anchored boat tied to the Coast Guard lifeboat. It had dragged its anchor across the harbor! It would have been less embarrassing if I hadn't been sounding off to the skipper of the fishing boat which took us to the island. He had been the bosun of their lifeboat, and I had told him about the many needless calls to which our U.S. Coast Guard had to respond.

We decided that we would like to have our Aries wind vane reconditioned at the factory in England. Our destination was Falmouth and we had a 36-hour sail across St. George's Channel, continuing around Land's End and the Lizard.

We arrived at Falmouth, England in the middle of the night and picked up a mooring. The next morning the customs boat cleared us into England and directed us to a mooring opposite the Royal Cornwall Yacht Club. Falmouth is an interesting city built on a narrow peninsula, with the great harbor on one side and resort beaches on the other. A 16th-century fortress castle, built by Henry VIII, guards the harbor entrance. We spent several days in Falmouth sightseeing and shopping.

The tides there were very high. We discovered this while we were having lunch at the Yacht Club with an American friend. We left our dinghy tied halfway up a long sloping ramp. We spent more time visiting than we had anticipated, and when we returned to retrieve our dinghy, we found it floating out in the water with the painter pointing straight down. We had to ask a man on the dock to row us out to our dinghy. We disconnected the painter and retrieved it after the tide had gone down.

We were bound for Cowes, the famous yachting center on the Isle of Wight, and on the way we visited several other famous harbors. We spent a night anchored in Plymouth harbor, a large naval port. The city of Dartmouth was the British equivalent to Annapolis. Castles on each side of the Dart River marked the entrance to the harbor. The British Royal Naval College overlooked both the harbor and the charming city with its Elizabethan buildings. Weymouth was a popular resort town. We stopped there twice. There was practically no dock space for yachts, so we became part of a ten-boat raft-up with only one boat tied to the dock. The entire raft drifted first one way and then another with the tide.

Boisterous winds buffeted us as we passed the Needles and entered the Solent, the passage between the Isle of Wight and the mainland. We passed the famous Royal Yacht Club. Here Queen Victoria watched the yacht *America* win the Hundred Guinea Cup, later known as the America's Cup. We tied up on a dock with hundreds of other yachts. Nick Franklin, the inventor of the Aries wind vane, reconditioned it while we were there.

With our wind vane repaired, we motor-sailed offshore and arrived back in Ireland, at the Royal Cork Yacht Club, on August 26. While we were preparing the boat for winter storage at a mooring, we were overwhelmed by Irish hospitality. One day Ken and Claire Dixon took us on a wonderful drive to the scenic lakes in Killarney National Park and then had us for dinner at their home. They offered to store our electronics for the winter, and we asked them if they would like to sail with us to Scotland next summer. They were very excited at the prospect.

We left our boat for the winter on a mooring at Drakes Pond in the Carrigaline River. The Yacht Club manager said that he would keep an eye on it for us. New Irish friends, Joan and Henry Jermaine, insisted that they would take us to Shannon airport on

September 2. What an amazing thing to have offered. They took us to their lovely home for the night and the next day drove three hours to the airport. We arrived back home on September 2.

Two days later, we drove to Annapolis, Maryland where we picked up the motorhome and drove it back home. During the years that I worked for the directory, we owned six different motorhomes. We never bought them at the same place. Four of them were purchased while we were traveling, when we found one that we liked at a dealer. We had specific things that we wanted in a motorhome which were quite different from those of the average recreational traveler. For one thing, we couldn't be overly large because we had to get in and out of our customers' parking lots without creating too much fuss. I needed a separate table for doing evening paperwork while Mary was preparing dinner. Our fifth motorhome was a Bounder. It had all these features as well as two comfortable single beds. Our biggest problem was that motorhomes were never meant to have as much mileage as we were putting on ours.

We stopped one morning at a large Alabama dealer's repair facility to fix a problem. I don't recall what it was, but while I was waiting, I looked at motorhomes in their sales lot. None of their new motorhomes fit our requirements, and I told the salesman that we just loved our Bounder. He said that he had just taken a Bounder in trade on a larger motorhome because the owner's wife wanted a washer and dryer. He went on to tell me that they had taken just one trip out west and the Bounder was in perfect condition. He said they were bringing it in that afternoon; we decided to wait and look at it. It was everything that he said, and we bought it. He took our motorhome in trade, and we spent the night at a nearby campground before we were to take delivery the next day. That evening I got into a conversation with a man who was purchasing used motorhomes. He asked me how much I was receiving from the dealer in trade, and when I told him, he said that he would give me $1000 more. The next morning, when I offered to make my purchase without a trade-in, the salesman agreed. The amazing thing was that the two motorhomes were identical, except that the newer one had a five-speed transmission, which turned out to give us two more miles per gallon. We parked the two motorhomes so that their doors were opposite each other, and when we moved our belongings, everything went exactly where it had been in the old motorhome.

In the spring of 1983, we had just returned from a business trip when the phone rang to tell us that Mary's mother had just died peacefully in her chair in a nursing home. She passed away less than a week before her 85th birthday. We were very grateful to have been there for her burial beside "The Judge," her husband, and for the memorial service at the Chagrin Falls Federated Church.

Celtic Cross's in Ireland

Skelig Lighthouse Trail

View From the Monk's Trail

Little Skelig Island

Approaching the Skelig Dock

6th Century Monastery Buildings

Dartmouth Harbor

CHAPTER 39

Scotland and Norway

On Sunday, June 5, 1983, we arrived at Shannon airport where Joan Jermaine met us and drove us to Crosshaven where the *Mary Constance* was tied to a yacht club dock. We spent three weeks working on the boat. We had a very social time during this period. A friend of Ken's, who taught refrigeration at a local trade school, worked on our boat refrigerator for hours, and absolutely would not accept any payment. Every page of Mary's journal has several names of people with whom we visited.

On June 24, our 39th wedding anniversary, we were about ready and fully provisioned for our trip to Scotland with Ken and Claire as crew. They were great company; Ken was a professional seaman who taught seamanship at a nearby school. Claire, on the other hand, had very little boating experience. She was a very experienced amateur radio operator who had talked to almost all of our states. During her time on the boat, she kept in regular contact with her brother in Tasmania.

Our trip that summer took us north, in the Irish Sea, to Scotland by way of Dublin and the Isle of Man. We stayed at a mooring at the Royal Irish Yacht Club while Mary and I spent a day in Dublin sightseeing. The club doorman wore tails! In the club register was the signature of Sir Thomas Lipton and his yacht, *Shamrock*.

The Isle of Man always had all the trappings of a typical British holiday resort. Ferries from England brought hordes of tourists. Douglas, the main city, had a horse-drawn street car running down the main street, which was lined with ornately faced hotels. We rode back to the harbor on a steam-powered narrow gauge railroad.

We found ourselves harbor bound, jammed in at the dock with fishing boats and all kinds of pleasure craft, for another day and a half waiting out a storm. At about 10:00 p.m. on the second day, the weather cleared, and we decided to sail overnight to Troon harbor, in Scotland, where we arrived at about 3:00 p.m. the next day. We all went to bed and slept for four hours. It was the Fourth of July, but no one was celebrating the holiday.

We left the boat on the mooring and took a one-hour trip, on a high-speed train, to the center of Glasgow. The Great Lakes Cruising Club had an exchange program with the Clyde Cruising Club in Glasgow. We had the name of the club secretary, so we called him and made an appointment to see him that afternoon. We hoped that he would be able to give us some guidance about cruising in Scotland.

In the morning, we took the subway to visit the Simpson Lawrence Company, which manufactured chain. We had found that in the deeper harbors which we were experiencing, we needed so much anchor line that we were making big sweeps of the harbor. Boats on chain didn't need to use as much. We made arrangements to have our new chain delivered to the ship's chandler in Inverness.

We found the Clyde Cruising Club that afternoon and were surprised to find that it was located in the Clyde River on an old schooner with its masts removed. Sandy Taggart, the club secretary, turned out to be a successful businessman, who took time off from work to visit with us. He met us with a large portfolio of charts and spent a long time showing us the best places to sail. Then he amazed us by saying, "Why don't you just take these charts with you as long as you're in Scotland and then return them to us." The detailed charts would have cost us more than $200.

We spent several days in the Western Isles, anchoring at night in beautiful harbors. Every day we visited with other sailors, on their boat or ours. As usual, they told us about their favorite places which we should really see. We shopped in small towns for provisions. In more isolated anchorages, we went ashore and walked on the moors.

We sailed west to the Outer Hebrides, which protect northern Scotland from the Atlantic Ocean. Wizards Pool on South Uist Island is described by world sailor Eric Hiscock as one of the three best harbors he has ever visited. We had it all to ourselves and climbed up in the hills to photograph our boat below.

We learned something about perception, when, in the fog, we approached the harbor of the remote town of Loch Maddy, on the island of North Uist. We were looking for a light at the entrance, and a fairly large structure appeared out of the fog so we headed toward it. Suddenly we heard surf and realized that the lighthouse was only about five feet tall and we were uncomfortably close to the shore. The fog had distorted all of our depth perception. We backed off and discovered the harbor entrance.

To take advantage of beautiful clear sailing weather, we returned to the Western Isles. As we sailed along the coast of the island of Skye, sunlight filtered through the ocean-born clouds creating beautiful constantly changing patterns on the sea and the mountains beyond.

Off the southwest tip of the island of Mull lies tiny Iona. It has been the home of Christian communities since the first monastery was founded by St. Columba in 563. What has been considered the most beautifully illuminated manuscript, the Book of Kells, was created here. Today the Iona community, a non-sectarian fellowship, operates a retreat center and maintains the 12th century church.

The 60-mile-long Caledonian Canal cuts through Scotland, from the Atlantic Ocean to the North Sea. Twenty-nine locks connect several lakes, the most famous of which is Loch Ness. The canal traverses the beautiful Scottish Highlands, following the great Glen. It was the third week in July when we entered the canal system. It took three days to complete the trip. Locks operated from 9:00 to 5:00 and never on Sundays. Four other boats accompanied us, two Scottish, one German, and another American boat. Some of the locks were 180 years old. The surging water which filled them sometimes resembled river rapids, sending boats in all directions as we fought to hold them off the walls. We traversed Loch Ness and never saw the monster. There were still snow patches on Ben Nevis, Great Britain's highest mountain.

Ken and Claire returned to Ireland when we reached Inverness, near the eastern end of the canal. Our new anchor chain was waiting for us when we arrived, and we were able to trade our 35-pound plow anchor for a 45-pound one. The man at the chandlery said he was going to Glasgow the next day and would return our charts to the Clyde Cruising Club. On Sunday, July 31, we passed through the sea lock at high tide and headed out into the Moray Firth. It is a 300-mile trip across the North Sea from Inverness to Bergen, Norway. We sailed for two and a half days. We had easy going for the first day, but we had to contend with force-seven winds on the second day. We reached the Norwegian coast at about midnight and spent the remaining hours in the dark trying to find the Bergen Sailing Club. Finally we saw a group of masts between two islands and picked up a mooring at the club at 8:00 a.m. We went to bed and slept until 4:00 p.m.

The next day, the club secretary drove us into Bergen, where we cleared customs and arranged to take a small freighter, named *Frieda,* on a two-day round trip up the Sognefjord. It is Norway's largest fjord, and it reaches 125 miles inland. We would have loved to take the *Mary Constance* up the fjord, but the water was too deep for anchoring and there was no room at the docks in the small towns along the way.

We were the only Americans among the 20 passengers on the small freighter. We were served three excellent meals a day, and the accommodations, while spartan, were comfortable. The first night we discovered that our cabin was just above the loading area of the boat, and the banging and bumping gave us a very un-restful night. When I asked for different accommodations, the purser gave us the VIP cabin. At first the freighter wound its way through very narrow passages, so close that sometimes it felt like we could reach out and touch the shore. Once we reached the great fjord, the water widened. We stopped at many of the small town docks, discharging and loading cargo and passengers. Along the shore, green farmlands reached back to the high mountains on either side, some of which were snow-capped. The trip cost very little and was a great experience.

Much of our passage south along the Norwegian coast was through channels behind off-lying islands. We had learned while visiting with Norwegian sailors that the small Lysefjord, near the city of Stavanger, was very beautiful and small enough that we could make a one-day round trip.

Early morning fog still shrouded the mountaintops as we entered the Lysefjord. The fog lifted as the day progressed. On the *Mary Constance,* we were able to motor close to the shore in the deep water. Several waterfalls cascaded down the mountainsides to the water. There were no towns until we reached the head of the fjord, where we tied up at a freight dock for lunch. Then we headed back in lovely warm sunshine.

As we traveled south and then southeast along the Norwegian coast, we would sail sometimes at sea, and then duck in, behind islands, through lovely, quiet passages. It seemed as if every obstacle was marked with a buoy. We felt that every Norwegian owned a summer cottage, which could be seen perched on shore or on an island. We were warmly welcomed everywhere we stopped and had many visits with people aboard our boat. As we rounded the tip of Norway, our course led us northeast.

On August 19, we sailed to the great Oslo fjord and reached the Royal Norwegian Yacht Club at about eight in the evening. We tied up temporarily. A little later, a man and his wife came down to the boat to visit and offered us the use of their slip.

We spent 12 days in Oslo, sightseeing and preparing the boat for the winter. We found the Herbrand Marina, in a well-protected cove, where we could leave the boat for the winter. It would be in the water all winter, but the water would not freeze because of the bubbler system. The boatyard manager told us that we would have to get a customs permit to leave the boat that long, so Mary and I went to the local customs office. A customs agent told us he could give us a permit but we would have to post a bond. Then I discovered that the bond would cost $10,000. I told the agent that we couldn't possibly afford to spend this much and asked if there was someone we could talk to who might be able to help us. He said maybe Mr. Nielsen (the name has been changed) could help us out and then sent us to a different location.

At a modern new building, when I asked the customs agent where I could find Mr. Nielsen, he replied, "I'll take you." We rode up a couple of floors in an elevator. When the elevator door opened, he pointed to an office door and quickly scurried back into the elevator. We found a reception area outside of Mr. Nielsen's office. His secretary, after I had told her about our problem, entered his office, then came out and ushered us in. Mr. Nielsen was most cordial and spent some time asking us about our sailing experiences in Norway. He seemed to understand our predicament. He thought about it for a few moments and said they could issue a letter of permission. He said they would seal the boat for the winter but we would have to leave the country next spring as soon as it was ready to go. He explained that this was the national office and that we would have to return to the local customs agent in order to have the letter issued.

After we reached the local office, the customs agent said once again that there was no problem leaving the boat but that we would have to post a bond. When I explained that Mr. Nielsen had said we could receive a letter of permission, he almost snapped to attention and said that if Mr. Nielsen had authorized this, he was sure it could be worked out. We discovered that Mr. Nielsen was the head of the entire Norwegian customs.

Before we left the boat for the winter, a young customs man and a woman in civilian clothes came to the marina where they "sealed" the *Mary Constance*. The sealing process amused us greatly. They wrapped a piece of string around the steering wheel and clamped it with a very official-looking seal. We thought it was funny because we still could have steered the boat anywhere while it was sealed, and we also still had access to the boat's interior. We flew from Oslo to Shannon airport and then back to the United States.

Ken and Claire

Hiking on the Moors

Wizards Cove

Caledonian Canal Lock

Bergen, Norway

Songe Fjord

Gustav Vigeland Statue

"Mary Constance" Winter Storage in Oslo

CHAPTER 40

Scandinavia

We started provisioning our yacht for a summer cruise in Europe while still in the United States during the winter and spring. We needed to buy replacement parts and supplies where they were available and then carry them with us. In 1984, when we boarded the plane in Cleveland, bound for Norway, we presented the ticket agent with a hanging bag, two large World War II duffel bags, a huge suitcase filled with engine parts and supplies, and a small suitcase for Mary's more delicate things. Mary carried aboard her train case and a large pocket book with our passports and ship's papers. I carried my camera case with two Nikons, four lenses and 20 rolls of film. Norwegian customs passed us through quickly. We had no cigarettes or liquor, and the engine parts didn't seem to interest them.

We found the *Mary Constance* ready for us when we arrived at the Herbrand Marina. The customs people came to our boat and cut the string that "sealed" her. It took us a week to clean, replace engine parts, rig and provision the boat before we were once again ready to resume our touring by sea.

We departed the marina on June 6, 1984, bound for Sweden. We were experiencing the very long summer days; we could read in the cockpit until well after 11:00 p.m. At about 1:30 a.m., we could see daylight on the horizon. In our first Swedish harbor,

Stromstead, we cleared customs and exchanged our Norwegian currency for Swedish.

The vacation season had not started, and we saw very few boats as we cruised south through the Swedish archipelago. We sailed most of this coast through the waters between and behind the islands, protected from the open sea. The four-color Scandinavian charts were a joy to use because they not only described the navigation marks but also indicated, with cardinal marks, to which side we should pass.

We stopped at small town harbors. Sometimes we anchored in unoccupied coves, where we found iron mooring rings driven into the rock. By dropping a bow anchor and tying the stern to one of the rings, we had a secure berth. As always, we visited with many people along the way. We docked at the Royal Swedish Yacht Club while we visited Gothenburg, Sweden's second largest city. For six days, during a windstorm, the *Mary Constance* remained secure at the Royal Danish Yacht Club just north of Copenhagen, while we made inland side trips by train. Mary and I celebrated our 40th wedding anniversary in Copenhagen with dinner on the terrace in the world-famous Tivoli Gardens. We later were able to motor with the *Mary Constance* through the Copenhagen harbor, where we photographed the famous "Little Mermaid" from the water. The European vacation season soon was starting, and we again shared dock space with other boats. No matter how far you were from shore, often alongside another boat, a harbormaster would collect harbor fees, usually about $5. It was a new experience for us to have boats tie alongside our boat without asking permission, but the large number of boats made this procedure necessary and we soon adopted it.

Mary and I found it difficult to maneuver our 48-foot sailboat in these small, crowded harbors. In Klintholm, Denmark, with 25-knot winds blowing, by the time we were secured to pilings, we had blocked six other boats. We also had one of our own dock lines snarled in our propeller! A professional diver had to cut it free and give us what was left of our 40-foot line. Denmark is a country of islands, ideal for boat tourists, except that they have very few natural harbors. Wherever possible we liked to anchor for the night, which gave us relief from the crowded harbors.

Dutch friends, whom we had met along the way, urged us to visit the Netherlands and told us that it might be a good place to leave our boat for the winter. We decided to take the German Kiel Canal from the North Sea to the Baltic Sea. The Kiel Canal is probably the most heavily trafficked artificial waterway in the world. With locks at both ends, it is largely water level for 61 miles. We passed through both locks tied alongside freighters, whose crew handled our lines for us. We made the passage under power and were never out of sight of large vessels coming and going.

Leaving the canal, our course took us down the Elbe River to Cuxhaven, and then west past the German Frisian Islands. We arrived at Borkum, last of the Frisian Islands, after dark with limited visibility. As we approached the harbor entrance, two fishing boats closely passed us from the stern, one on each side, yelling at us. Some of their wakes sloshed into our cockpit. We learned later that our stern light was not functioning. We were lucky they had been able to avoid us. At Borkum, a young Dutch couple changed our plans when they showed us how we could sail through the Dutch canals with our masts up.

The harbor at Delfzjl, our first Dutch port, was located outside of the dike. A gate, which could be closed, led down below sea level into the city. The very best way to tour the Netherlands is by canal. For centuries, the lifeblood of Holland has flowed through these arteries. Today, they are still the focus of commercial, cultural and recreational life.

All of the canals through which we passed had lift bridges. Passing through a city could be a very slow trip. At each street crossing the canal, we waited until the bridge tender decided enough boats had accumulated to stop the automobile traffic and lift the bridge. Sometimes the same bridge tender served several bridges, riding his bicycle from bridge to bridge.

With favorable winds, we spent one whole day under sail, along with dozens of other sailboats. Using just our genoa jib, we simply furled it at the bridges and then unrolled it again until the next bridge.

We entered the Ijsselmeer at the town of Stavoran. The Ijsselmeer was once known as the Zuider Zee. It was separated from the North Sea, in the 1930's, by a long dike. Gradually, over the years, the lake cleansed itself of salt and today it is fresh water. As salt-water fishing ended, the small fishing villages along the shore of the Ijsselmeer stopped growing, frozen in time; they remain untouched today as popular tourist sites.

In Stavoran, we found a marina with a large undercover storage shed where we could leave our boat for the winter. I had discovered some small blisters on the hull which concerned us. I contracted with the yard to store the boat inside all winter. This would make sure it was well dried, before refinishing of the bottom with epoxy and paint was done.

With our winter arrangements completed, we sailed to Amsterdam where we tied up at Six Marina just across the canal from the city, which we reached by free ferry. By now we had decided that we would like to sail to London. We have always enjoyed visiting large cities, and we still had time left in the summer. We spent several days in Amsterdam, sightseeing and purchasing the necessary charts for our crossing to England.

The busy North Sea Canal connects Amsterdam to the English Channel. A wonderful overnight passage, sailing on a broad reach, took us to the entrance to the Stour River, where we found a good anchorage. We went to bed at about 8:30 a.m. The next day we sailed to Ipswich where we cleared British customs.

We were now back in an area of very high tides, and like the sailing vessels of old, we needed to ride the flood tide up the Thames River. So we spent the night anchored in the Roach River, just off the Thames estuary. We left at 4:00 a.m. to wend our way through the estuary that is crossed and re-crossed by well-marked channels. Every obstacle was not only marked on our chart but was named; one name that still sticks in my mind was "Foulness Shoal."

Riding the flood tide, our trip up the Thames to London was exciting. We passed the huge floodgates that protect the city from flooding in very high tides and winds. We motored past Greenwich, the location of the Prime Meridian. We finally arrived just off the Tower Bridge, where we had to wait for almost three hours to pass through the lock at St. Catherine's Dock Marina. St. Catherine's Marina is located in the old "Dickens" part of the city and was once the port for the Ivory House.

When the gates opened at high tide, the departing boats had to exit first, followed by the larger craft waiting to enter. Finally it was our turn and we were assigned a dock. Our boat became part of the tourist attractions. We spent six days in London and had a wonderful time. The dock was very convenient to the "tube" (subway), so it was easy getting around the city. We attended two theater performances, *Singing in the Rain* and *Noises Off*.

On Tuesday, August 14, Mary's birthday, she received a very unusual bunch of presents. We bought several charts, three pilot books, Greek and Yugoslavian flags, and two new large 23-pound propane tanks. Ah, the life of a sailor!

Five days later, we left London at 7:00 a.m. on the high tide and rode the ebb tide all the way out into the North Sea. We motored all the way across the English Channel and arrived at Ostend, Belgium at 2:00 a.m. We tied up at the first dock we could see. The next day the dockmaster told us to move to the main dock where we cleared customs.

We rested for one day at Ostend and then made a quick passage back to Stavoran, where the boatyard removed our masts and moved the *Mary Constance* inside for winter storage and repairs. Before we left, we told the boatyard that we wanted our masts fastened horizontally on deck for a trip through the French canals. That summer we had been in seven countries!

We used a ferry and a train to reach Amsterdam, then flew from Amsterdam to Oslo and then home to the United States. During the winter we asked Stan and Joey if they would like to crew for us on our trip through the rivers and canals from Amsterdam to Marseille in the Mediterranean. They immediately agreed to go with us.

Student Graduates celebrate in Copenhagen

Village in Denmark

Transiting The Kiel Canal

Sailing with local boats
on the Canals of Holland

Waiting for bridges in a city in Holland

Town on the Ijsselmeer

Tied-Up in a Park on the Canal

CHAPTER 41

Through Europe on the Canals and Rivers

In 1985, about ten days before we were due to arrive in Holland to pick up our boat, the boatyard called to inform us that someone had broken into our boat over a weekend and stolen a lot of things. I called our insurance company and they informed me that I would have to have a copy of the police report about the burglary. I would have to file this report, in person, in Holland. The last place in the world that we would have expected to have a break-in was in this little town in Holland.

Stan and Joey, Mary and I, flew together to Amsterdam and then took a train and ferry to Stavoran. We arrived on May 30, and the next morning we went to the boat to find out what had been stolen. The boatyard had moved the boat from the shed to the dock and left it there over the weekend, when the burglary had taken place. The most surprising thing we found was that a thief had taken our Aries steering vane right off the transom! We were happy to find that he had left the compound curved mounting blocks in place. The other happy fact was that we had stored all of our electronic equipment in the marina's storage locker. The thieves had cleaned out the storage area, which had been a quarter berth in the pass-through to the aft cabin. Gone were the Avon dinghy, boom vang, bosun's chair, some electrical tools, 250 feet of line, and many other things. They also had stolen all of our flags and charts, as well as two sail bags to carry away some of the loot.

I filled out the necessary police report and mailed it, with a complete list of the stolen items and their value, to the insurance company. They were very generous in reimbursing us for the loss.

In an odd sense, the thieves almost did us a favor. We didn't need most of the items they took for our trip through the canals. They missed our outboard motor, which was stored in a seat locker beneath the pile of life preservers. We were able to store our sails in the now empty pass-through shelf, instead of on deck as we had planned. We felt bad about the courtesy flags, but we could acquire new ones along the way. The charts that they took were all ones which we had already used. We had brought the new ones with us. We did not need a dinghy in the canals.

During the mid-19th century, Europe experienced explosive growth in navigable inland waterways. Entrepreneurs and governments built dams and locks to control the rivers, and dug canals to connect them. Most of the waterways have been maintained to this day.

We were fortunate that Europe was having normal weather in 1985. If there is too much rain, boats can't get under the low bridges. Too little rain would have meant that many of the canals would have been too shallow for our boat.

We left Stavoran on June 6. The first part of our trip took us to Amsterdam, then south on the Maas-Meuse River and its parallel canals through Holland and Belgium. In France we cruised west on the Canal des Ardennes and the River Oise to the River Seine and Paris. We really needed Stan and Joey with us, because we expected to pass through 323 locks before we reached the Mediterranean. We paid no fees for the use of the French and Dutch canals and only a very small amount in Belgium.

Where we could, we liked to tie up for the night at docks in the cities and towns along the canals. We could sightsee, and, in France, buy delicious French bread and croissants some mornings. Often I felt as though I was traveling back in history. In Belgium, the cities along the Meuse had suffered the ravages of both world wars; every town had its war memorials. The bridges under which we passed had been destroyed and rebuilt several times. The town names recalled great battles.

We crossed the French border at Givet. The customs agent gave our boat a perfunctory examination and cleared us into his country. Leaving the Meuse, we entered the narrower Canal des Ardennes where the locks were smaller and in most cases hand-operated. We sometimes felt obligated to help open and close the gates and sluice controls because the lock keeper happened to be an elderly woman. By now, we had refined our locking technique. One person stood on the foredeck, another on the stern, and usually a third was dropped off on the shore as we entered the lock to handle the lines. Mary stayed at the wheel to steer the *Mary Constance* into the lock.

The city of Confluence, at the junction of the Oise and Seine rivers, was a favorite stopping point for barge families. A chapel on one of the barges was tied up there. We spoke to several families who lived aboard their barges. Some of the owners were second and third generation skippers. During school season, their children often boarded on shore during the week, and then joined their families for the weekend when ever possible.

We all were excited as we traveled up the River Seine below Paris. Mary and I had visited Paris 20 years before, but Stan and Joey had never been there. What a thrilling way to enter Paris! The Seine is crossed by 30 bridges. The river bisects the "city of light"—great buildings lining its right and left banks. Our destination was the St. Martin Canal which entered the Seine off the right bank, in the northeastern part of the city. Our course took us right through the center of Paris. We passed close by Notre Dame Cathedral on our way to the canal.

An entrance lock lifted us almost ten feet into the St. Martin Canal anchorage. A modern marina, located at the entrance to the canal, provided a secure berth for the *Mary Constance* while we visited Paris. We had water and electric connections at the dock, and in those days it cost us only $82 for the week. Our berth was only five minutes from the subway.

Stan and Joey, new to the city, visited it differently than we did. We had seen many of the usual tourist attractions and spent more time wandering in some of the neighborhoods. In one, we stumbled upon a wonderful neighborhood street dance. All four of us took a trip by bus to visit the great Chartres Cathedral.

While we were in Paris, we called home and received the sad news that my father had died. He'd been gravely ill for some time. Our daughter Connie took care of him in the nursing home at Shell Point and was with him during his last month.

He was 90 years old and had insisted that there be no memorial service, so there was no need for us to return to Florida.

Once again under way on the Seine, we were in the suburbs only a few kilometers from the marina when our propeller fouled and the engine stalled. We coasted to a barge where, unbelievably, we found a scuba diver aboard another sailboat tied alongside the same barge. He removed a heavy ball of plastic from our propeller and we were under way again in less than an hour. Maybe it's better to be a lucky sailor than a skill-ful sailor.

On the Fourth of July, we observed a *Mary Constance* tradition and dressed the ship with all of our signal flags. Later that day, the entire crew of a British yacht lined up on deck and saluted us as they passed by. That same day as the Seine turned north, we headed south on the River Yonne.

Two days later on July 6, we entered the Canal de Bourgogne. This small canal winds its way through Burgundy. One hundred and ninety locks, in about as many kilometers, lift boats up to a two-mile-long tunnel at the summit, then down again to join the Saône River at Dijon.

We met people in interesting ways. I was ashore, tying up the boat to a dock in the small town of Brienon, when an elderly man approached me. It was impossible for me to understand what he was trying to tell me, but I smiled and tried to be friendly. Then a younger man, who spoke perfect English, stopped by and asked if he could help me. I thanked him for his help. The old man had seen our American flag and wanted to tell me that he had worked for the American Army during World War II.

Stan and Joey had gone into town, so we were alone when the man who had interpreted for me, Bernard Gadget, and his wife Colette arrived at the boat and asked us if we would like to visit their home. It had been in the family for 600 years. We found it fascinating. It was located on the town square and consisted of two ancient buildings that had been connected to make one residence. The furnishings were all genuine old French Provincial. Bernard introduced us to his mother, who was of our generation. Using him to interpret, we had a great conversation. At the end of our visit Bernard said, "I've saved the best room for last." He took us down a flight of stairs to his wine cellar, a most impressive room. He surveyed the rack, selected a bottle of wine, blew off the dust and handed it to me to take back to the boat. We learned that Bernard and his wife actually lived in Paris, where he worked for IBM. They were home for a holiday visit with his mother.

On July 11 we set a record by passing through 37 locks in 23 kilometers. The next day, one day before we expected to reach the summit of the canal and the tunnel, we overtook another American boat. We were pleased and surprised to discover it was *Pilgrim,* from Cleveland, Ohio. Aboard were Drew Peretzky and his wife Cathy Brugett. We recognized Kathy because she had been doing a program on Cleveland television. Drew was a professional photographer. We decided to travel together for a while.

The next day, July 13, we reached the summit of the canal and a two-mile-long, water-level tunnel through a mountain. The tunnel was one way, and we needed clearance from the tunnel authority to enter it. When we entered the tunnel, far off in the distance we saw what looked like a star, which actually was the "light at the end of the tunnel." *Pilgrim* led the way because there were no lights in the tunnel. We had a powerful searchlight, which lighted the way for both boats. One tension-filled hour later, we emerged from the dark tunnel into bright daylight.

The next day, July 14, was Bastille Day, a French holiday. Kathy suggested that Château Neuf, a medieval walled village, would be a good place to spend the holiday. We tied up on the canal bank and dressed our ships for the occasion. That evening we climbed the long path to the beautiful ancient village, where the villagers were celebrating with a carnival. We joined a torch-light procession to the castle gates, in a symbolic storming of the Bastille. Kathy said, "It's just like a Fellini movie."

Kathy and Drew decided to stay another day at Château Neuf, because they were doing short TV programs along the way for a Cleveland station. They videoed a program about the four of us, who were all Greater Cleveland residents.

We continued down the canal to the beautiful Saône River, which meets the mighty Rhône River at Lyon. We found a dock in the heart of Lyon, France's second largest city, where Stan and Joey left us to return home, via train to Rome.

We had about two knots of current with us as we motored down the scenic Rhône River toward the Mediterranean. We passed through five huge locks, the largest of which lowered us more than 90 feet in ten minutes. The locks seemed easy because they had floating bollards, to which we could tie as the water lowered.

When we approached the first lock, we found we had to wait for it to fill. We headed toward some pilings, to attach a line while we waited, when Mary discovered that neither our forward nor reverse gears were working, so we drifted. To our port was a mean-looking spillway with river water flowing over it. Fortunately, a 20-knot wind was blowing up the Rhône against the two-knot current. The two forces canceled each other and we remained almost stationary. Some distance away I could see a Dutch motorsailer approaching us, and I waved my arms frantically. He tied alongside our boat and towed us through the lock, which had opened by this time, and we tied beside the lock entrance wall.

The Dutch sailor wouldn't let me touch anything, as we examined the driveshaft to discover that it separated from the engine coupling. He said, "I can fix that," and managed to insert the driveshaft into the coupling and tighten one bolt to hold it in place. A critical key and two other bolts were lost in the bilge. All during this time, the lock tender had been advising us that we were not allowed to tie up there.

The temporary repairs meant that we could no longer use reverse because we would pull the shaft out of the coupling again. But we could go forward because the pressure from the propeller held the shaft in place. We had passed a marina a few miles upriver, so we entered the lock again and headed up the river to the marina. When we arrived, I told Mary that she might get one spurt of reverse before the shaft pulled free again. She did a magnificent job of maneuvering the boat into a slip and used the last spurt of reverse to stop us. The marina mechanic replaced the key and the bolts. We spent the night at the dock, decompressing from our experience and visiting with dock mates.

We stopped at the walled city of Avignon, home of the Papacy during much of the 14th century. We passed the Roman Bridge, "Le Pont d'Avignon," and tied up alongside another boat at the yacht quay. We were delighted to discover that we had arrived during the famous Avignon Festival. We walked through a narrow winding cut in the rock that led into the city. The Papal Palace and large residences, built for the Cardinals, face the Great Plaza. That night it was filled with performing artists and crowds. We had a wonderful meal in town and met an interesting couple who were there to study the festival. They were the organizers of the Sydney, Australia Fine Arts Festival.

On July 29 we arrived at Port St. Louis, at the entrance to the Mediterranean Sea. Late that afternoon, the highly skilled boatyard stepped our masts. We spent two days finishing the rigging and getting the boat, once again, ready for sailing.

While at the port, I found three teenage boys who were delighted to take our four inoperative, surplus Amsterdam Fleamarket bicycles. I had a difficult time convincing them that they actually were free. The next day they appeared on the dock to show us two of the bikes that they had already repaired.

On the first day of August 1985, we cleared the short St. Louis Canal and entered the Mediterranean. We hoisted sails and headed for Marseille. It was wonderful to be sailing the *Mary Constance* again!

Two rocky islands form the outer harbor of Marseille. They were connected by large breakwalls. We rounded a protective fortress and tied up, at Port de Frioul, with a "Mediterranean mooring." We accomplished this by coming in with an anchor dropped off the stern and the bow then tied to the dock. Marseille was spread out behind us. The next day we took a small ferry to the Inner Harbor at Marseille, where we purchased charts and a new Zodiac dinghy.

During the summer, someone had suggested that the Balearic Islands would be a good place to leave our boat for the winter and suggested the yacht club in Palma Majorca. So we "harbor-hopped" west along the French and Spanish coasts. We cleared Spanish customs in a resort town that looked just like southern Florida.

We left the next morning for the Balearic Islands, but very strong headwinds and rough seas forced us to return to the harbor. The next day our attempt was much more successful, with almost perfect wind for the 24-hour crossing. We arrived at sunrise and rounded Cape Fermenter, on the northern tip of Majorca, the largest of the islands. There we anchored for a day in a beautiful harbor. Majorca is a very popular cruising ground, and as we made our way to Palma de Majorca, we were surprised to meet, and visit with, a number of American boats.

We left our boat for the winter on land at the Club Nautical Arenal, a very modern yacht club located near the beach of Palma. Perhaps we overreacted to the "break-in" in Holland, because this time we left the *Mary Constance* on land, in a guarded storage area protected by a 13-foot fence.

When we describe our unusual lifestyle, people often ask us how we could stand being in such close proximity in both the boat and motorhome. While cruising on our boat we actually had a social life, many days visiting with new acquaintances on boats and onshore. We also had established routines; Mary cooked while I worked on maintaining the boat. We were constantly visiting new and interesting places. We were actually tourists on the boat.

Back at work, Mary was very good at reading maps and noting our day's calls, then directing me to my funeral home customers. In most cases, while I was visiting the funeral home, Mary had time to read or to do needlework. In some places, the funeral director's wife came out to the motorhome for a visit. We also met many people in the campgrounds and parks. We had the opportunity to discover many interesting things in the parks in which we spent our weekends. At the end of the day, while Mary prepared supper, I worked on the paperwork from the day's calls. We had a television in all of our motorhomes, and when they became available, we purchased a DirecTV dish that I set up outside our motorhome. This gave us a wide choice of programs.

When we started sailing, I merged two hobbies, sailing and photography. On each leg of our trips, I took hundreds of Kodachrome slide pictures. When we returned home, Mary and I arranged the pictures to illustrate our summer cruise. Then I wrote a script so that we could add narration to the slides and finally put it all to music. We used two projectors and a dissolve unit that controlled the projectors, the narration and the music. A finished program ran automatically, from a cassette tape recorder, for 45 minutes. Before we finished cruising, we had produced nine programs that we showed in all kinds of places: churches, libraries, civic organizations, campgrounds, retirement communities and, a few times, for funeral home customers. Before our equipment got too old and tired, we had shown our programs more than 100 times. These programs were very much a shared activity.

Launching the "Mary Constance" In Holland

Approaching Paris

Barge Traffic on the Mass River

Tied-up in Liege, Belgium

"Mary Constance under power

On The Canal De Bourgogne with "Pilgrim"

The Plaza at Avignon

Large Rhône River Lock

CHAPTER 42

Islands of the Mediterranean

In 1986, we arrived at the boat in Palma Majorca on June 5. We found the *Mary Constance* still parked among the palm trees, where we had left her, at the yacht club. Everything in the boat was exactly as we had left it. It took us three weeks, I sanding and painting the bottom, installing a replacement Aries wind vane, and working on the rigging, replacing many of the lines that we had lost in the robbery of the previous year.

To sail the Mediterranean is to live with history. A sense of antiquity pervades the atmosphere. We learned that in most of the cities and villages we visited, beneath the outer skin of modern civilization, are layer upon layer of ancient civilizations, going back to early history. The same elemental forces of wind and sea that we contended with were there when the ancient Greek and Roman trading vessels plied these waters. Without sea trade, there would have been no civilization. The very winds with which we sailed are still called by ancient names. The Mistral, Meltemi, Sirocco, and Bora affected us, as they have all sailors through recorded time.

We spent the summer cruising east through the islands of the Mediterranean Sea and ended up in Turkey. Our trip took us to Corsica, Sardinia, Sicily, and the Ionian and Aegean Greek islands and Cofu. Each of the islands was fascinating in a different way. We were very fortunate to have cruised these islands when we did. Today they are much more crowded with boats. We had to check in and clear customs in each new country, and today the European Union has eliminated this. However, we had little trouble leaving our boat for the winter, no matter where we ended up. Now, much more stringent regulations make this more difficult to accomplish. Often we were able to tie right up to a dock in the center of town. In most places where we had to pay for dockage, the fees were small.

Several things stand out in my mind about that summer, one of which was our passage through the Straits of Messina, which separate the toe of Italy from Sicily. The straits were once reported to be the location of the whirlpool Charybdis, described in the Odyssey. On our passage there were still strong tidal currents and winds, but reportedly, earthquakes have altered the bottom, smoothing the passage of the water. The greatest danger was from crossing ferryboats.

We cleared Greek customs on the island of Corfu, situated between the Ionian and Adriatic seas. Its recorded history dates from around 1200 B.C. We anchored in lovely protected water beneath a large fortress and were able to use the fortress moat to reach the center of the city by dinghy. This island has been occupied by Minoans, Corinthians, Athenians, Romans, Byzantines, Normans, Sicilians, Turks, Venetians, French, and British. Each culture has left its mark. We came to clear customs, but stayed almost a week.

We left our boat at the dock at Galaxidhi, a small town on the Gulf of Patras, and took a taxi to the ruins of Delphi, whose spectacular location high in the mountains makes it particularly fascinating. Its largely intact amphitheater was built for crowds attending the Pythian Games, the first of which occurred in 776 B.C. Delphi was one of the few places where citizens of competing Greek city-states could meet in peace. Delphi was also where people came to visit the famous Delphic Oracle.

We motored through the three-mile-long Corinth Canal. It is hewn out of solid rock, rising precipitously on either side. It connects the Ionian and Aegean Seas and separates the Peloponnesus from the rest of Greece. Nero, using 6000 Jewish slaves, first undertook the canal's construction. He failed. It was not until 1893 that a French company completed the project.

In the summer, the strong Meltemi winds originate in the Alps and flow down the river valleys to the Mediterranean. The wind often blows from the north, night and day, for days at a time. This meant that we had to make quick dashes between islands whenever the winds diminished. However, the winds caught up with us on the popular tourist island of Mykonos.

We were able to set our anchor in a patch of weed-free sand close to the beach and let out lots of chain. We didn't have to worry about drifting ashore because the winds always blew from the same direction. For two days we had to stay on the boat. We were afraid that if we took our dinghy to shore and the engine failed, we would not have been able to row back against the very strong winds. We watched, as several boats had no success in setting their anchors. We were particularly amused by one very odd-looking powered catamaran, whose crew dropped their anchor off the bow, let out a little bit of anchor line, and disappeared below decks. Their boat must have drifted a quarter of a mile offshore when the crew reappeared on deck. With much waving of arms, they set their anchor again, just as before, with the same result. Finally, they just gave up and motored away.

Mykonos was a beautiful place to be trapped by the winds. It is certainly the most photographed island in all of Greece. Whitewashed buildings and narrow shaded streets lead up from a very colorful harbor. It was once a fishing village, but today its only industry is tourism.

The Meltemi winds diminish in the fall. We were on the island of Samos, on September 9, when we awoke to find no wind at all. After untangling our anchor line from those of two other boats, we set out across the Samos Strait for nearby Turkey.

Kusadasi, where we entered Turkey, has a modern marina with just about every convenience. The city is a popular port for cruise ships because of its proximity to the ruins of Ephesus. This small town had over 40 Oriental rug shops. A taxi driver took us into town and showed us where to go to clear customs, and where to find immigration, the harbormaster's office and the bank, all of which were in different locations. Back at the marina, I gave the taxi driver what I thought was $10 in Turkish currency. He refused it and took out the correct Turkish money, from his wallet, laying it beside mine to show me the mistake. I had offered him the equivalent of $100 US. Imagine what would have happened if I had made this mistake in New York City.

We sought out the same driver for our trip to view the ruins of Ephesus. The site is impressive for its size and for the clarity with which one can picture life in the ancient city. One can walk down the marble roads, once lined with shops, protected from the sun by colonnade-covered sidewalks. It was exciting to walk down the same roads that St. Paul used in 53 A.D. The city is important because it was one of the first places where the evolution from paganism to Christianity took place.

Close to Ephesus are the remains of the large Byzantine basilica of St. John the Beloved, where the disciple is reputed to be buried. The ruins of this large building give evidence of the rapid spread of Christianity in the area. We found it ironic that today Turkey is a Muslim country.

We cruised south along the rugged, scenic Carian Coast of Turkey, to the city of Bodrum, ancient Halicarnassus. While walking in town, we discovered a sandwich-board sign with a picture of a modern Travel Lift. We climbed the stairs to a second-floor office, where we asked a man if they could haul and store boats for the winter. He said that he could. A South African sailor, who was sitting in the office, said that he had left his boat there for several winters with no problems. We made arrangements to leave the *Mary Constance* for the winter.

Now that we knew where we were going to leave the boat, we were able to relax and spend ten leisurely days cruising the beautiful unspoiled Gulf of Gokova. We spent our last sailing days of the summer in those lovely Turkish waters.

There were chickens and goats in the boatyard at Bodrum and no facilities, but they used their modern Travel Lift to move our boat out of the sea. We spent our nights in a small hotel while we prepared the boat for the winter.

We started our way home on a small ferry to the Greek island of Kos. The same afternoon we took a large ferry overnight to Athens. We flew home from there. It seemed fitting that we spent a final day of our trip in Athens, visiting the Acropolis. We had visited many of the islands that classical Athens had controlled.

In May of 1987, our daughter Beth married Tony Parkes in our Federated Church. They are both dance callers and had met at a dance week. Members of Tony's band and several of their caller friends came to the wedding, so there was dancing at the reception.

Soon after the wedding, we left for Turkey.

The Boys and our Old Bikes

Iinner Harbor at Marseilles

The Scenic Coast of Majorca

Corsica Coast

Bonifacio, Corsica Harbor

Cagliari, Sardinia

Corfu Anchorage

Corfu Fortress Moat

CHAPTER 43

The Eastern Mediterranean

Our trip would take us from Bodrum to Mamaris, in Turkey, then south to the Greek island of Rhodes. Next we island-hopped to Karpathos, Kasos, and Crete. We sailed northwest, to Kithira and the city of Methoni, on the southwesternmost point of mainland Greece. From there, we sailed north through the Greek Ionian islands on the way to the Adriatic Sea. From Corfu we bypassed Albania, keeping well offshore, to Yugoslavia, where we spent two months following the coast northward. Finally we crossed the Adriatic to Venice.

While making plans to return to our boat in Turkey, we discovered we could save a lot of money by flying to Istanbul and then taking a bus to Bodrum. We thought the bus trip would give us a chance to see some of inland Turkey. We arrived in Istanbul on June 2 and spent three days doing all the things that tourists do. When we picked up our bus tickets, we discovered that our bus would leave at 8:30 p.m.

The bus trip was excruciating; the bus itself was not bad, but the trip was mostly after dark so we saw little of the countryside. The roads were rough, making sleep almost impossible. The bus stopped at a rest stop every three hours. The toilets were primitive, consisting of a hole in the concrete with footpads on either side, with no flush and no paper. One stop at 3:00 a.m. was out of this world. Brightly lit, with music blaring, it had a "farmers' market" spread out on tables, and a wine shop. It was alive with people, lots of old men, and the passengers from several buses. It was hard to believe that that it was the middle of the night! The entire trip lasted 14 hours. From the Bodrum bus station, we took a taxi directly to our boat in the boatyard. We found the *Mary Constance* exactly as we had left her. We loaded most of our baggage aboard and then took a small suitcase to the hotel, where we fell gratefully into bed.

We spent nine days getting the boat ready to leave. Our trip south along the Turkish coast was fun. Sailing during the day, we spent each night at anchor. The scenery was spectacular, and we discovered that this was a popular cruising ground. Many nights we were joined by a number of Gulicks, Turkish-crewed charter boats, or by flotillas of small charter sailboats escorted from harbor to harbor by a "mother duck" boat. In some anchorages we found attractive restaurants that served visiting yachts during the season.

Strong Meltemi winds blew us into the harbor of the Greek island of Rhodes and kept us there for a week. We were incredibly lucky to secure a place on the dock, which was crowded with charter and excursion boats, leaving little space for visiting yachts. In 280 B.C., one of the seven wonders of the ancient world, the famous Colossus of Rhodes, a huge bronze statue of Apollo, had stood astride the harbor entrance. The medieval walled city was a delight.

We reached the island of Crete on the Fourth of July. We tied to the dock at Iraklion, the capital of Crete. Just outside the city are the ruins of Knossos, the most ancient city in Europe. Four thousand years ago, Minoan kings built a civilized city so powerful that it needed no fortifications. The huge palace is thought to be the labyrinth in the Greek myth of Thesus and the Minotaur. We walked on the oldest road in Europe, 2000 years older than Rome's Appian Way.

The village of Methoni, on the farthest west of the Greek Peloponnesian capes, is dominated by a huge fortress protecting this important headland. Over the centuries it changed hands many times. The Turks imprisoned Cervantes here. His tale of the prisoner in *Don Quixote* was probably inspired by this experience. When we visited the fortress, we found that the only building still in use was a small chapel. Wildflowers had taken over the courtyard.

In the same village harbor, another sailor spotted a Greek fishing boat whose anchor had broken loose and was drifting. Using my dinghy, we motored over to the boat, boarded it, and set the anchor again, using chain that was lying in a heap on the bow. The next morning, when we awoke, I found a plastic bag full of very nice fish in our cockpit. There were far more than we could use, so we shared them with a number of boats in the harbor. Mary fried ours for supper and they were delicious.

As we journeyed north through the Greek Ionian islands, we crossed our track from the previous year. We anchored at Corfu in preparation for our trip to Yugoslavia. At that time, Communist Albania was a very closed country and we were advised to stay well out of their territorial waters, which extended 15 miles out from the shore. Communist Yugoslavia, on the other hand, welcomed foreign yachts.

During our overnight sail, we witnessed a constant lightning display from behind the Albanian high mountains. We entered Yugoslavia at Bar, whose large commercial harbor was perhaps the cleanest we had ever visited. We discovered that the modern appearance of this old city was the result of extensive rebuilding after a devastating earthquake in 1979 that had leveled most of the buildings.

We had obtained our visas at the Yugoslav consulate in Cleveland. The immigration official who boarded our boat was overweight and gruff, almost a stereotype of what we expected of a Communist official. He had obviously never seen a visa issued in Cleveland. Finally he stamped our passports and asked if we had anything to drink. I took a cold beer out of the refrigerator, snapped the top and handed it to him. He took one sip and said, "Too cold," set it down and left.

The Adriatic coast of Yugoslavia offered some of the finest cruising waters in the Mediterranean. Parallel off-lying islands provided sheltered sailing along much of the coast. We had a leisurely sail north, stopping at places that interested us.

The Gulf of Kotor would be called a fjord anywhere in the North. It winds its way 15 miles inland to the city of Kotor, an ancient walled city, whose walls climb up the mountainside to surround the city. It had been another earthquake victim. A UNESCO grant was helping to pay for the restoration of the beautiful old buildings. Miraculously, an old church was undamaged. Other buildings also had survived untouched and were occupied, as they had been for centuries.

It is possible that Dubrovnik was Europe's best-preserved medieval city. It was certainly Yugoslavia's most popular tourist attraction. We put in at a modern marina north of the city. The marina, built on the waterfront property of a former summer estate, featured outdoor dining in the formal gardens and an impressive restaurant in the old villa. One could circle the entire walled city of Dubrovnik on top of the battlements. We found Dubrovnik amazingly free from the usual street vendors, with their tourist wares, which helped to preserve the medieval ambience of the town.

At Split, the Dalmatian coast's largest city, we joined the Adriatic Club Yugoslavia. Our membership gave us free docking privileges at their 16 modern marinas, strategically placed along the coast. Our membership, which seemed expensive, actually was not, because it included free winter storage on land.

At Split we had the *Mary Constance* hauled on the slipway, where a mechanic fabricated a new propeller shaft and coupling which solved the coupling problem that we had experienced several times. It never gave us trouble again, as long as we owned the boat.

North of Split, the islands of the Croatian coast are more arid, with the great white mountains of the mainland looming over them. The Trogir Marina, like many other ACY marinas, was located in the center of a fascinating old city. This full-service marina had a store, restaurant, duty-free shop, mechanical service, and water and electricity at the dock.

We had been experiencing difficulties with our Johnson outboard motor. In the duty-free shop we found one identical to the one that had served us so well for years. When we tried to purchase it, we were not able to, because the clerk couldn't find the paperwork. What's more, he really didn't care. The communist government employee had no incentive to make the sale. The Yugoslavian government encouraged entrepreneurs. This was very evident in the farmers' markets. There, competition and service were the rule, in contrast to the disinterested attitude of the state store employees.

The Kornati Islands were different in a fascinating way; they were almost completely barren. However, they have many protected anchorages among the islands. Their desolate landscape and clear warm water have a unique appeal. We found a full-service marina located on one of these uninhabited islands. The marina operator said, "At night after we turn off the generator, it's so quiet here that you can hear the cats walking."

Ruins of Delphi

Where we anchored at Delos

White buildings of Mykinos

Mykinos Harbor

Corinth Canal

Pizza with Feridun in Kusidasi

Saint Paul probably walked on This Road In Ephesus

Shrines at Ephesus

Library at Ephesus

Turkish Charter Gulet in Bodrum

Boatyard at Bodrum

Carving of Greek Vessel in Lidos

With Rental Car in Crete

Restoration at Knossos

Cervantes was Imprisoned Here

CHAPTER 44

Venice

At Rovinja, on September 11, we cleared Yugoslavian customs for Italy and left for Venice at three in the morning. We had such a quiet passage that I spent a good deal of the trip polishing lifelines and stanchions. In mid-afternoon we passed the unusual squat black and white checkered lighthouse which marked the entrance to Venice. It was a thrill to sail into Venice. If there's any city that should be approached by water, "The Queen of the Sea" is it!

We had learned from someone along the way that there was a small boat club on the island of San Giorgio, just across the Grand Canal from St. Mark's Square. We very carefully inched our boat into the narrow entrance to the club and tied up at a dock. If the *Mary Constance* had been one foot longer, we could not have made it. We were docked under the campanile of the island of San Giorgio Maggiore. The view from our boat was unbelievable. Mary could do the breakfast dishes while looking out at the Doge's Palace and St. Mark's Campanile.

We discovered that the vaporetto (water bus) made frequent stops at the island. A kind tourist gave us the money to ride across the canal into the city. We exchanged our currency and joined hundreds of others walking the streets. We had a delicious meal that night in a charming restaurant. We only stayed in Venice for a few days, but the September weather was delightful and we revisited places we had seen years ago, and discovered new wonderful churches and museums which we had not seen.

We enjoyed walking on the streets and plazas, but much of the city may only be seen from the canals. A gondola ride is still the best way to get an intimate view of Venice. During our previous visit the winter weather was not propitious for a gondola ride. This time the two of us hired a gondola for a very interesting ride through the small canals among buildings that could only be reached by water.

We reluctantly left Venice early in the morning, in what we thought was a light fog. It thickened considerably as we made our way out of the Grand Canal, along with many other boats and vessels. We used our handheld radar to avoid other boats, and at one time we were able to follow a pilot boat on its way out to a freighter. Once we reached the open sea, the traffic spread and we had an uneventful sail in the fog to Yugoslavia.

I think that emotionally, our summer's trip ended in Venice. We traveled south along the Croatian coast, spending nights in ACY marinas. On September 23 we arrived at Vodice, where we had previously made storage arrangements at the ACY marina. Four days later, with the boat safely hauled up and secured on shore, we left for home. With us, we carried a list of 28 things to bring back from the States the next year.

Island Monastery In The Gulf of Kotor

Dubrovnik

ACY Marina

Kornati Island Climb

Lighthouse at Venice

View from our boat Docked in Venice

Gondola Ride

Rigging in Ravena, Italy with Mario

CHAPTER 45

West Toward the Atlantic Ocean

After cruising for six summers in Europe aboard the *Mary Constance,* we decided in 1988 that it was time to turn west toward the Atlantic Ocean and home. Our trip that summer took us from Yugoslavia to Ravenna, Italy, then back across the Adriatic and south along the Dalmatian coast of Yugoslavia. Once again we crossed the Adriatic and sailed around the boot of Italy, then up the west coast to the Italian and French Rivieras. We sailed to Gibraltar, at the entrance to the Mediterranean, by way of the Spanish Balearic Islands.

I haven't written much about the constant maintenance which we faced in our travels, so this may be a good time to talk about just one trip. Our list of things to bring with us when we returned to Yugoslavia follows:

1. Parts for Shur-Flo water pump
2. Grommet set
3. Heavy-duty extension cord for tools
4. Waterproofing compound for canvas
5. Scotchgard
6. Rubber galley apron for the cook
7. Rubber floor mat for foot wiper
8. Volt-ammeter
9. Flame tamer for galley
10. Epoxy resin

11. 5-inch low-profile dorade ventilator
12. Small Whale floor pump
13. Screen material
14. Contact cement
15. Groco K repair kit
16. Refrigerator gasket material and foam mat for over the freezer
17. Electric shower water pump
18. 1 amp fuses for Furuno Loran
19. Anchor shackles
20. Hacksaw blades
21. Power sander
22. Fram C1191A fuel filters
23. Fram CAV296 fuel filters
24. Photo prints of work at ACY yard in Vodice
25. Two 12-inch drop-leaf table braces
26. Oil changing pump
27. Water bilge filter
28. Electrical connectors

In addition to all these things, during the winter we decided to buy a new 4 hp, two-cylinder Johnson outboard for our dinghy. By this time radar technology had advanced enough to produce small radars that could be mounted on the mast. The prices had come down enough so we thought we could afford one. I had been assured by Yugoslav customs that as long as this equipment was going to be installed immediately on the boat, it could come in duty-free. We packaged all this for shipment to Yugoslavia. The outboard came in a great shipping crate, and we were able to stuff many of the smaller items around the motor. The radar, when we purchased it, was equally well packed for shipment. We sent all of this ahead of us in care of the ACY marina.

We also made arrangements with a North Sails franchise in Florence, Italy, to replace our 15-year-old standing rigging, which we felt was old enough to need replacement. They also said that they could add roller furling on our genoa jib and club jib. We wanted to make these improvements before our return trip across the Atlantic. We made all of the arrangements with an American North Sails employee in Florence, who assured me that they could provide a good rigger to install the new equipment.

In 1988, we left Cleveland on May 31 and flew, in the wrong direction, to Chicago. We had a two-hour wait for a KLM flight to Amsterdam. There we waited six hours at the airport for a flight to Zagreb. We once again waited two hours for a flight to Split, where we arrived on June 1 at 6:30 p.m. I rented a Volkswagen van and we found a hotel where we crashed for the night.

The next day, after breakfast, we had a beautiful drive along the coast to Vodice, where we found everything on the *Mary Constance* in good order. The marina informed us that our packages had arrived, and they assigned a young man who spoke English to accompany me to customs. The customs agent was very friendly, but we had to open up every package and carton so that he could do a quick inventory of the contents. At one point he looked up and said, "It's almost like Christmas."

It was very convenient having a van to bring things back to the boat. The next day we returned the van to Split and returned to the boat by bus. For the first seven days, we lived aboard the boat on land, in the boatyard, while we prepared her for the water. We had to get in and out on a ladder. I was asleep one night when Mary shook me awake and said, "There's someone on deck." Just then, I looked up and saw a pair of legs go by our aft cabin porthole. I rushed forward, opened the hatch and yelled. Someone took a flying leap off the boat and ran off. Our deck was a good eight feet off the cement pad, and I was concerned that whoever it was might have been hurt. We learned later that teenagers valued American flags and he was probably going to take ours. I'm certain that he had no idea that someone was sleeping on the boat.

On June 8 the boatyard launched our boat. When we got her into the water, we were pleased when our diesel engine started quickly and began pumping refrigerant through the refrigerator and freezer. At the marina dock we had water and electricity, so we were able to charge batteries and wash down our decks. I spent four hours in a bosun's chair on the mizzenmast while I installed our new radar, and several more hours the next day installing a new Loran C antenna at the top of the mizzen. All this time spent at the marina wasn't just work. We had plenty of time to visit with other sailors from several countries, including the U.S.

When our work was completed at the yacht club, we cruised north along the Yugoslav coast, stopping at ACY marinas. A long day's sail took us to the harbor of Ravenna, on the Adriatic coast of Italy. We docked at the Ravenna yacht club. We expected to be there for one week, but it actually took us four weeks to get the work completed.

The new rigging required changes to our sails. We rented a car and delivered them to the sailmaker in Florence. There we discovered that the American employee who had made all our arrangements was leaving the company in about a week. We also learned that the sailmaker did not have the proper size roller-furling drums and had ordered them from the United States. They explained that they had made arrangements with a rigger in Ravenna to install our new standing rigging.

Since we had learned that we were going to be in Italy longer than expected, we spent two nights in a hotel located in a beautiful old villa and spent our 44th wedding anniversary visiting wonderful Florence.

On the way back to our boat, we stopped at the medieval city of Assisi, renowned as the birthplace of St. Francis. It seemed ironic to me that the tiny church that he had built by himself, where he had lived in self-imposed poverty, was ensconced in a huge ornate basilica.

After several days' delay we were able to move our boat to a boatyard, where they removed our masts. We left them in the boatyard on sawhorses and returned the boat to the yacht club. Our experience with the "rigger" was extremely frustrating. He was a small, heavily muscled young man whose name was Mark. He spoke no English and was pigheaded and not very bright. Aboard the boat we had enough new rigging wire and expensive Norseman fittings to replace the permanently attached ones on the old rigging. I had provided detailed instructions showing how to install the new fittings, complete with pictures, but Mark couldn't seem to understand them and, to make things worse, rebelled at doing them the right way.

There was a very nice marine store not far from the yacht club, and I made the very happy discovery that the owner spoke fluent English. With his help, I found out what my problem was with Mark. His entire boating experience had been as a winch grinder on an Italian America's Cup boat the year before. He knew nothing about how to rig a boat. From then on, I was the rigger and Mark was my helper.

We had more problems. We discovered that the new roller-furling gear could not be used with our new forestay, so the marine store had to order the metric equivalent. This meant six more days of waiting. While all this was going on, we ran out of propane and I discovered that the Italian fittings would not fit into our British propane tanks. When one of the yacht club members heard about our predicament, he came to my rescue. Fortunately I had a male fitting for our tanks. He took that with him, disappeared for several hours, and reappeared with a large Italian tank of propane and our fitting attached to an Italian male fitting by a piece of propane hose. We literally poured liquid propane from the Italian tank to ours. I had heard somewhere that if you kept the full tank in the sun and put the empty tank in the shade, the extra warmth of the sunlight would help vaporize the full tank and force it into the other. We managed to fill both of our propane tanks.

Finally our rigging was completed and we were ready to leave. When I paid the final bill at the club, the manager gave us two little dishes and a very beautiful key fob, both emblazoned with the yacht club flag. It was a difficult month, but the warmth and friendship of the people at the club was something we'll never forget.

We decided to return to Yugoslavia and sailed south along the beautiful coast. That way we could take advantage of the free ACY marinas. We motored in thick fog under way to Trogir. I had a chance to use our new radar, which gave us the assurance that we could spot other boats and navigation marks well before we reached them. The fog lifted just before we reached the city.

In the distance we saw another sailboat trying to sail with practically no wind. When we reached them, we discovered that they had lost their propeller, a very unusual thing to have happened. They were trying to make their way back to Trogir, where they had chartered the boat. It was a new Austrian-flagged boat and they were just starting their vacation. We towed them back to the marina. After both boats were secured at the dock, the captain, who spoke excellent English, came back and invited us to dinner. We joined him and his wife, another man and four children, from 12 to 3 years old, for a very pleasant dinner in a courtyard in the old city. We learned that they owned a small hotel in Switzerland, and we left with their invitation to come for a visit if we could possibly do it. Unfortunately, we never got to Switzerland.

On August 3 we left Budva, and Yugoslavia, at 8:30 a.m. for a passage southwest across the Adriatic to the town of Otranto, located on the instep of the boot of Italy, where we arrived at 7:00 a.m. the next day. A few days later we once again motored through the Strait of Messina, this time heading northwest.

In the strait we saw an amazing sight; motoring back and forth across the strait were several 40-foot fishing boats, each equipped with a very high tower, much taller than the boat was long, shipped, amidships. On the top of the tower was perched a man. A forest of wire stays supported the tower and a bowsprit, which was longer than the boat. His job was to spot fish. In the pulpit on the bowsprit was a man with a harpoon. We learned that these were swordfishing boats.

We traveled north off the Italian coast, through the Tyrrhenian Sea, which lies between the west coast of Italy and Sardinia. Sailing through the Aeolian Islands, we timed our arrival to pass the island of Stromboli after dark. We watched as an active volcano spewed brilliant eruptions several times. These eruptions have occurred through recorded time, and ancient mariners used them as a lighthouse.

It was vacation time in Italy, and the docks were crowded and noisy. Mary and I decided to take a vacation from our vacation. In Agropoli, we booked a very inexpensive Italian charter flight from Rome to New York and return. We would leave on August 27 and be back to the boat on September 10.

We sailed just offshore, from the famed Amalfi drive that hugs the cliffs along the scenic coast. Certain cities will always be vividly etched in our memories because of their enchanting appearance from the water. The ancient city of Amalfi is tucked into rugged mountains rising precipitously from the city. We were fortunate to find a place at the crowded dock. Amalfi was an early Italian maritime power rivaling Pisa and Venice. The buildings around the small harbor seem to have an organic relationship to the mountains as they grow out of the rocks, tier upon tier. Narrow streets, alleys, passages and stairways, some carved out of the cliff face, rise level upon level.

In the town of Formia, as we were preparing to tie up alongside a large freight dock, Mary discovered that we had no reverse gear. This was a real problem, because reverse not only makes the boat go backwards, but also acts as a brake to stop the boat. Mary did a wonderful job of bringing the boat into the dock slowly enough so that I could get a breast-line from the boat around a cleat and stop our movement. We decided that we had to head toward Rome, where we had the best chance of getting some mechanical help. We sailed to visit Civitavecchia, the port of Rome, where we coasted to the side of a large fishing vessel that looked as though it had been laid up for a while. I contacted two marine service facilities, each of which sent a mechanic to look at our transmission. Both men said they would have to take the engine out of the boat in order to get at the transmission. Because it was vacation time, one of the mechanics said he could probably start sometime in September and the other said it would probably be October. I don't know who suggested that we take our boat to a marina in the Fiumare Grande, the yacht center located in the mouth of the Tiber River; it turned out to be an excellent choice.

Our charter flights to the United States taught us a lesson. We saved a lot of money, but it wasn't worth it. At 5:00 a.m. we took a taxi to the nearby airport and were greatly overcharged because of the early hour. There we discovered that our flight had been changed to a different airport. The flight finally departed at 11:00, four hours late. The seats were extremely close together and we couldn't recline our back; I couldn't even cross my legs. Imagine a planeload of Italian tourists with no cabin attendants who spoke Italian. Our return trip was even worse; it was eight hours late leaving New York and we arrived in Rome nine hours late, only to discover that we had landed at the other airport instead of the one convenient to our boat. A $50 taxi ride took us to our boat.

Our time at home was wonderful. Mary attended eight of her meetings.

We were both able to attend the "Red Book" annual sales meeting, which was a day of fun and visiting with people we enjoy. I phoned the Paragon transmission distributor, gave them the model number and serial number, and asked them to send me, as quickly as possible, everything needed to repair a reverse gear. I was able to take the parts back to the boat on our return flight.

I don't know who suggested calling the Perkins diesel dealer in Rome. They sent two mechanics who spent a good deal of time in the engine room and emerged to tell us they could remove the transmission without removing the engine. They spent most of the next day in the engine compartment and appeared on deck with the transmission, which they took back to the shop. I gave them the repair parts. Two days later, sooner than we expected, they completed the job and we were free to resume our cruising.

We cruised northeast along the Italian coast and then through the Tuscan islands, largest of which is Elba. Portoferraio is located in a superb natural harbor. Napoleon was exiled to here in 1814. A large palatial building, located in the center of the city, was his residence for a year before he escaped British naval patrols and returned to France.

We made several long passages along the Italian Riviera coast, stopping in Portofino and San Remo, where we cleared out of Italy. Harbors along the French Riviera were expensive, so we avoided staying in as many as we could. We circled the harbor at Monaco to look at the mega-yachts and found the famous casino dwarfed among the tall buildings.

We were in the last weeks of October and needed to get to Gibraltar for the start of our return Atlantic crossing. We made a 42-hour offshore passage to the Balearic Islands. From there we sailed southwest for two days to the Spanish mainland. The Costa del Sol, the Spanish Riviera, has a scenic coastline, often with the background of snowcapped mountains. Villages cling to the rugged shore. Unfortunately, the harbors were mostly man-made resorts, one very much like another, and all expensive.

On October 30 we reached Gibraltar. As we approached, the face of the great rock was hidden; but as we rounded the point and entered the harbor, "the rock" assumed its familiar "Prudential" face. We tied up at the customs dock and when the formalities were completed moved to the yacht harbor, where we found the two marinas jammed with boats waiting for better weather. We were extremely fortunate to find a place at the dock at Shepherds Marina. The affable Scottish dockmaster checked us in. We found ourselves part of the dock community of sailors, almost all of whom were preparing for an Atlantic crossing.

CHAPTER 46

Sailing in the Trade Winds

Each year, in the late fall, hundreds of sailboats congregate along the west coast of Europe. Like flocks of migrating birds, they await the end of the hurricane season before heading south and west across the Atlantic Ocean to the West Indies. Following exactly the same course that took Columbus to the New World, they head south to the Canary Islands off the coast of Africa. In November and December they start their migration. In pursuit of the westward flowing trade winds, boats head south toward the Cape Verde Islands. When, at last, somewhere near the islands the clouds begin to form little puffs of cotton balls and the winds are steady into the northeast, they know that they have found the trade winds that will propel them unerringly to the New World.

In 1986 *Yachting World,* the British yachting magazine, sponsored a race from the Canary Islands to Barbados. With so many cruising boats crossing in early winter each year, they reasoned that a strictly amateur race might offer camaraderie and a sense of security. It was a resounding success; over 200 boats participated the first year. It became an annual event. It was intended to be a strictly amateur race. The boat's owner had to be on board, and no sponsorship was allowed. Boats could even run their engines as long as they logged the time and distance. We decided to join what had become "The Atlantic Rally for Cruisers" (ARC) in 1988.

Friend Dick London from Sarasota, Florida and his friend Mickey Koniky, young men in their forties, wanted the experience of an Atlantic crossing and agreed to meet us in Las Palmas, Gran Canaria Island, in late November. Mary and I had planned to make the 800-mile trip to the Canaries alone. However, when we met Canadian swim coach Jim Ritchie, who was looking for a passage home, we decided at the last minute to take him along as far as the Canaries. What a fortunate decision it was!

After waiting ten days for a break in the weather, we left Gibraltar on November 1, 1988 and cleared the busy shipping channels by the next day. However, the winds, which we had expected to move into the northeast, remained out of the southwest directly on our course. They blew from 25 to 30 knots for eight days, and the south-flowing equatorial currents raised steep unpleasant seas. Unfortunately, the rough seas made Mary seasick. Jim took over the cooking.

By the sixth day, Mary had decided not to make the rest of the crossing. Jim would take her place. We had discovered by this point that Jim could cook! With the exception of myself, all of the crew was young enough to be Mary's children and they didn't need "Mom" to tell them what to do on the boat, even if she had much more experience than they did. Jim really wanted to crew all the way across.

The winds had moderated by the time we made landfall in the northern Canary Islands. We found an anchorage between the barren volcanic islands of Lanzarotte and Graciosa. After a day of rest, we had an easy overnight passage to Las Palmas, on Gran Canaria Island. We found the harbor crowded with boats from many nations planning to join the ARC rally. They assigned us a dock next to a floating bar, and we joined almost 100 other boats preparing for the race.

Mary helped Jim plan our provisioning and shopped before she left to fly home. I had an unending list of things to do but there was fun, too. Crews from the 26 nations represented in the race hoisted their country flags along the dock. A local folk dance group performed for us, and local bands marched along the docks. Tents, housing bars and restaurants, blossomed at the head of the dock. The rally organizers had a captains' meeting, and the amateur radio operators arranged for a schedule of daily check-ins.

We had time to visit with many of the crews on other boats. The sailboats ranged in size from a 120-foot Saudi palace to a very small catamaran that would carry a young couple and two large dogs safely across the ocean.

The morning of November 26, the day of the race arrived at last. Boats began slowly to leave the dock, and at noon we cast off our lines and headed out into the harbor to join the fleet of 157 boats for an exciting 2:00 p.m. start. A Spanish naval vessel provided one end of the starting line, with a hotel on shore the other. We were not the first boat across the starting line, by any means, but when we looked behind us, we saw a satisfying number of boats. The winds held into the evening as we passed the end of the island and headed out into the Atlantic, for Barbados 2700 miles away.

The crew took two or three days to get their sea legs, as we sailed south toward the Cape Verde Islands. The boat sailed herself down the wind, under polled-out genoa jib and mainsail, wing on wing, with our Aries wind vane steering. Two hundred miles north of the Cape Verde Islands, the wind settled into the northeast and we turned west under trade wind skies. We tightened the club jib hard amidships to help dampen the rolling motion of the boat.

Radio contact was an important part of every day. We kept in touch with other hams in the race and with the Transatlantic Amateur Radio Network. It was controlled by Sheila in the Turks and Caicos Islands. We all talked to home, via amateur radio phone patch, at least twice a week.

Jim, as cook, and I, as captain, stood one watch. Dick and Mickey had two watches. This meant that I was able to be available for consultation on every watch if needed. We did not rotate watches but stayed on the same schedule for the entire trip.

Almost every morning we found flying fish on deck; they can fly amazingly long distances over the water. What a cruel turn of fate: after millions of years of evolution, they had learned to escape their marine predators only to end up on the deck of the sailboat.

With winds 15 to 25 knots on our back, we covered 171 miles in 24 hours, an average of over seven knots and a new record for the *Mary Constance*. The winds don't always blow in the trades. We experienced 36 hours of calm seas. We were fortunate to have a good engine and plenty of diesel fuel. We had been running our engine an hour a day for refrigeration and battery charging. Now, for the first time in quite a while, our batteries came up to full charge. It was easy to imagine how terribly frustrating and discouraging this kind of calm must have been for sailors without engines.

Navigation was easy with our satellite navigation receiver. We plotted regular fixes on our chart. I took some sun lines with the sextant, but they were really redundant. About half the time, we could see a sail or a running light in the distance. The only boat that passed close to us was an Austrian sailboat that was not in the race. We saw no large vessels until we were close to Barbados.

We had a very easy trip. Jim served a delicious sit-down dinner every night. We did have to conserve water, and the pressure water system was turned off for the trip. We bathed in warm salt water from the sea, with a very limited rinse of fresh water from the hand pump.

Early in the morning of the 19th day, we spotted land and I hoisted the Barbados courtesy flag and the Q flag. As we approached the harbor to Bridgetown, we found ourselves in a head-to-head race with another boat. After 19 days at sea, we were approaching the finish line neck and neck. It added a lot of spice to the end of our trip. But they won! We were the 47th boat to cross the line, one of the earlier boats in our class, but by the time judges applied the penalty for our hours of motoring, we ended up near the bottom.

We were met at the dock by two pretty bikini-clad women with a basket of goodies and a rum punch. Dick and Mickey took off the next day for the United States.

Two days later, Jim and I made the 100-mile hop to the island of St. Lucia, where we laid the boat up on shore until the following spring. We both got home for Christmas.

Amalfi From The Sea

Amalfi Harbor

Tied Up in Rome's Commercial Harbor

Jim Richie and Mary

Boats in Palmas Waiting For the ARC

The Crew-Ted, Mickey,Dickand Jim

Downwind Sails

Flying Fish

CHAPTER 47

West Indies Island Cruising

On June 4, 1989 we once again boarded the *Mary Constance,* which had wintered on shore in beautiful Rodney Bay, St. Lucia. We didn't know at the time that this year was going to provide another turning point in our lives.

Once we had the boat in the water, we sailed against the trade winds to Barbados, where we picked up new sails made for us at the Hood loft on the island. The trade winds made for great sailing as we sailed overnight to Martinique, where we celebrated our 45th wedding anniversary with dinner in a very nice French restaurant.

On our way to Dominica, well offshore, we almost hit a fishing boat. We were under sail and Mary was in the cockpit facing aft when she heard voices shouting. I was below and came up quickly and we were able to veer off, just in time to pass within ten feet of the small boat. We had never expected to see a small fishing boat that far away from land. We were guilty of not keeping an adequate lookout.

We stopped at Guadalupe. At English Harbour, Antigua, we had repairs made at the famous old boatyard and "dressed ship" for the Fourth of July in this ancient British stronghold.

We had made plans to meet our daughter Connie and her two children, Kate and Bob, in St. Croix in the Virgin Islands. They would sail with us aboard the *Mary Constance* in these lovely cruising waters. Most of the time during our island cruising in the Caribbean, we had had good sailing winds, although afternoon and evening rain squalls were common.

We stopped at St. Kitts before leaving there for an overnight sail to St. Croix. We didn't leave St. Kitts until late afternoon because we wanted to arrive at St. Croix in daylight. At about midnight we had a sudden squall, with 35-knot winds, which caught us with our sails up. Seas were only six or seven feet high, but because we were sailing on the Saba Bank, they were very steep. We took on board the largest wave that we had ever had in all our years of sailing. It caught us with all our ports open: the head, the galley, the one over the chart table, and the main hatch. I was standing at the mainmast and the water came up to my waist. Mary was at the helm, and with the cockpit filled, she was absolutely soaked. As soon as the boat righted herself, the cockpit drained rapidly, but we still had a lot of drying out to do in the cabin. The squall passed quickly and we arrived at St.Croix, as we had hoped, at about 7:30 a.m.

We were still mopping up below when a voice called out to me. It was Gordon and Shirley Thorn who were living aboard the *Donna X*. They were working on a large sailboat, as captain and mate, and had left their own sailboat in St. Thomas. We had first met the Thorns at the top of Newfoundland in 1979, then again in 1983 in the Daytona Beach Marina. Now here we were together again in the Virgins. Several times in our cruising years we had this experience, where sailing friends turned up repeatedly in unexpected places.

CHAPTER 48

The Virgin Islands with Our Family

On July 10 our daughter and her two children, Bob and Kate, arrived on schedule at the St. Croix airport. The next day we left for our cruise through the Virgin Islands. We all had a wonderful time. In the British Virgin Islands, we anchored off the caves at Norman Island where we went snorkeling in the water-filled caves. In Tortola, BVI, I bought a new Avon dinghy to replace our Zodiac, which had turned out to be a piece of junk. It was wonderful to have a slightly larger dinghy that didn't leak.

The baths of Virgin Gorda are scenic grottoes that are open to the sea. Huge partly submerged granite boulders lie along the shore. The largest boulders are about 40 feet long. We all enjoyed wading in the grottoes and snorkeling over the beautiful coral gardens in the area. That night we picked up a mooring at the Bitter End Resort and had dinner on shore.

We later anchored in the harbor of Charlotte Amalie and I took Connie and the kids ashore, where they went shopping and had lunch. We went to the Yacht Haven Marina and talked to several people about the possibility of acquiring a new power anchor windlass. In the dinghy, on our way back from the marine store, we stopped and visited with Tim and Sue Stein and their teenage son Timmy on *Tri-Umph*. Young Tim went ashore in their tender and brought Connie and the kids back to the boat. Soon the three teenagers went back to town for some teenage fun.

In the early morning of the next day, the last day they were going to be with us, we anchored in Lindberg Bay, as it was very close to the airport. Mary, Connie, and the kids walked to a 10:30 a.m. meeting. When they returned, they discovered that young Tim Stein had arrived by dinghy to give them an audio-tape. Tim stayed aboard while everyone packed to go. Then at 2:00 p.m. Tim and I took Connie, Kate, and Bob, with all their duffels, to the shore. We were able to walk to the airport and left them in the check-in line for their flight back home.

During the last days of July we spent most of our time working on the boat. One of our water tanks was leaking, and I had to remove it to have it patched. This was a difficult job. It seemed as if our refrigeration system had been repaired in every country we visited. This wasn't actually the case, but over the years we had spent a lot of time having it fixed. The basic problem with it was that when it had been installed, they had used flexible hose to bring the refrigerant from the compressor on the engine to the refrigerator and freezer. Over the years it had become permeable, which allowed the refrigerant to seep out slowly.

Even in those days there were large charter fleets based in the Virgins. We found a company whose specialty was servicing marine refrigeration systems, and we contracted with them to have our entire refrigeration system redone. We also arranged to purchase and install a new anchor windlass to replace our old hand-operated one, which had become very hard to use.

The first of August, we moved the boat to the dock at Yacht Haven Marina so that the refrigeration man could work on it. We had all been watching the weather reports concerning Tropical Storm Dean, expected to become a hurricane. The refrigeration work was almost complete when, at 1:00 p.m., a man from the marina came to our boat and told us that the Virgin Islands and Puerto Rico were under a hurricane watch. We would have to leave the dock for a safer anchorage.

We joined at least 200 other boats and headed for Culebra, Puerto Rico, a small island halfway between the Virgins and mainland Puerto Rico. In an article in the April 1983 *Cruising World,* author Brian Rees had surveyed a "dozen best shelters in the Caribbean" and had selected Ensenada Honda, on Culebra, as the best all-around hurricane hole in the Caribbean.

We arrived early enough to tie into the mangroves along with many other boats. Boats with multiple lines in the mangroves stay put like a spider in a web. Mangroves are extremely tough and offer a reasonably soft cushioning against which to tie. However, in a major hurricane, only boats tied very securely stay put. Even these boats are at the mercy of other boats that break loose from their moorings.

We tied up as if we were at a dock with bow and stern lines, crossed spring lines and breast line to an anchor across the channel. It's a measure of our combined ignorance that almost none of the boats, including ours, were adequately secured. One hundred or more other boats, many of them charter boats, were anchored in the harbor.

We removed everything movable, including the dinghy, to below decks. At about 10:30 that night we heard on the radio that the storm had been upgraded and was going to go right over the Virgin Islands and Puerto Rico, so we removed all of the sails and running rigging and stored them inside the boat. We went to bed as soon as possible because we felt we would have a rough day ahead of us.

When we awoke, later than we had expected the next day, we found clear skies, soft winds and birds singing. At the last minute, the hurricane had veered north and missed the islands completely! It took us most of the day, with trips to the top of both masts, to get everything ready to sail. Amazingly, we still had time that day to sail back to the Yacht Haven Marina, where we tied up in the same slip. The next day the refrigeration man completed his work and his boss came to the boat to fine-tune the system.

We had purchased a new, highly recommended Maxwell power anchor windlass. Shortly after that, while walking down the dock beside a large charter fleet, I saw a line of four or five Maxwell windlasses lined up on the dock. I asked a man working on one of the charter boats how they happened to be there, and he told me that they all had burned-out motors. He went on to say that the manufacturer had ordered some Chinese motors that were just not able to take the strain. I just hoped that this problem had been fixed before I received mine.

Installation of the anchor windlass was much more difficult than we had anticipated. The man I had hired to mount the windlass proved to be very hard to work with and tried to extract as much money from us as he could. The work progressed very slowly, and even after we had the windlass installed on deck, we had to wait for the chain gypsy to arrive from the distributor in California. When the gypsy arrived, I discovered it was the wrong size for our chain, so I had to pack it up and send it back to California for the correct size.

We had originally planned to sail the boat to Venezuela, which is well outside the hurricane belt, and to leave it there for the winter. But with all of the delays we were experiencing working on the boat, it became obvious that this would be impossible. Jack, at the "Red Book," was particularly anxious to have me attend the annual Labor Day sales meeting because he had a number of new men attending and wanted to have an experienced man there as well.

On August 24 we were at last able to leave Charlotte Amalie and sailed into the harbor at Culebra, where we planned to leave the boat for the winter. We arranged with Bruce, an expatriate American, to take care of our boat. He had a small canvas shop and some heavy duty moorings in the harbor, where we could leave the boat. Bruce and his wife lived on their boat *Katrina,* on another mooring close to where the *Mary Constance* was to be located. He would also watch our boat and check the mooring chain from time to time. The mooring which we planned to use was still occupied for a short time, so we left our boat on bow and stern anchors in the lee of a small island in the harbor. Our decisions to leave the boat in Culebra and to hire Bruce were both great mistakes.

CHAPTER 49

Hurricane Hugo

We arrived back in Chagrin Falls for a good time at the "Red Book" sales meeting. We hadn't seen Beth and Tony since their wedding, and we found that our friends Ann and Phil Hermann in Maine had just about completed a major renovation of an old house on the water. So we decided to drive our motorhome to visit with our children near Boston, and then to see the Hermanns in Maine. We were with Ann and Phil when we heard the news that Hurricane Hugo was headed directly for the Virgin Islands. On Sunday and Monday, September 17 and 18, 1989, Hugo passed directly over Culebra with sustained winds of 150 miles an hour. This definitely was a major turning point in our life. We waited and watched, in horror, the news on TV of the damage done to St. Croix, St. Thomas, and Puerto Rico.

We drove the motorhome directly back to Cleveland and waited. On Wednesday night, CBS TV had an hour-long special, which we taped, on the hurricane on *48 Hours*. At one point they made a photographic fly-over of the harbor at Culebra. The place behind the little island, where the *Mary Constance* had been anchored, was vacant. Most of the boats were gone from the harbor. Boats were piled up on top of each other on the shore, and we saw many flattened houses. I made a reservation to fly to Puerto Rico on American Airlines on Monday, September 25.

On Thursday, September 21, Hugo ravaged the coast of South Carolina and especially Charleston. Our son Jim called to say that his house was okay but that many of the seashore homes in Myrtle Beach, where he worked, were damaged or destroyed. Finally, on Saturday morning, September 23, Sue Stein reached us by commercial radio and said that they had seen the *Mary Constance* on the shore. It was located near the bridge, with several other boats on top of it. She said that Tim had walked around it and that it didn't seem to have too much hull damage. At last we knew that our boat had not sunk and could be re-launched and repaired. Sue said their boat had survived on five anchors, almost unharmed. She said that I could stay with them, on *Tri-Umph,* when I got to Culebra.

I assembled a "kit" of things to carry with me to the boat. I had a couple of dozen granola bars, a hand-held VHF ship-to-shore radio, a flashlight with extra batteries, and as much clothing as I could stuff into a carry-on bag. One week after the storm hit the islands, I was on an American Airlines flight to San Juan, Puerto Rico. I think almost everyone else on the flight was involved with relief agencies.

In San Juan I rented a car to drive to Fajardo, where I hoped to catch the ferry to Culebra. When I arrived at Fajardo, I found the ferry high and dry in the center of the town square. Next I drove to the small airport nearby, where I was able to catch a free ride, in a small plane, to the Culebra airport. The buildings at the airport were destroyed, and the wreckage of small planes littered the airport. Most of the island vegetation had been stripped of its leaves.

As I walked into town, all that was left of many houses was the concrete slab. The road led along the head of the harbor and along the shore, where boats were stacked up helter-skelter everywhere. I saw Bruce's *Katrina* on its side on the shore. No wonder I hadn't heard from Bruce. There were only a few boats anchored in the harbor; hundreds were piled up along the shore. The town dock was gone, so I stood on the shore and called *Tri-Umph* on my VHF radio and Timmy took me out to their boat in their dinghy.

Tim and Sue Stein were wonderful to me. They provided me with a bunk and insisted I share meals with them in the evening; I ate my granola bars for most breakfasts and lunches. They even let me use a dinghy and motor that someone had left in their care after the hurricane.

As soon as I could, I went to look at the *Mary Constance*. Only 30 feet or so from our boat, the storm surge had sucked boats into the entrance of a small stream that bisected the island and had jammed them up against a low bridge in a large pile-up.

Fortunately, our boat had avoided this fate and had landed on dirt. She was lying on her side with three other boats stacked beside her, with their rigging tangled with ours. The hull had been scratched and gouged in places, but not penetrated. Our anchor chain extended from the boat's bow, which had gone through a chain-link fence. The chain led to the side of a house that apparently had been lifted by the surge and dropped on our chain. The stern anchor line led down into the water. Our Aries wind vane, on the transom, was twisted but looked like it could be repaired. Only one lifeline stanchion was intact. The bow pulpit was badly distorted, but not enough to interfere with the roller-furling drum. The mizzenmast was leaning sideways and pulled from its base. The mizzen deck fitting was shattered, so we wouldn't be able to use the mast until it could be replaced. The mainmast and all of its standing rigging were intact. The heavier rigging, which we had purchased in Italy, had done its job.

When I climbed aboard the boat, I discovered a very ripe three-foot barracuda in the cockpit. Chalk circles on the hatches indicated that the boat had been checked for possible survivors. In the cabins I could see no evidence that salt water had entered the boat, but some fresh water had been blown inside.

Fortunately, Lloyd's of London insured our boat. I had told them, by phone before I left home, that our boat had been blown ashore at Culebra. Only a few days after I arrived, Culebra telephone service had been restored to one payphone. We discovered that we could call free to anywhere! Due to the change in time zones, I was able to converse with the insurance company in London in the early morning without waiting in line for the phone. I was able to talk to Mary almost every day.

The people of Culebra were wonderful, in contrast to the riots that occurred in St. Croix. The small island community pulled together to serve the more needy. On the driveway, in front of one of the cement block houses which had survived the storm, was a card table with a large coffeepot and a sign reading "Free Coffee." On a badly damaged church was posted "Pampers in most sizes available." The undamaged island stores were open, and none of their prices had been increased.

An anchored American naval vessel ferried tanker trucks, filled with fresh water, to shore. Navy men repaired the town generator and the island desalination plant. One of them told me that they were fixing many things that weren't damaged by the storm. The National Guard set up headquarters in what was left of the hospital and helped to clear streets of rubble.

The boating people also pulled together to help one another. Club Seaborne, a small hotel, served as a refugee and communication center with several VHF radio broadcasts each day. Around the building were piles of items that owners had salvaged from their boats. Sadly, many of the owners lived aboard their boats in the harbor. When they lost their boats, they lost everything. Because many were retired or traveling out of their savings, most of their boats were uninsured.

It was amazing that only one person was lost in the storm. An older couple stayed on their boat when the storm hit. When it was obvious that they had to leave, they swam to shore. The husband was able to climb out of the water and reached to his wife to pull her up behind him, when they lost their grip and she was swept into the surging water.

A few days after I arrived, the first of several salvage boats entered the harbor. A typical salvage boat consisted of a small tug towing a large barge with a crane on board. They were usually accompanied by a smaller, more maneuverable boat. For obvious reasons, they were interested at first in salvaging insured boats, so uninsured boat owners gathered at the soccer field grandstand to create a committee to negotiate for reduced group rates.

A Lloyd's surveyor, who had been inspecting a large vessel in Puerto Rico, was sent to Culebra to inspect their insured boats. He negotiated with the salvage boat to move the *Mary Constance* into the water. His inspection of our boat proved to be very pleasant and very thorough. He made a list of all of the things that had been damaged, both on the exterior and in the interior. He thought of things that would never have occurred to me. For example, he checked to see that the engine was still properly positioned on its mounts. He checked the entire hull with the sounding hammer to look for possible hidden damage.

While I was waiting for the salvage crews to get to our boat, I circled the harbor. It was impossible for me to identify the mangrove channel where we had taken our boat for Hurricane Dean. A number of boats tied up properly in the mangroves had survived the hurricane only to be tossed up into the mangroves, but a number survived in the water and were undamaged. There were 200 boats in the harbor when Hugo struck; 175 ended up on the shore and another 25 or more were sunk. Almost all of the anchored or moored boats had dragged across the harbor. One survivor reported seeing a multi-hull boat cartwheel across the entire harbor. A large boat broke loose from its anchors and carried several smaller craft with it to shore.

An amazing number of boats had left their furled sails on the boat. Wind-shredded sails were everywhere! In some places, sailboats had been carried across roads and deposited on the other side.

With insurance adjusters' approval for two boats in our pile to be moved, our turn came on October 7. It would cost Lloyd's $6000 to put our boat back in the water. In our pile-up, two boats, which had housed full-time live-aboards, were damaged beyond repair and not insured. *Mary Constance* and *India Rosa,* a large charter sailboat, were salvageable. They removed the *India Rosa* first. The salvage crew removed the broken mast from our rigging and then, with straps from the crane in place, the actual lift was not difficult. I watched as the keel and rudder emerged from the sand. They placed the boat in the water, where she righted herself. As salvage men towed the boat out to the anchorage, I called out, "Try the steering." A voice called back, "Seems okay." I was greatly relieved because until then I had no way to determine whether the rudder was damaged.

Boats tied Into the Mangroves

Culebra Airport After Hugo

Destroyed Home- Only Palms Survived

"Mary Constance On Left after Hugo

Lifting our boat from the Rubble

Back In the Water!

Repairing our Aries Wind Steering Vane

CHAPTER 50

North through the Islands

With a working engine, mainsail and foresails, we decided to sail the boat north to Florida for repairs because many of the marinas in the islands were damaged and those that survived were jammed with work. In order to insure us for our trip to Florida, Lloyd's required that we have a third person on board. This was impractical for us. We decided to make the trip without insurance.

Mary flew to the St. Thomas airport on October 17. Repair parts for our Aries wind steering vane arrived from England on the same day. We moved our boat to Charlotte Amalie, so that we could provision it for our trip north. Finally, ten days later, we left for our trip to the United States. We had wonderful sailing with the wind behind us all the way.

We sailed along the south coast of Puerto Rico and then made a 24-hour overnight trip to Samana, in the Dominican Republic. Then another overnight passage took us to the Big Sand Cay in the Turks and Caicos Islands, where we anchored and were all alone! We rested for a day.

The next day we sailed across the Caicos Bank. The entire 48-mile trip was in water 10 to 12 feet deep. We sailed for hours and hours in flat calm water, but we did have to watch out for the occasional coral head which rose from the bottom. They look something like a great bull's-eye, with a clear circle of sand around each one of them. We just steered around them and resumed our course. We anchored at Providenciales on Provo Island, Caicos. It was a nearly perfect day!

Leaving in early light, we sailed north to anchor inside a huge reef on the south coast of the island of Mayaguana, where we had dinner aboard and sat in the cockpit in the bright moonlight. We then sailed north through the Bahamas, spending some nights off beautiful white sandy beaches, absolutely all to ourselves. We traveled along the coast of Long Island to great Exuma Island.

At Staniel Cay we anchored off the town and took our dinghy to a nearby cay that has a National Park cave. We snorkeled through a short passage under rocks, and in the cave we saw many varieties of the most wonderful tame fish surrounding us. A scene for one of the James Bond movies was filmed there.

We anchored in the harbor at Norman's Cay, where a fairly large airplane, partly submerged, was resting on the bottom. This is where we had had our close encounter with the drug cartel years before. We took our dinghy to the large dock and walked a short distance to view the wreckage of what had been a beautiful round building, where we had eaten dinner years before. The resort was overgrown and vandalized.

At Allen's Cay we went snorkeling at the "coral gardens." We enjoyed the beautiful coral and many bright colored tropical fish so much that we spent another day there so that we could go again.

On Thursday, November 23, Thanksgiving Day, we had an almost perfect sail across the "yellow bank" to Nassau. Then at Chubb Cay we woke up at midnight and decided to leave and go across the "Great Bahama Bank," starting in the dark. It was a

75-mile trip, and this way we could get to Gun Cay and Cat Cay by early afternoon. There we planned to clear customs, only to discover that all we had to do was mail our cruising permit to Nassau.

On Monday, November 27, we motored with our sunshade up across the Gulf Stream. We had misjudged the current, and so we reached the coast north of Miami and then sailed north to Fort Lauderdale and Port Everglades. We tied up at Pier 66 Marina. We didn't have harbor charts or cruising guides, and this was the only place that I had heard of. It cost us $100 for the night. We were able to do two loads of laundry and had dinner at the Café 66, on the terrace where we looked out at our boat. After supper we walked the docks looking at all the "gold-plated yachts." I made up for our exorbitant dock fees the next morning, when I purchased a $100 chart kit for the East Coast which had a price tag of $10.

CHAPTER 51

Repairs

All along the way we met people who, when they saw the condition of the *Mary Constance,* said "We know where you came from." I asked a number of people familiar with repair facilities for their recommendation in South Florida. Several people suggested the River Bend Marina in Ft. Lauderdale. So we left "Pier 66" and motored up the New River to the River Bend Marina, gawking at the mansions and yachts which lined the river's banks.

I had previously told Lloyd's where I planned to have the boat repaired and asked them to send me a name of someone to inspect the boat while it was out of the water. The yard foreman had already received a fax from the insurance company for me, with the name of the man who would supervise the work on the *Mary Constance.*

Friday, December 1 was a big day! The boat was out of the water by 9:00 a.m. and the insurance surveyor arrived at 10:00. It took him several hours to complete the survey. I thought he was very fair, listing the things that had been damaged or had to be replaced. Once he looked at our bed pillows and said that he thought they needed to be replaced because of water damage. I didn't see anything wrong with them but went along with his decision.

Between the time of the survey and the results, we took down the sails, deflated our dinghy, and arranged for a storage locker in which to leave the contents of the boat while the yard worked on it.

The surveyor came back with the figure of $50,000. It allowed us to contract for just what we wanted to have done by the yard. We authorized the yard to repair and paint the entire hull with Imron Hatteras white paint, and to remove the antiskid surface on the decks and replace it with light yellow paint with an embedded antiskid surface. We would get all new lifelines and stanchions as well as a new bow pulpit. The repairs were to be completed by June 1, 1990. With all the arrangements completed, we flew home and stayed until after the holidays.

Right after New Year's in 1990, we once again set out in the motorhome for our business sales calls. When we had finished working in my northern Florida territory, we took time out to drive to Fort Lauderdale and the River Bend Marina. We were discouraged to find that they had done practically no work on the boat.

We learned from people on other boats that just before we left our boat for repairs, the original owner had sold the boatyard and marina. The new owners were inexperienced in managing a repair facility and had spent a great deal of money in upgrading the marina, but had paid little attention to the boatyard. Little by little, the very experienced workmen left for other jobs and were replaced by less qualified people. We told the yard manager that they would have to have the boat ready by May.

We arrived back at River Bend Marina in the motorhome on May 20 and stayed in a nearby RV park. We were surprised when we saw the *Mary Constance*. The workmen had reversed the colors. The hull had been painted a soft yellow and the decks were painted Hatteras white. We had specified the paint, by numbers, and where the colors were supposed to go, so we could have forced the boatyard to repaint the boat. Mary and I decided that we really liked the yellow hull. From that time forward, whenever we gave directions to somebody to locate our boat, we told them to look for the yellow-hulled ketch. The boatyard had many things to complete and the workers were not skilled. One of them had actually installed the cables that ran from the steering wheel backwards, so when the wheel turned in one direction, the rudder would have taken the boat in the opposite direction. We moved all our belongings from the storage locker back to the boat. This was a mistake because later we found several of our possessions missing.

After the last year's summer Caribbean cruising, we decided to head north and back into the Great Lakes. Finally, on Thursday, June 21 we had our boat put back together. We left the River Bend at 6:00 a.m. and had all the bridges lift perfectly for us, and reached the ocean by 7:30. We motored for several hours, charging the batteries and refrigerator, then hoisted our sails. We sailed the rest of the day in 15-knot offshore winds and calm seas.

We re-entered the waterway at the St. Lucie Inlet and anchored close to Stewart, Florida at 6:00 p.m. Mary wrote in her journal:

It was a wonderful day! And so good to be sailing. The "old girl" just sailed like a dream all day in less than 15 knots; close to 75 miles, with no water aboard, and all the ports open. Both Ted and I felt the hot weeks in the boatyard were worth it.

We celebrated our 46th wedding anniversary at the Chart House in Daytona Beach, where the restaurant gave us a huge ice cream dessert to celebrate the occasion.

We were anchored in the waterway, not too far from Charleston, South Carolina, when we discovered that our windlass had failed. It obviously had one of those Chinese motors. We were able to bring the anchor and chain on deck by repeatedly pulling up small sections attached to a line on our sheet winch. We put into a marina in Charleston, where they sent the windlass to the Maxwell distributor in California for repairs.

We rented a car and spent the early days of July topping off our provisions, shopping the boat stores and sightseeing in Charleston. We were able to replace our dinghy inflation pump, which was among several of the things taken off our boat while at River Bend.

During these July days, we made frequent phone calls along the waterway to find out how things were progressing with my brother Doug, who was suffering from terminal congestive heart failure. With his time running out, he had been given the opportunity to undergo some new experimental heart surgery. On July 12 we learned that he had undergone the operation on his heart. When we reached Elizabeth City, North Carolina on July 16, we called our answering service to get the sad news from his wife Nancy that the operation had not been successful and Doug had died the day before at 3:15 p.m. All this would have been so much easier with today's cell phones.

When we reached Annapolis, Maryland on Monday, July 23, we had completed our circumnavigation of the North Atlantic.

We spent several days in Annapolis, and during that time I was able to complete a long telephone call with Doug's widow, Nancy. She told me that Doug had requested that he be cremated and that we have a peanut butter and jelly picnic at Lake Lucerne, near where we lived. After that, he wanted his ashes distributed in Lake Erie. Lake Lucerne is a private community. Fortunately, Stan and Joey Orr lived there and said they would be happy to arrange for us to have picnic tables by the lake in the fall.

We had an uneventful passage to the Chesapeake and Delaware Canal and then down Delaware Bay to Cape May, New Jersey. We waited several days, at anchor in the harbor at Cape May, for suitable weather to sail offshore to New York City. Finally, on August 3, the weather changed, and after getting water and fuel at the dock, we left at 11:00 a.m. for our overnight sail north along the New Jersey shore.

It was a delightful trip, with a full moon, as we watched the twinkling lights of various resort towns. Even in the middle of the night, Atlantic City was brightly lit. We reached the New York Harbor area just as it was getting light, as we had hoped, so we could see the complicated lighted navigation aids as well as the shore.

We furled our sails and started the engine just before we rounded Sandy Hook. Several boats were anchored in a small cove behind the Hook. This protected anchorage had been recommended to us by sailing friends. As we headed toward the cove, I was on the bow, at the anchor, and Mary was on the wheel when I called out to Mary, "Are those seagulls ahead of us standing or swimming?" The words were hardly out of my mouth when the boat went hard aground. Our chart showed nine feet of water where we hit the bottom. We had not only grounded, but on the falling tide, with a full moon.

Reversing the engine did no good, so I launched the dinghy, carrying a stern anchor. I put the anchor line on a winch and tried to pull us off with the anchor. By this time our boat had started to heel to one side. The Coast Guard had a station right on Sandy Hook, so I called them. They answered quickly and I had to answer a list of prepared questions. When they had determined we were in no immediate danger, they asked me if I wanted them to call a commercial towing service. I told him "Yes," and Sea Tow answered immediately. I am certain that they had been listening to our entire conversation on their radio. They arrived quickly with two boats, one of which took a line to our mast and pulled us over on our side, while the other towed us off the sandbar. Three hours later we anchored behind the break wall at Atlantic Highlands, where we slept and spent the next day resting.

We left Atlantic Highlands on what turned out to be a beautiful clear warm day, and motored into New York Harbor, past the Statue of Liberty and Ellis Island. Then back around the Battery to pass the South Street Seaport, to view the tall ships and Pete Seeger's *Clearwater,* in which he was leading a campaign to clean up the Hudson River. As we once again passed the tip of Manhattan, I was able to take a picture of the skyline with the twin towers rising above it. I still have that photograph. We found a place to anchor for the night close to the Statue of Liberty.

We enjoyed our trip up the scenic Hudson River and eventually arrived at Catskill, New York where I made arrangements at a marina to have our masts removed in preparation for our trip through the Erie Canal to Lake Erie. It took us only seven days to complete the canal passage. It was a relaxed and enjoyable trip this time, in contrast to the trip we had made on *Golconda*.

We had our masts stepped in Waddell's Boat Yard at Tonawanda, near Buffalo. His equipment was as ancient and rickety as we had remembered, but with his son doing most of the work this time, they accomplished the task with amazing ease. After a hard day's work putting on the sails and running rigging, the next day we left early in the morning for a two-hour trip through the canal leading to the Buffalo harbor and Lake Erie. With stops at Erie and Fairport Harbor, we arrived at the Vermilion Yacht Club Guest Dock on Friday, August 17. We were assigned slip 1-W, where we remained for the rest of the summer.

We had Doug's memorial picnic, complete with peanut butter and jelly sandwiches as Doug had requested. His widow, Nancy, and a number of her children came from the East. Our brother Bob and his wife Allie flew in from California. After the picnic, we all piled into automobiles and drove to the Lake Erie shore, where we took turns scattering his ashes in the lake.

CHAPTER 52

Lake Sailing

During the winter we anticipated revisiting our favorite cruising grounds in Lake Huron's Georgian Bay. This time we would be traveling on our much more comfortable *Mary Constance*. After our usual weeks of fitting out the boat, we left the Vermilion Yacht Club at 8:30 a.m. on June 22. We put a reef in our mainsail before we left and had a fabulous sail in 15- to 20-knot winds, reaching Put-in-Bay in only four hours, a new record for us. After a blustery day in the harbor, the next day, June 24, turned out to be warm and calm. We hoisted our new radial geniker (an anniversary present to each other) and sailed across the lake into the Detroit River at about five to six knots, occasionally seven knots, even though the wind was less than ten knots all day. The new sail was wonderful for just this kind of day. We motored up the Detroit River on a very pleasant clear, cool and fresh day. Mary said that she could not think of anything that she would rather be doing for this, our 47th wedding anniversary.

We spent the summer of 1991 visiting our favorite places in Lake Huron and Georgian Bay. We looked up old friends, and because we were sailing in the summer vacation waters, we visited with other sailors, on their boat or ours, almost every day.

We also had days of solitude when we anchored alone. We enjoyed the Fourth of July all by ourselves in McRae Bay, on

Bois Blanc Island. Mary baked bread and sticky buns. Later we sat in our cockpit and watched a beautiful sunset and wonderful fireworks, over the water, from Mackinac Island and St. Ignace City.

We sailed under the Mackinac Bridge and then south along the coast of Lake Michigan to Harbor Springs. Mary's cousins, John and Fred Emery, and their wives drove to the boat. We took them for a sail across the bottom of Little Travis Bay and back in a couple of hours. We had perfect weather, sunny with 12- to 15-knot winds on our beam both ways. The Emerys drove us to their cottage for a picnic dinner, then back to the boat.

We spent two days anchored in the harbor at Mackinac Island. This popular tourist island was crowded with people during the day. After the ferries left, there were still lots of people, but they were the young people who worked on the island during the summer. I guessed that the average age of the people on the street had been cut in half after the departure of the ferries.

During our summer of cruising we passed through hundreds of small islands. Most of them were unoccupied. We anchored in small tight anchorages where we climbed up the rocks and picked enough blueberries for Mary to make blueberry shortcake.

At the small town of Gore Bay, on Manitoulin Island, we joined the fleet of boats at the Great Lakes Cruising Club Rendezvous. The Rotary Club of Gore Bay held a fish fry for us. This was a great success, with good food and a large crowd of boaters. We talked and talked with people for hours! After we got back to the *Mary Constance,* we had a young couple visit us and ask us all kinds of questions about crossing the Atlantic.

In one anchorage we met a very interesting couple who had shipped their boat overland from Alaska. He was a real pioneer who built his own log cabin single-handedly. He had participated several times in the Iditarod dog sled race. He met his wife, who was from England, in the Netherlands, where they were invited to participate in a "Celebration of Transportation." When I asked her how she ran the dogsled in England, she answered "Wheels." This couple had spent their honeymoon in the middle of the Alaskan winter, on a trip into the wilderness with their dog sleds. They planned to ship their boat to Portland, Oregon at the end of the summer and then sail up the Inside Passage to their home the next summer. I was fascinated with this, and it led to an experience that I will write about later.

The culmination of our trip was revisiting Parry Sound and our former cottage. We arrived at Parry Sound early in the morning and tied up at the big government dock. We walked around town to see the many changes that had occurred. Mary found out about the meeting that we had attended the first year at Dobote, and for many subsequent years.

The next day we motored down the South Channel and anchored off "Grandma's beach." A short dinghy trip around the point took us to the Dobote dock. The new owners greeted us warmly and showed all the improvements that they had made to the camp. It was wonderful to once again smell the lovely pine-scented air that I have always associated with the cottage. It was heartwarming to visit with people who were enjoying the camp as much as we had.

We returned to Parry Sound so that we could attend the original Sunday night meeting which in 1954 had had only seven people, including us. A lone woman had started it only two years before. This time there were more than 25 people in attendance from all over the area.

Perhaps a good way to describe the cruising that we were doing in these familiar waters is to start on Mary's 69th birthday, August 14, 1991. We motored from the Sound past Killbear Point, then south in the small boat channel to Frying Pan Island and the town of San Souci. There we anchored just off Henry's Famous Fish Restaurant dock. We had a delicious pickerel meal, with blueberry pie à la mode for dessert.

On August 15 we made our way from San Souci up the South Channel to Parry Sound. The bridge tender swung the bridge for us for the last time. We tied up again at the big town dock. We went to the drugstore, then to the A&P for another basket of Ontario peaches. We left the Parry Sound dock and motored to Depot Harbor, where we anchored for the night.

On August 16 we started north in the small boat channel and spent the day carefully motoring from buoy to buoy. We ate a soup lunch under way in the Shawanaga Channel. We left the channel at Pointe au Baril, through Armstrong Rocks, and back in behind Mares Ledge, through the Hangdog Channel. This was fun but demanding passage making.

We were sad leaving these waters, which we had learned to love while exploring them in the *Ellie B*. We realized that we would probably never see them again. We had some great sailing days on our voyage back to Lake Erie. We stopped overnight in favorite anchorages and spent time on the docks in villages we always had enjoyed. We reached the Vermilion Yacht Club late in August.

CHAPTER 53

The Voyage That Didn't Happen

We were fascinated by the description of the Alaskan inner passage, described during our brief encounter with the Alaskans during that summer. We decided we would like to make that trip. I made arrangements to have our boat transported overland to Seattle by a man with a large trailer designed for hauling large boats. He said he would make the trip in the spring. I gave him a $500 deposit to reserve the time. I found a marina in Seattle which would receive the boat and store it until we arrived.

When I called the trailer owner in March, he told me that he had sold his trailer and now was a boat transport broker. He said not to worry because he had already arranged for another boat hauler to move our boat. When I asked him when we could expect them to pick up our boat, he told me the date would be contingent upon the completion of another boat, under construction on the West Coast. The hauler would deliver that boat to the East Coast and return west with our boat.

We had enough experience with boat builders to know that their completion deadlines were usually very optimistic. We faced the probability that our move could extend well into the summer. This would make our cruising plans impossible. We reluctantly canceled the move. We never did get our $500 back! Sometimes the guiding spirit that seemed to watch over us simply said "No." This was another turning point, and it was probably a good one because Mary would turn 70 that summer and I was already 71 years old.

CHAPTER 54

We Do It All Over Again

We decided we would retrace our earlier trip down the St. Lawrence Seaway to Nova Scotia. Then we would spend the next two years retracing our cruising paths in Newfoundland and Labrador. We had laid up our boat for the second time, ashore at the Marina in Huron, Ohio, on Lake Erie. Preparing the boat for winter storage on land takes time. Even though we were usually able to leave the masts up, we removed all of the lines leading to the mastheads, with the exception of one halyard on each mast. I would use these halyards to hoist myself to the mastheads in the spring using the bosun's chair. Inside the boat, we winterized the engine. I always changed the oil before layup, and made certain that the fresh water cooling system contained sufficient anti-freeze. I emptied the water tanks, opened all the faucets, and blew out the lines. I winterized the toilets by pumping anti-freeze through them. We made certain that the batteries were fully charged, and then disconnected them. I found that our batteries, prepared this way, survived even very long cold winters.

The boatyard went bankrupt over the winter. After some negotiations, we were able to have the *Mary Constance* launched in the spring. We took her back to the yacht club to prepare for our Seaway trip. Almost immediately I discovered that I had forgotten to winterize the toilets. As a result, the porcelain bowl in the aft head had cracked, so I replaced it. My winterizing system worked well, but only when I followed it. The rest of our preparations went smoothly, and by late May we were ready to leave.

It had been exactly 15 years since our previous trip down the Seaway, and we expected to find many changes. We learned that the Welland Canal was now strictly enforcing their requirement that boats must have three persons aboard. Fortunately for us, our grandson Bob McPeak was graduating from high school at just the right time, and agreed to crew for us through the canal. On June 2 he joined us at Fairport Harbor, fresh from his graduation activities.

At 6:00 the next morning we left for our trip across Lake Erie to Port Colbourne, at the entrance to the Welland Canal. The lake was calm with no wind, so we used a motor all the way. The autopilot steered. Bob was able to catch up from his graduation celebrations with a long nap. Mary and I also took turns napping. Mary even cooked a celebration meal: roasted chicken with dressing and peas, and peaches and cream for dessert. We tied up at the Port Colbourne small craft dock at 11:00 p.m.

It took us only five hours to traverse the Welland Canal the next day. We left early in the morning and passed through all of the locks alone, no longer having to wait and enter with a large vessel. I asked one of the lock tenders if perhaps a small boat had been scrunched by a big boat, and he nodded his head. The canal cost us $80 this time, but it was worth it.

We sailed to Youngstown, New York on the Niagara River, and picked up a mooring opposite a marina. Bob and I went ashore in the dinghy. There I purchased some new and used charts to supplement those we already had. We also made inquiries about how we could get Bob to Buffalo, where he wanted to attend a

Grateful Dead concert. We met Bob Finn, publisher of *Yachting World* magazine, who offered us the use of his car.

We drove Bob to the Buffalo Stadium in Orchard Park. It was fun to see the "Wharf Rats" and "Deadheads" assembling with their gaily painted vehicles and different tents. Bob told us later that he had a wonderful time and had no difficulty getting a ride directly to his house near Cleveland.

We had been noticing the odor of diesel fuel, and it seemed to be getting stronger. I spent most of the day trying to locate the source, with no success. So the next day we motored out of the Niagara River at 6:45 a.m. and used the radar to pick up the outer buoy in light fog. After about 20 miles we hosted our geniker and sailed the rest of the 50-mile downwind trip, so flat-out and comfortable that we agreed it was almost a perfect sail. We traveled 12 hours to reach the Rochester Yacht Club, but neither of us felt tired.

After dinner, I found the source of our odor. Against one of the stringers in the bilge was a small pool of diesel oil. We had a slow leak in our main fuel tank. We moved the boat to a nearby boatyard, where they discovered that the leak was in an inaccessible spot against the hull. They pumped out almost 80 gallons of diesel fuel into the temporary drums. We watched as they dismantled the seat locker, which was over the tank, and cut our beautiful Monel metal tank into small pieces, which they removed from the boat. Workers then built a wooden pattern for a tank that would fit through the seat locker. A stainless steel fabricator built this new tank. They installed supports for the new tank, fiberglassed them to the hull, and fastened the new tank in place. All of this took ten days.

We returned our diesel fuel to the new tank, five gallons at a time, so that I could mark a dipstick. The new tank was only 20 gallons smaller. We still had 100 gallons of tankage, enough fuel for us to motor almost 170 miles between fills.

We sailed along Lake Ontario to Ogdensburg, on the St. Lawrence River, where we picked up our 17-year-old grandson, Thomas Boynton, to join us on our trip through the St. Lawrence Seaway.

In the Eisenhower lock, the lock keeper told four elderly people aboard a small aluminum powerboat to tie up against our boat. Instead of passing us a line, one of the men reached out for our gunnel and held on. With his hands on our boat and his feet in his boat, the light boat moved away from us and he found himself suspended like a bridge over the water. He let go with a splash! After he climbed back on his boat, the lock keeper announced that everyone, on any of the boats in the lock, must don a life preserver.

We found staying in both Montreal and Quebec City easier this trip because both had new marinas close to the center of the city. In Montreal we tied up in a marina, so new that we felt lonely in its complex of floating docks. The Quebec Marina reminded us of Paris, where a lock maintained a constant water level at the docks.

Thomas purchased a pair of "John Lennon" sunglasses in Montreal, to replace those that he had forgotten to bring. We all went to an IMAX show, *Antarctica,* at 6:30 p.m. Tom went back at 9:30 for an IMAX Rolling Stones show. We spent two days sightseeing and enjoying some excellent French restaurants.

We continued to have high tides and strong currents as we motored and sailed down the river. At Trois Rivières we set our alarm clock for 3:45 a.m. to leave at high tide and ride the strong tidal ebb current down the river to Quebec. With our normal seven-knot cruising speed under power, aided by the river current, our GPS showed us that we were actually making ten knots over the bottom. We reached Quebec and tied up in the marina shortly after noon. We all took naps and then went sightseeing. In the evening, we went to bed and Tom went to a folk rock concert.

The second day, we did our usual large city chores. We went to the supermarket and stocked up on groceries. At a marine store we purchased a cruising guide for the St. Lawrence. Tom visited the numerous street festivals.

We discovered, as we continued down the river, that most of the larger towns had new small-boat marinas. This was a big change from our previous trip, where we had to tie up alongside fishing boats and other commercial craft. We still preferred to anchor where we could.

We were about seven miles downstream from the village of Pointe-au-Pic when our diesel overheated. We turned it off and hoisted our sails, but there wasn't enough wind to move the boat back upstream to Pointe-au-Pic. So we tied our rubber dinghy alongside the boat, and used its 5 hp outboard to push our 34,000-pound *Mary Constance* against the current. Five hours later we tied to a dock with a large "condemned" sign posted on it at Pointe-au-Pic. A couple in another boat pointed out that we were not supposed to tie to a condemned dock. When I explained our predicament, they helped us contact a local mechanic, who was able to build a replacement part.

The next morning, while we were waiting for the mechanic, a Canadian Coast Guard man arrived to tell us that it was illegal to tie up to a condemned dock. After I explained our problem, he said to move as soon as we could. When the word of our presence arrived in the village, we had several people come down to the dock to see the American yacht. A mechanic arrived with the new part in the early afternoon. As soon as the engine was functional, we moved to an anchorage.

In 1984, to celebrate the 450th anniversary of the discovery of the St. Lawrence River by Jacques Cartier, the Canadian government had subsidized the construction of small-craft harbors and marinas along the river. This made the beauty of the lower reaches of the St. Lawrence accessible to many more boats. Where we had experienced a mostly solitary trip on our previous passage, this time we often found ourselves in company with several boats.

There is a small marina at the town of Tadoussac, at the entrance to the Saguenay River. Even though it was larger, we found it completely filled with small boats. We anchored in Tadoussac Bay. We discovered that the beautiful, scenic, fjord-like Saguenay River had become a popular destination for large cruise ships. Much of the land on either side of the river was still reserved and undeveloped. We took a two-day trip up the river. By stopping overnight and arriving early in the morning, we were able once again to secure a mooring at the Saguenay River National Park, where we found a substantial new nature center. There were beautiful hiking trails in the park. We walked some of them, and Thomas did the more strenuous ones. After we returned to Tadoussac, we made bus arrangements for Thomas to return to his home in Manassas, Virginia. We continued our trip alone.

We decided that we wanted to take a different route back to Nova Scotia. After rounding the tip of the Gaspé Peninsula, we made a quick visit to the city of Gaspé. There we found that a beautiful new marina and yacht club had replaced the one long dock and the one-room yacht club shack. We continued along the coast to the town of Grand Rivière. The weather forecast was unfavorable, so we decided to stay in the harbor. While there I was able to make telephone arrangements for our winter storage. When I called the boatyard owner in Baddeck, where we had left the boat years ago, I discovered that he required that the masts be removed and stored separately. In addition, we would be required to pay him to cover our boat. Faced with these requirements, combined with a substantial increase in his rates, I decided to find another place.

Someone recommended a boat yard in Lunenburg, Nova Scotia. I did not remember the name of the boatyard, but I did have a telephone number for a marine store there. When I called, the lady who answered said yes, their store was still in business and at the same location. I explained what I was looking for and she immediately replied, "Oh, you want the Lunenburg Foundry." She gave me their telephone number. When I called the foundry and explained I was looking for a place to leave my boat for the winter, they transferred me to the boatyard manager. He said that they did store boats and they had a 75-ton Travel Lift. He then quoted what I thought were very reasonable rates. Our winter storage problems were solved.

We decided to sail to Cape Breton by way of the isolated Magdalen Islands, in the Gulf of St. Lawrence. We waited for two days and were rewarded with almost perfect sailing winds. We started our passage at seven in the morning on a beautiful clear day and sailed all day and into the night, with our genoa, mainsail, and mizzen. Our wind vane steered. It was such a comfortable trip that Mary baked bread and sticky buns which, fresh out of the oven, make wonderful snacks.

Later in the night, the winds increased and we furled the genoa and sailed the rest of the trip with staysail and main. A fabulous display of northern lights added to the beauty of the night. We reached the turning light at Entry Island, the southernmost Magdalen Island, and then continued 30 more miles to the harbor at Havre Aubert Est. We arrived at dawn, almost exactly 24 hours after our departure, and dropped anchor in the harbor, in 15 feet of water at high tide, and went to sleep. This was our first overnight trip in two years. This kind of passage is what makes sailboat cruising worthwhile.

When we woke up at about 10:30 a.m., we found our boat nearly surrounded with mud flats and shallow water. A number of pleasure and fishing boats passed by and anchored in the bay, so we moved the *Mary Constance* out with them. More and more boats came in and anchored. We thought this must be the thing to do on a Saturday afternoon. At about 2:00 we went ashore in the dinghy to a sand flat, where a man asked us, "Have you seen the sand castles?" Then he indicated the direction we should walk. When we reached the top of the large sand dune, there before us on the ocean side of the spit was a long wide beach with throngs of people. Large beautiful sand castles were spaced about 25 feet apart for at least half a mile. We were flabbergasted. This was the last thing we had expected to find on this remote isolated island.

The next morning, after a restful night, we visited the town and discovered that the Acadian Festival des Iles de la Madeleine had just begun. When the British deported the Acadians from the Maritimes, they did not reach the Magdalens. Many of the residents on the islands consider themselves first Acadians, then French, and finally Quebec Canadians. They have even created their own flag, which is a French flag with a gold star on the blue stripe.

The festival was fun, with flags flying, all the shops open, and people of all ages dancing in the street to music provided by a local fiddler. We left the festivities at about 3:00.

We then departed the anchorage and sailed very slowly to Cap aux Meules, on the next island, where we found a huge harbor and a marina. We tied up at the dock and walked ashore, purchased groceries, and climbed high up the cliff overlooking the harbor. The Gulf of St. Lawrence winds were forecast to be 25 to 35 knots, which would mean rough sailing, so we decided to stay another day.

It was fortunate that we decided to stay, because early the next morning a young man and his five-year-old son came to see the boat. After a quick visit on the boat, he announced that he was going to take us on a tour of his island. I think he was interested in practicing his English and had seen our American flag when we came into the harbor. His name was Serge Arseneau, and his son was Emanuel. He was a wonderful host and drove us to see many of the interesting viewpoints along the shore, as well as attractive old buildings, one of which was a beautiful old wooden Gothic church that had been lovingly restored. We didn't only sightsee! He took us to meet his 70-year-old parents. We stopped at Serge's home, where he left his son with his sister-in-law, and the three of us went to lunch at an attractive restaurant located in a converted convent building. He returned us to our boat at 2:30 p.m. He would not let us pay for anything.

We left for Cape Breton, in the dark, at 3:45 the next morning. A full moon was still in the sky. The sunrise was lovely, as the sun cleared the horizon and the moon disappeared into the clouds. We realized that the dark blue horizon ahead of us was actually the high cliffs of Cape Breton, 60 miles away. We continued to sail and motor the 90 miles to Ingonish Harbor, where we anchored for the night.

We cruised along the shore the next day and watched tiny automobiles traveling along the famous Cabot Trail. The *Mary Constance* entered the Bras d'Or Lakes through the north entrance. We reached the harbor at Baddeck in the early afternoon and paid for a mooring.

CHAPTER 55

Baddeck Again

We were anxious to see the changes that occurred in Baddeck, which we had gotten to know so well 15 years before. Many of our favorite places remained the same. The city dock was still as we remembered it. The Chinese restaurant still had our favorite sweet and sour fish on their menu. Henry had added a small marina to the Cape Breton boatyard. When we told him that we would not be able to leave our boat with him that winter, he simply replied "Good" as he turned and walked away. Henry had not changed a bit! I always felt he had two handicaps to overcome as the boatyard operator: he didn't like people and he didn't like boats!

In the boatyard we met Bill and Eleanor Spunar, a couple in their sixties who had motored their large twin-screw, gasoline-powered Chris Craft yacht named *Ol Watzzernam* from Detroit, out via the Seaway, all the way to Cape Breton. We wondered how they managed to find enough gasoline on their trip. Bill explained that they were leaving in the morning for a final cruise before the boatyard laid up their boat.

August 14, 1992 was Mary's 70th birthday, and we started the day by taking a large load of dirty laundry to the new Laundromat in town. I had a haircut and Mary stopped in several of the new gift shops that had emerged like weeds in this tourist town. We had lunch at the High Roller Deli. On this warm summer day, we had luncheon outside. I picked up our laundry and took it to the dinghy at the dock. I was surprised to see *Ol Watzzernam* still at the dock. I visited with Eleanor Spunar while I waited for Mary.

Mary had been trying to find a contact for her program in Baddeck. After she joined us, I saw a village policeman on the dock and walked over to ask him if he knew of a contact in town. He did not; however, Bill, who had joined his wife, asked if we had some sort of trouble. With a glance of approval from my wife, I told him that Mary was looking for a meeting. Bill replied, "Yes, there's one tonight and I'll take Mary there with me." Bill had decided to wait a day and attend the meeting that night. Another small miracle!

We returned to the *Mary Constance* with our laundry in our dinghy, to discover, attached to the lifelines, a one-foot-high, ten-foot-long banner reading "Happy 3 Score & 10 Mary Boynton." Bill had gone to the store and purchased Magic Markers and paper to letter the sign. We learned later that he was a graphic artist.

That evening I visited with Eleanor aboard her boat while Bill and Mary attended the meeting. When they returned, Eleanor surprised Mary with a birthday cake complete with 70 candles and the message "Happy Birthday Mary." It was a birthday that neither Mary nor I will ever forget!

The next morning we used Bill's car to provision the boat at the supermarket. Then we brought the *Mary Constance* to the town dock and filled our water and fuel tanks. We left for Lunenburg in the afternoon.

CHAPTER 56

Lunenburg

Aware of probable periods of bad weather, we allowed enough time for a leisurely trip down the coast. We stopped at favorite anchorages, spent two days in Halifax, and arrived in Lunenburg on August 26, the day before the annual Fishermen's Exhibition and Reunion. With changeable weather in the forecast, we immediately removed all the sails and running rigging and stowed them below. It was fortunate that we did, because that afternoon dense fog filled the harbor and stayed for four days.

I took the dinghy ashore and made final arrangements with the boatyard. I learned that the Lunenburg Foundry had been owned by the same family, at the same location, for several generations. It was still an active foundry and had hundreds of patterns for marine applications. In addition, the family owned a shipyard with slipways large enough to haul large off-shore trawlers. They had purchased the Travel Lift to service smaller boat customers. The yard scheduled our haul-out for August 31, 1992.

I had an embarrassing experience returning to the boat in the dinghy. I couldn't find our boat in the thick fog! I moved around in the harbor to no avail. I finally headed back toward the shore. This was easy because I could follow the noise. As soon as I could see the shore, I motored over to a fishing trawler anchored nearby and asked him if he could find my boat with his radar and direct me to it. He obliged and pointed the way. I always carried a compass after that.

The next day we watched the Fishermen's Reunion festivities. One by one, the large trawlers passed by, as a priest on the dock blessed them. When they were finished, sailors threw wreaths in the ocean to commemorate their fellow crewmates lost at sea. Onshore, we enjoyed a typical hometown parade, with floats, marching bands, and many bagpipes. Small children scurried along the route picking up candy.

The yard hauled out the boat on schedule on August 31. By 11:30 a.m. the boat was secured on land for the winter. After a quick lunch I climbed aboard the boat and started the winterizing process. Finally we moved the last of our possessions to a rented van and checked into a bed and breakfast for the night. Our meal that night was at Magnolia's Grill, our favorite eating place, and was delicious as usual.

On September 1 we drove a rented van to the Halifax airport. We had an easy flight, via Toronto, to Cleveland. On the last leg of our flight, we met a young woman from Chagrin Falls who had left her car at the airport. She saved us a 20-mile taxi ride and kindly drove us to our house.

CHAPTER 57

Back to Newfoundland

In 1993 we drove the motorhome to the boat. On the way we made several stops. We attended our grandson Thomas's high school graduation and helped Beth and Tony move from an apartment to their new house in Billerica, Mass.

We spent a wonderful day at Mount Desert National Park. Another day we walked the docks and streets of Bar Harbor. We put the motorhome on a large ferry for Nova Scotia, which saved us many miles of driving.

We arrived in Lunenburg on June 9, where we parked the motorhome in the boatyard and went immediately to check out the boat. We had learned that during the winter someone had broken into the boat. After inspection, it became apparent that a person had spent some days aboard the boat. One of our sleeping bags had been unrolled and probably used. There were pots and pans on the stove, and there were empty food cans from our stores.

Whoever it was had taken a number of things with him when he left. Our small portable Honda generator was gone. He had found our Nikon underwater camera, which I had mistakenly left in a drawer. We discovered a few days later, to our surprise, that he had also taken one of our 22.5-gallon propane canisters. This was one of two canisters we installed in London. These tanks had British fittings that we found difficult to fill on this side of the ocean. In many of the ports we visited, hardware stores would exchange empty 20-gallon tanks for filled tanks. A local propane service installed new tanks for us, along with a pressure gauge and a new line from the tanks to our stove. The new gauge would help warn us of propane leaks.

It took a little more than two weeks for us to prepare the boat for our trip to Newfoundland and Labrador. We were able to stay in the motorhome, in the boatyard, with occasional overnight trips to a nearby campground to empty the holding tank and fill our water tank. The weeks of preparation were not all work; Mary attended meetings, and we made new friends on the dock and in the yard. Peter Kinley, the younger of the two brothers who were currently managing the business, was responsible for the boatyard. He arrived for a visit to the motorhome on our first night.

One afternoon while we were working on the boat, Jim Kinley, the Foundry chairman of the board and the two brothers' father, invited us to come to his house for one o'clock Sunday brunch. We had a delightful luncheon under the maple trees in his backyard. The next year Jim was appointed Governor General of Nova Scotia, the Queen's representative. His first job after moving into the governor's mansion was to house and entertain President and Mrs. Nixon on their visit to Nova Scotia. Certainly, the Lunenburg Foundry was the friendliest place we have ever left a boat.

On our way to Newfoundland we stopped at many of our favorite places. We stayed for two days in Halifax and lingered for a while in Baddeck. We sailed nonstop overnight to Channel-Port aux Basques. After two days of rest, we started our trip eastward along the southern coast of Newfoundland.

That afternoon we anchored in Dublin Cove, as we had 15 years before. However, this time we were not greeted by exuberant young fishermen. In 1992, the year before we arrived, the Canadian and U.S. governments had banned all ground fishing within their fishing waters, extending 200 miles from the shore. The northern cod had almost completely vanished from the Grand Banks. The governments, in spite of the warnings from inshore fishermen, had actually subsidized the building of many more large draggers to work the waters that they controlled. Within these waters were the codfish spawning grounds. Their experts recorded the increased catches, not realizing that the increases were due to more fishing boats, in spite of the rapidly declining fish population.

The next morning we made our way through the narrow pass into the harbor of Les Petites. Two men on the shore waved to us to tie up at the fishermen's pier. My first impression, when we entered the harbor, was that the village was more beautiful than I had remembered it, but I then realized that almost all of the houses were freshly painted in new bright colors. The fishermen, who were now being paid not to fish, had time on their hands, so they painted their houses. Norman Strickland came down to the dock and greeted us by name after 15 years. We learned that his wife had died, so we invited him to dinner aboard the *Mary Constance*. We were warmly greeted by many fishermen who visited with us in the cockpit of our boat. For us it was a bittersweet reunion to see these self-sufficient fishermen reduced to the government dole. We learned recently that the village residents have been moved and the village no longer exists.

We visited Rencontre Bay, where we had an interesting time exploring the totally abandoned village. The remains of the village pier, where we had tied up before, were completely gone, but we were pleasantly surprised to see smoke coming from the chimneys of several buildings. People from some of the larger communities had restored six buildings as summer homes. We never went ashore.

In the town of Gaultois, we docked on the fishermen's wharf. Almost immediately after we tied up, we had the first of many visitors who stopped by the boat. The next morning we invited a man aboard our boat. He told us that he had walked from an abandoned town, Piccaire, which was having a "Come Home."

We discovered that this was a reunion of descendants of residents who had lived there and of some people who had been there in 1966 when the town was vacated by government edict. He invited us to attend the celebration, so we took him back in our boat to the harbor where the village had once existed. The reunion committee had built a new white fence around the cemetery and mowed the grass. They constructed a platform and bandshell on what had been the schoolhouse foundation. A row of outhouses had been erected. Families had placed their tents where their homes had once been located. Food was being prepared at several different places. Concerts and dances were scheduled for each night, with various games for both adults and children during the day.

The day had started bright and sunny, almost the first day that it felt like summer. Unfortunately, at about noon the weather changed abruptly, as it often did in Newfoundland, and heavy rain started falling. By late afternoon the campsite was covered with sticky mud. We spent the night aboard our boat in the harbor. It rained hard all night. The next morning, when we awoke, people were already dismantling their tents in preparation to leave. The committee had canceled the reunion. We left immediately after breakfast to clear space in the tiny harbor.

Gaultois was also having a "Come Home," which ran for a week. Gaultois was one of the places to which people had been relocated. People came to it not only from Newfoundland but from all over Canada. We tied up on the town dock, which was the center of many activities. The children's fishing contest was conducted on the dock just in front of our boat. We watched the dory race and the evening fireworks from our cockpit.

During that summer we revisited most of our favorite anchorages on the south coast. It was a rainy summer, but we had periods of sunshine that we enjoyed even more because of their scarcity. The scenery was as beautiful as ever, and the people everywhere we went were just as cordial.

We visited St. Pierre again on a lovely warm summer day. We did a lot of walking and eating the delicious French food. We had hoped to stay a day or two more, but the weather forecasts indicated we would have one more good sailing day before windy, rainy days were anticipated. So we left the next morning and had a fast easy passage back to Nova Scotia under sail.

We enjoyed a week in Baddeck on our return trip to Lunenburg. We once again left the *Mary Constance* in the foundry boatyard for the winter. We had learned that the ferry from Halifax to Portland, Maine charged half price for motorhomes on Mondays. We took advantage of this discount and had a very pleasant six-hour trip on this large vessel, which again saved us miles and miles of driving.

CHAPTER 58

Preparations

When new sailors approach us with questions about what it requires to do long-range cruising on a sailboat, I always try to determine if they are able to fix things. While I was never considered mechanically inclined, I have always done household repairs. I am still not able to go beyond the basics in engine maintenance and mechanics, but I have learned to fix many things on our boat. I do believe, however, that without some mechanical aptitude, cruising in a sailboat can prove to be a very difficult endeavor. I think, in our cruising, hardly a week went by without something in need of fixing.

Often we have been asked about how we handled our correspondence and paid our bills when we were cruising. Today, with the Internet and cell phones, this is much easier. For mail, we had a post office box in our hometown, and a young local housewife was happy to be paid to pick it up and to read our mail to us when we called her. I was able to pay our bills through our bank, using the touch-tone telephone. There were mail-forwarding services that also could pay bills, but our arrangement worked well for us.

I believe that our experience while preparing the *Mary Constance* for our trip to circumnavigate Newfoundland will illustrate the type of repairs we constantly faced. By this time, the *Mary Constance* had survived two Atlantic crossings; she had various repairs made in many countries and survived a major hurricane. She was 18 years old and beginning to show her age. It is our observation, however, that even new boats are often not exempt from regular problems.

We returned to Lunenburg in our motorhome on June 3, 1994. We discovered that repairs to a vertical crack in the topsides were already under way in our absence. This had not been a structural problem, but its appearance had bothered us. I started to work getting a new fiberglass patch on one of the cockpit coamings. This project took several days.

June 8: A workman sanded the entire bottom of the boat below the waterline to prepare it for a new coat of anti-fouling paint.

June 9: A man from Covey Island Boat Works finished the patching on the topsides.

June 10: I sanded and painted the repaired cockpit combing and rub rails.

June 11: I finished painting the boot stripe.

June 12: I painted the bottom with a new coat of anti-fouling paint.

June 13: I arranged to send our life raft to Dartmouth for inspection and re-packing. I discovered our Espar cabin heater was not working. A man from the yard installed our new engine heat exchanger that we had brought with us.

June 14: I repaired a bad electrical connection and the cabin heater works.

June 15: We moved most of the staple food that we had brought with us from the motorhome to the boat.

June 16: We filled the water tanks on the boat, and I put the Aries wind vane back on the transom and ran the lines to the drum on the new wheel that I had just installed.

June 17: I replaced the flexible engine shutoff cable that runs from the helm to the engine. The old one had become impossibly corroded and no longer worked. Late in the afternoon the boatyard launched our boat. We remained in the boatyard travel lift slings for the weekend. We were taking on water and discovered that the problem was a through hull fitting that wasn't properly closed.

June 18: Early in the morning I went to the mastheads and installed the running rigging. Before lunch we had both foresails in place. In the afternoon we pulled both the main and mizzen sails up their slots on the mast, then furled them and put on their sail covers.

June 19: We moved the clothing and bedding from the motorhome to the boat.

Monday, June 20 was a discouraging day. The yard moved the boat out of the launch slip to a dock. When the refrigeration man arrived on schedule, we could not get the engine started; he waited almost two hours and then left. The mechanic from the yard determined that the problem was the starter. We took it to Bridgewater and left it with a generator and starter repair service. On the way back to the boat in the motorhome, I purchased a good battery tester and found that our boat batteries were almost fully charged.

June 21: It took us a long time to get the pilot light on our cookstove burning; it was taking a long time for the propane to travel from the tanks in the back of the boat to the tiny pilot light. At noon we drove to Bridgewater and picked up our reconditioned starter motor and another identical one that we would keep as a spare. I installed our starter in the afternoon and the engine started.

June 22: We drove the motorhome to the foundry and parked it outside the gate. We then motored the boat to the museum dock. The refrigeration man arrived at 10:00 a.m., and within a couple of hours the fridge was working well so we finished getting everything out of the motorhome and into the boat. I bought a new deck wash pump. We drove the motorhome to the Hay Wagon campground. We hooked it up temporarily and took showers, then emptied the tanks and moved it to the storage area for the summer. The last thing we did before we closed the door was set off a bug fogger. The lady from the campground drove us back to the boat.

June 23, the next day, would be our 50th wedding anniversary and we planned to spend it in Halifax, so we did a few last-minute things ashore. I started the engine, and we were beginning to remove the sail covers when the engine stopped. It wouldn't start again! The boatyard mechanic spent two hours before deciding that the fuel injection pump was broken. He removed it and sent it to Halifax. We, of course, had no way to keep the boat refrigerator and freezer cold. The manager of the Fishermen's Museum was nice enough to say that we could park the motorhome on the pier next to the *Mary Constance*. I was able to get a ride to the campground, where I filled the motorhome water tank, turned on the propane, and started the refrigerator. At the dock we moved all of the contents of the boat refrigerator and freezer back to the motorhome refrigerator.

June 24 was our 50th wedding anniversary! I installed the new deck wash pump. A radio repairman picked up our amateur radio transceiver and returned it later in the day. I was able to run an extension cord from the motorhome to the boat battery charger and use the motorhome generator to bring our boat batteries up to full charge. We had dinner at our favorite Lunenburg restaurant, Magnolia's Grill. We were each presented with a cupcake with a candle on it, and everyone in the restaurant stood and sang "Happy Anniversary to You."

Saturday, June 25, we found ourselves faced with the weekend before we could expect the return of our injection pump, but several things occurred which made for an eventful two days. Friends from Mary's meeting stopped by the motorhome and asked us if we would like to see the sinking of the cruiser *Saguenay* in the ocean off the town of Blue Rock. This was a planned event where a decommissioned Canadian naval cruiser was going to be scuttled to create an artificial reef for recreational divers. On this beautiful sunny day, we sat on the rocks and watched the demolition charges go off on the ship. Old Navy vessels can be difficult to sink, and she settled, stern first, with her bow protruding from the water. We learned later that it took another day to get the bow settled on the bottom. That evening other friends invited us to join them for a potluck fundraiser at a firehouse.

Sunday, June 26, we awoke to find the parking lot filled with trucks for the movie production of Stephen King's *Dolores Claiborne,* a movie starring Kathy Bates. We spent much of the day watching the moviemaking. Nancy, who owned Magnolia's Grill, was the stand-in for Kathy Bates. They photographed scenes of Kathy walking to the bank, and all the cars on the street had "Maine 1974" license plates. In the boatyard we had watched a young woman carving large blocks of Styrofoam that would be painted to look like rocks. Earlier the foundry had built an elaborate $18,000 device to support a car on a flatbed trailer so that they could make moving scenes as it drove down a road. Several of our friends had rented their homes to the movie company. They chartered dozens of boats for a nautical scene that never appeared in the movie.

June 27: We shopped in the village. I purchased some flexible tubing that I hoped to use to fix the slow leak in the pressure water system. I ordered a large new hand bilge pump, which was expected to arrive from Halifax on Wednesday. We learned that the reconditioned injector pump would be returned the next day.

June 28: I worked all morning removing the old bilge pump; it was a messy and difficult job. The mechanic arrived with the injector pump and installed it on the engine. Nothing changed! The pump was still not delivering fuel to the injectors. The mechanic worked most of the afternoon trying to repair the problem and finally gave up.

June 29: I took the injector pump to the service facility in Halifax myself. I waited while they checked it again. They ran a test while I watched, and it was working perfectly. We also picked up our newly inspected and repacked life raft. Driving back to Lunenburg, I think we were the only motorhome in North America carrying a six-man inflatable life raft. We picked up the new bilge pump and discovered it would not fit in the locker where the old pump had been located.

June 30: We returned the new bilge pump, and I bought some different caulking compound and was able to fix the old one and put it back in its place. The engine still would not start and the yard mechanic was becoming desperate. Finally, they called a mechanic who had worked in the yard, and he had the engine up and running in less than an hour. The problem, as everyone suspected, was an air leak. The injector pump was slanted on our engine, and an air pocket had formed at the high point in the pump. The new mechanic fixed the problem by lifting the lid and allowing the air to escape and fuel to flow into its place. We found that air was entering the system through a slightly loose fitting at the fuel tank.

July 1: We once again moved everything from the motorhome into the boat and took it back to the campground, again for summer storage. We hoisted our dinghy out of the water and secured it on the foredeck, then walked to Magnolia's for dinner.

CHAPTER 59

Bound for Newfoundland and Labrador

On July 2, almost exactly one month after we arrived in Lunenburg, we started our summer cruise, heading for Halifax. The fog lifted as we left the Lunenburg harbor, and it was easy to get by Cross Island and Duck Island. The wind dropped and the fog closed in as we motored through the Sambro Ledges with practically no visibility. I picked up the buoys on the radar and gave Mary the course to the next buoy. She then held the course until we either saw or heard the buoy. We repeated this procedure several times. The wind came up and the fog cleared as we reached the Halifax harbor, and we were able to sail all the way to the back of "the arm," where we picked up a mooring for the night. We both enjoyed the challenge of the trip.

We once more crossed the Cabot Strait to Port aux Basques and sailed north along the scenic west coast of Newfoundland. The fish were gone, so many of the small summer camps were closed. Lobster fishing, which had always been carefully controlled, flourished during the defined times when they were allowed to set traps. We spent one night on a dock with several large shrimp fishing boats and were asked to move to the other side of the dock in the middle of the night so that additional boats could come in. We left the next day with a bag of delicious freshly caught shrimp, presented to us by the man who had asked us to move.

We had an interesting experience at Port Saunders. It was a cold rainy day and we decided to stay in the harbor. Mary was baking bread when three teenage boys came down to the dock to look at the boat. They were still there when I returned from telephoning, and we told them about some of our adventures on the *Mary Constance*. We learned that they were attending a summer school intended to teach them about possible jobs in the tourist industry.

Later in the morning the same three boys returned to say that their teacher had asked them to invite us to talk to their class that afternoon. We said that we would and they escorted us back to their school at 1:30. There were 16 high-school-age boys and girls in the class. I do not remember exactly what we talked about, but I am certain that we told them how beautiful Newfoundland was. They seemed interested and asked lots of questions. When we left, they gave us jars of canned moose meat and pickled beets.

On July 26 we awoke to a foggy day, but it was a warm day for these latitudes so we left to cross the Strait of Belle Isle to Red Bay, Labrador. We saw nothing at all; no boats appeared on the radar screen. I did think that I saw one iceberg, but it was well off our course. We arrived early in the afternoon and took our dinghy across the harbor to visit a new museum that had recently been opened. In the 1500s the Basques had sailed here from Spain to catch whales. They established a fishing camp on Saddle Island. Archaeologists had uncovered a number of interesting items that were displayed at the museum.

We spent two days in Red Bay, waiting for strong winds in the strait to abate. Almost immediately after we left to sail down the Labrador coast, we were once again enveloped in thick fog. Our destination was Temple Bay, where a sailing friend had told us we would find good protection from the southwest winds. As we headed for Temple Pass, the sea fog lifted and we were amazed to see, above the remaining ground fog, the top of a large iceberg. This berg was obviously grounded in the shallow water, so we cautiously headed toward it. As we neared it, the fog lifted and I was able to take pictures of it. We continued through Temple Pass into beautiful isolated Temple Bay. There was very little left of the town of Château, indicated on our chart. We were very, very alone in this vast land. The nasty, biting black flies found us immediately, so we screened up and stayed below for the rest of the afternoon and quiet night. In the morning there was a large whale playing around our boat.

The next day the fog had lifted and we could see the huge expanse of the Labrador coast. There were numerous icebergs in the Straits of Belle Isle. Mary counted eight of them as we sailed well offshore, along the immeasurable Newfoundland coast. None of the villages we passed that day were occupied. The fishing moratorium had emptied them—their occupants had moved to larger communities.

We tied up at the dock in the village of Battle Harbor. There we discovered that they were rebuilding many of the original Grenfell Mission buildings to commemorate the first Grenfell Clinic in Labrador. We had been told that there was a small freighter that spent the night at the dock at Battle Harbor, so we knew we would have to move. We were visiting in the home of a couple who had remembered us from our previous trip when the freighter's horn sounded above the village. We rushed down to the dock. With the help of half of the men on the dock, we backed off and made a hasty departure.

We went west along the side of Caribou Island into the Caribou Run and tried to anchor in a place recommended to us by an experienced Newfoundland sailor. We found it too windy for comfort. So we went back behind Indian Island to Shoal Tickle and anchored in the middle of the tickle there was a lovely little town in the harbor. We took our dinghy to shore and met the only residents, Doug and Doris Bradley, who had lived there all their lives. They spent their summer there but wintered at their home in Dodge Bay. Doug had been the village storekeeper and did some fishing. They had a lovely two-story home where they had raised five children, who were now scattered throughout Canada.

It was a short distance, on a clear day, to St. Louis Sound, where we found a large iceberg that had drifted in and grounded. I took my camera, and from the dinghy I photographed the *Mary Constance* while Mary steered in front of the iceberg several times. Each time I motioned to her to get closer to the iceberg, she shook her head "No." After I was back on board, Mary told me that she could hear the water lapping on the iceberg and could see the huge submerged part of the berg very close to the boat.

We continued down the Labrador coast to the town of Mary's Harbor. I have used the term "down the Labrador coast," instead of "north along the coast," because this is the maritime way of describing this direction. This usage goes back to the days when sailing vessels sailed downwind to go north along the coast. The small coastal freighter *Duke of Topsail* was tied up in the harbor, and we were introduced to the captain, Lloyd Bugden. His freighter made regular round trips to the far north, serving small villages and Inuit settlements. We would have liked to make this trip with him but discovered that it was necessary to make reservations well in advance.

We wanted to revisit L'Anse aux Meadows, the site of an authenticated Viking settlement, which we had found so interesting 15 years before. We tried to tie up in the village of Ship Cove, but strong winds made anchoring or docking impossible, so we went on to the city of St. Anthony. The next day we rented a car and drove to the Viking settlement site. It certainly was much more developed than we had remembered, now featuring a reconstruction of houses and a welcome center where we watched an interesting film.

That afternoon, back in St. Anthony, we drove to the Grenfell House, Sir Wilfred's home, which was now a museum. A young guide took us to the Grenfell Dock House Museum. It housed the mechanism for the Marine Railway and pictures of the boats that had gone down the Labrador Coast for the Medical Mission. Next we drove to the hospital to see the wonderful mosaic murals in the lobby. We asked the hospital receptionist if Dr. Ann Roberts still worked there. She told us that she did and directed us across the street to the Grenfell Regional Health Service. Dr. Roberts remembered us well, probably because it was on her first assignment in Labrador that we met her. We learned that she was now the Director of Medical Services for the Grenfell Regional Health Service, now run by the Canadian government. We had a short visit with her in her office and asked her to come down and see us on the boat that evening. The next day she invited us to tea at her house.

We spent another day at the dock. In the morning, the First Officer of the Canadian Coast Guard cutter *Harp* came to visit us on the boat and invited us to have dinner aboard the *Harp* at five o'clock. We walked to Ann Roberts' home at about two o'clock and had tea. Next we went for a hike with Ann, through a beautiful spruce forest up the hill to see the Grenville plaques at their burial site. That night we went to dinner on the *Harp* as the guests of Captain Michael O'Brien. We were served salad, a delicious large steak with baked potatoes, and Rice Krispie squares. We were asked to stay and watch the CBS news from Detroit, Michigan on their television. It was quite a day!

I believe it important to repeat that almost all cruising sailors will say that the most enjoyable thing about the cruising life is the chance to visit with people along the way. This was true even on our 1994 trip to more remote areas. I counted the calling cards and signatures in Mary's journal and discovered that we had more than 40 people visit with us aboard our boat that summer.

On our passage southeast along the Newfoundland coast, we saw many icebergs, large whales, dolphins, seals and numerous varieties of seagoing birds. We were seldom alone. We stopped in favorite anchorages and returned through the Bras d'Or Lakes and Baddeck to Lunenburg, where we had left our motorhome for the summer.

For one last time we left the *Mary Constance* in the foundry boatyard for the winter. It took us less than a week to move all of our belongings into the motorhome and prepare the boat for winter storage. Before we left, we contracted with a couple who owned a sail loft and carpentry shop to build us a wooden frame and cover for the boat. It would make it possible to completely cover the boat with all of the rigging and mast in place. We left the boatyard, in the motorhome, on September 7.

CHAPTER 60

Sailing with Kate

The summer of 1985 was a big change for us. We planned to return to United States waters for the first time in many years. In the early spring our granddaughter Kate McPeak called us to ask if she could go cruising with us. Mary and I discussed this and called her back with the stipulation that if anytime during the summer she decided she wanted to go home, we would get her there. We also said that if anytime during the summer we felt she should go home, we would send her there. As a result, when we left for the boat in the motorhome, we had a beautiful 20-year-old granddaughter with us. We soon found out that she attracted young men like a magnet attracts iron filings.

When we arrived at the boatyard, we found the *Mary Constance* wrapped in her new cover. Kate helped me remove two sections of the three-part cover so that we could check the cabin. We found everything exactly as we had left it. We had a number of busy days as we removed the rest of the cover and carefully numbered each piece of the wooden frame before we dismantled it for storage.

While we were working on the boat, Keith, the owner of *Eastern Star*, stopped by to invite us for a sunset sail that evening on his charter boat. There were six of us aboard his boat: the three of us, Bernice of *Windrider*, and Dale and Ray, two young crewmembers from the schooner *Bluenose II*. It is a replica of the famous fishing schooner whose image is on the Canadian dime. We had a lovely sail, and when we returned, Dale and Ray invited Kate for coffee aboard the *Bluenose II*. From that time on we saw very little of Kate. She spent most of her time with the college-age kids on the famous schooner.

Finally the *Bluenose II* left and we thought we would have our granddaughter back with us again. We couldn't have been more wrong. That day the *Tree of Life,* a beautiful and very large schooner built for a wealthy man who planned to sail around the world, arrived for some major modifications in the shipyard. The next thing we knew, Kate was aboard the *Tree of Life,* helping the crew move things from the boat to a cottage they had rented in the nearby town of Le Havre. She spent the night there with the rest of the crew. We were concerned at first that her interest was the middle-aged captain, Kelly, who was also the owner of the boat. However, we soon learned that it was actually the handsome young Swedish first officer, Frederick. She "got stuck" on the schooner while it was being hauled up on the ways, but later brought Freddie and Kelly to meet us. They invited us to the cottage for dinner the next night. Kate returned to the cottage with them for the night.

The next morning we moved the last things from the motorhome to the boat and left the motorhome in the campground storage area. We had a lovely 20-mile sail to Le Havre, where we anchored off the bakery dock. We had a marvelous feast cooked on a barbecue grill with chicken, steak, potatoes and corn, and a salad, with watermelon for dessert.

We left early the next morning. Frederick was at the dock as the three of us boarded our dinghy after purchasing fresh warm bread at the bakery. We stored the dinghy on the foredeck and waved to Frederick as we started our trip along the Nova Scotia coast, headed for Maine. It was June 24, our 51st wedding anniversary.

We stopped at two harbors as we cruised southwest along the Nova Scotia coast. We had a rough passage around Cape Sable on our way to Yarmouth. There we shopped for groceries, and while I made some repairs on our Espar furnace, Mary cooked a large stew. Kate made a phone call to Frederick at the cottage, as she had done at each harbor along the way. She returned somewhat downcast, as once again she had not been able to make contact. After supper, the evening weather forecast called for light southwesterly winds in the Gulf of Maine. We all dressed in warm clothing and left for an overnight passage to Bar Harbor. At 1:00 p.m. the next day we anchored in the bay, behind the bar, at Bar Harbor. We all went to bed until dinner when we enjoyed Mary's precooked stew.

The next morning we secured a mooring in the main harbor, went ashore in the dinghy, and went our separate ways. That afternoon, a radiant Kate joined us. She had talked to Frederick on the telephone. I had ordered a new autopilot that was going to be delivered in Bar Harbor, so we spent several days there until it arrived. The weather was clear and warm during our stay.

We were in the harbor for the Fourth of July, so we "dressed" the ship and hoisted all of our flags. We went ashore and watched the large town parade that lasted two hours. It was a good old-fashioned celebration! In the afternoon, we walked to the ballfield where the Kiwanis Club was serving lobster dinner.

We had a wonderful strawberry shortcake, which the YMCA was selling.

We awoke the next morning to find the *Queen Elizabeth 2* cruise ship anchored in the harbor. It was a large, beautiful ship. Tenders traveled back and forth, carrying passengers between the vessel and the dock, all day long. She left right after supper. My new ST 4000 Autohelm arrived by UPS that afternoon. We stayed in Bar Harbor for another day while I finished installing the new autopilot. Kate went ashore and talked on the phone to her father, Frederick, and Kelly. Then she went to a concert in the park with a man and his little girl whom she had previously met.

We felt it was too soon to start our trip south, so we decided to explore some of the Down East coast of Maine. In each harbor where we stopped, Kate went ashore to find a telephone. One day, when she returned from one of these excursions, I asked Kate, "Are the fires still burning?" She replied, "Boy, are they!" Not long after that exchange, she returned from another phone call and told us that she had been asked to crew on the *Tree of Life*. They told her that she would be paid and they really needed her help. We asked her if she was certain she wanted to do this, and she made it clear that she wanted to do this very much. In keeping with our agreement, we said that we would help her get back to Nova Scotia. We sailed in the fog to Saint John, New Brunswick.

Since we were going to be in Saint John, we decided it would be interesting to go through the Reversing Falls and up the Saint John River. The huge high tides from the Bay of Fundy create a large tidal bore as the water surges through the gorge at the entrance to the Saint John River. The direction of this phenomenon changes at the turn of the tide. We had to wait until 5:20 p.m. before we received permission from the harbor control to go through the gorge with the Reversing Falls.

The passage through the falls was much less difficult than we had been led to believe. We continued upriver to the Kennebecasis Yacht Club, where we picked up a mooring. I helped Kate consolidate her belongings, and on July 15 we moved to a slip at the Yacht Club early in the morning so that Kate could get her bags off the boat. The taxi arrived at 8:00 to take her to the ferry to Digby, Nova Scotia, where Frederick would meet her when she arrived. We sailed alone for the rest of the summer. We missed her company, but were grateful that she was on her own "great adventure."

CHAPTER 61

Heading South Again

We sailed up the river as far as Fredericton, where we could go no further because of a low bridge. We anchored there and took the dinghy into the town. We stopped at interesting anchorages in the river, both coming and going. For the first time in years, we swam off the boat in the fresh water.

After we left Saint John, we once again headed south, making long fast passages from harbor to harbor. We took advantage of the strong current, many days making as much as nine knots over the bottom. We tied up against a fishing boat in Welshford Harbor on Campobello Island. We walked a mile and a half to visit the Roosevelt Cottage. We watched an interesting video at the Visitors' Center and then walked through the "cottage," which we thought was a peculiar name for a 35-room house. It was here that the future president contracted polio, which crippled him for the rest of his life.

We continued south and reached Bar Harbor again on August 8. We cruised for a week in Penobscot Bay exploring some of the many lovely anchorages. One week later we reached our daughter Connie on the telephone to learn that Kate was going to marry Frederick. The wedding would take place on October 7 in the Friends Meeting in Cleveland. This changed our plans.

Sometime before, our friends Mike and Kay Arms had offered us the use of a mooring opposite their house in the Sassafras

River if we ever needed it. The river flows into Chesapeake Bay. Now we did need it as a place to leave the boat while we went to Kate's wedding in Cleveland. As a result, our destination was suddenly the Chesapeake Bay.

We enjoyed our passage south along the coast, where we stopped at numerous famous old harbors along the way. On August 30 we made our way through the Woods Hole passage and sailed along the Martha's Vineyard coast, where we picked up a buoy in the harbor of Edgartown.

We had just finished our lunch when Rex Kaiser came alongside, in his dinghy, and called to us. He had recognized his old boat. We asked him aboard. He was very interested in the modifications we had made to the old *Claire*. After he returned to the new *Claire,* he called us on the radio and asked us to come for drinks at 5:00. We had a warm and friendly visit with Rex and Claire, quite different from the frosty reception on our previous visit after we had purchased Claire's boat and summer home out from under her.

We spent another day in Edgartown, waiting for the southwesterly winds to change. Rex and Claire stopped at our boat again because Rex wanted to show Claire how we had converted our club staysail to roller furling. Mary was able to show Claire her old boat.

When we awoke on Saturday, September 2, Labor Day weekend, we discovered that the wind had shifted into the north. It was time to leave. We were under way at 7:00 a.m. to start south again. We had favorable winds when we turned west into Nantucket Sound and made good time. When we got to Vineyard Sound and turned south, the winds lightened and we put up the geniker. We continued along to the north side of Block Island and down into Long Island Sound. There were thousands of sailboats in the Sound this holiday weekend but very little commercial traffic.

It was a beautiful fall sailing day, with good winds, clear visibility, and quite calm water that made it easy to move around on the boat. It was also easy for Mary to prepare dinner. We had macaroni and cheese and canned zucchini, with gingerbread for dessert. We sailed on into the night. We did not turn on the engine until we were almost in the East River, heading into New York City. Our timing on the whole trip was good, with almost slack water at The Race and again at Hell Gate. We enjoyed our trip through the great city. We motored down the East River, then through New York Harbor and under the Verrazano-Narrows Bridge. We followed the buoys across Raritan Bay to the back of Sandy Hook, where we dropped the anchor in a little cove, at 3:00 p.m. We had traveled more than 200 miles, mostly under sail.

We stayed in the little cove on Labor Day. It was filled with boats coming and going on a beautiful fall holiday. By nightfall only eight sailboats remained in the Cove, some of them headed south, as we were. The next day we moved to Atlantic Highlands Harbor, where we provisioned our boat with water, diesel fuel, and groceries in preparation for our next long hop.

We left the next morning at sunrise. Soon we were sailing south along the New Jersey coast in light winds. The winds rose as the day progressed, and we passed offshore of the lights of Atlantic City as the sun dropped behind the horizon. We reached the harbor of Cape May, New Jersey at 2:00 a.m. By 3:00 we were anchored and in bed.

We woke up the next day at 8:00 a.m. We needed to ride a floodtide for the next part of our journey, and I determined from the tide tables that we needed to leave Cape May at 2:00 p.m. in order to pass under the low bridge on the Cape May Canal. This would also enable us to ride up the Delaware Bay with both the wind and current behind us. It all worked perfectly, and we arrived at the Chesapeake and Delaware Canal at slack tide and then rode the ebb tide current through the canal into Chesapeake Bay. It was a wonderful warm night again, and we wore shorts until midnight. We both had short naps. Even though the autopilot steered much of the trip, we had to keep a close watch because we were experiencing heavy barge and commercial traffic the entire way. We anchored at 1:00 a.m. in a cove on the Bohemia River. There were three other anchor lights in the cove.

The next morning we moved to the Sassafras River, where we picked up the mooring opposite Mike and Kay's house. When we were settled, Mike came out in his dinghy to tell us that we were invited to a birthday party at a neighbor's house that evening. We had a good nap, then showered and took our dinghy to the dock. We walked up to the house, and Mike and Kay took us to the party. It was great fun and we had a chance to meet many of their neighbors and sailing buddies.

On September 11 Kay drove us to BWI Airport for our flight home. Two days later I left for Nova Scotia to retrieve our motorhome. I was back home in Chagrin Falls six days later. We were home for one month before returning to the boat.

Kate and Frederick were married "under the care" of the Cleveland Friends Meeting, as planned, on October 7 in the meeting house. We all sat in silence until the bride and groom stood up and said their wedding vows to each other, after which they resumed their seats. We had more silence, which was soon broken by loving comments of friends and relatives. After the wedding everyone in attendance signed a large ornate wedding certificate. The meeting provided a potluck supper for the reception. Kelly paid for transportation and housing for two of Freddie's crewmates from the *Tree of Life* so that they could attend the wedding. Shortly after the crew returned to the ship, as a wedding present Kelly paid for a trip for the bride and groom to visit Frederick's parents in Sweden.

At the wedding reception, Kelly said to me, "You ought to come and sail with us sometime." I replied, somewhat facetiously, "When you get to Tahiti, let me know." He replied, "I will." I had no idea that I would actually join the crew there later.

After almost exactly one month at home, we arrived back at the *Mary Constance* on its mooring in the Sassafras River. Mike and Kay graciously offered to store our motorhome for us while we resumed our cruise south. We hoped to reach the Bahamas in time for Christmas. For the first time, we joined the migration of cruising sailors headed south for the islands.

On our way south we anchored in the Inner Harbor of Baltimore. After lunch we took the *Mary Constance* east to Fells Point, where we found the *Tree of Life* and tied up next to her. Kelly had told the harbormaster to expect us. Kate gave us the royal tour of her "new home." The next day their boat was going to participate in the Great Chesapeake Schooner Race starting from Annapolis and going to Norfolk. We had dinner ashore with Kate, Frederick, Kelly, and Donna and Ozzy, who had been at Kate's wedding.

We left the side of the *Tree of Life* at 7:40 a.m. and slowly motored around until the 40 schooners were lined up in parade formation, led by the *Pride of Baltimore*. Then we motored quickly to just south of the Bay Bridge where the race formed up. The race start was at 3:15 p.m. After that, we sailed into Annapolis Harbor where we picked up a town mooring right across from Steve's Boat Yard.

Our friends Steve and Audrey were now the owners of a full-service boatyard. We spent several days using their facility for various repairs on our boat. Audrey drove Mary to see their new home. They were no longer living aboard their Friendship sloop.

We were members of the Waterway Radio and Cruising Club. The club controls an amateur radio network at 7:45 each morning. It acts as a meeting point for cruising boats that call in, in a designated sequence depending on location. Cruisers wanting to talk to each other move to a different frequency. Individual boats can also file a trip plan; this is a particularly good idea for boats cruising offshore in the Atlantic. The "net controller" calls them each morning and, if he does not receive a reply, asks boats in different locations to try to make contact. If this is not successful, he telephones a previously designated contact to report the failure.

We were still in the Chesapeake, headed south, when we received a call on the net from Ken and Jean Moore, who had crewed with us on our Atlantic crossing. They said that

Shearwater was anchored in Indian Creek. It was a great surprise. We didn't know that they were anywhere near that part of the world because we hadn't talked to them in the year. We had a great sail in their direction, averaging seven knots. When we arrived at the Creek, we contacted them on the VHF radio. They said that they were in a little cove farther up the Creek. When we arrived, we couldn't find their sailboat because they were actually aboard their new Albin 33 trawler that they had owned for more than a year. They were also headed south and we traveled with them for several days.

CHAPTER 62

The Intracoastal Waterway

The Intracoastal Waterway provides protected water between the Chesapeake and Florida. We entered at mile marker 0.0, just out of Norfolk, at the Elizabeth River. In a sense, mile markers are more important indicators of progress than geographical locations. The mile markers measure distance in statute miles, while most ship's instruments are calibrated for nautical miles. However, one gets used to translating the distance rather quickly. In long sections of the Waterway, there is a mile marker every mile. Southbound, they start at zero and end at mile marker 987 in Stuart, Florida. Headed south, distinctive yellow signs mark the course with a triangle for port and a square to mark starboard. It is necessary to stay within the marks because in many parts of the Waterway, the water is very shallow. This means that someone must be steering the boat all the time. Experienced boatmen say, "If anyone tells you that he has traversed the entire Waterway without going aground, he is probably a liar."

Bridge openings become a major factor in planning trips. While most bridges open on the hour and half-hour, some change their schedules to accommodate rush-hour vehicle traffic. Many bridges will open on demand when contacted by radio, even at nonscheduled times. However, we found that bridge tenders usually waited until a number of boats arrived. Because the *Mary Constance* was a fast boat under power, we often arrived at bridges first and had to wait for the rest to catch up.

The Marine Corps base at Camp Lejeune, between Wilmington and Morehead City, North Carolina, posed another problem. It closed a five-mile section of the Waterway from 8:00 a.m. to noon and again from 1:00 to 5:00 p.m. for military maneuvers. Not many boats travel the Waterway after dark, and we were no exception. We solved the problem by leaving a nearby anchorage at 6:00 a.m. and cleared the restricted area just a few minutes before it closed for the morning.

On November 15 we awoke to find ice on our cockpit cushions and deck. A reminder that it was winter! This was an exception, and for most of the trip we were comfortable steering from our open cockpit.

We celebrated Thanksgiving in Fernandina Beach, Florida. We arrived the day before, and while we were ashore, we canvassed the restaurants to find one that was going to be open to serve a traditional turkey Thanksgiving dinner. There was only one, Maggie's Diner. Shortly before we planned to go ashore for our dinner, a cruising sailboat named *Imagine This* entered the harbor and dropped anchor. Filled with the holiday spirit, we stopped by their boat in our dinghy and asked them if they would like to go ashore and have dinner with us. They did.

We had a very nice traditional Thanksgiving buffet dinner. Sitting in the diner, Don and Tonya told us their tale of woe. Don had spent several years restoring a beautiful Swan sailboat in Annapolis, Maryland. Finally, he and his girlfriend Tonya departed on their dream trip to Nassau, in the Bahamas, where they planned to meet his children for Christmas. We soon learned that Don was totally unqualified to make this trip; he had never learned anything about navigation. I discovered he could not even read the chart. When I asked him how he found his way this far, he said that a friend had put all of the waypoints in his GPS. They had made several long offshore passages between waypoints. On one of these passages, at night, they hit a whale and bent their propeller. Trying to sail into an inlet for repairs, they ran aground and ultimately were towed into the harbor by the Coast Guard. Why the Coast Guard allowed them to continue their trip I will never know.

We continued down the waterway, and on December 15 we arrived in Miami. We anchored in an area called Marine Stadium Bay because there is a stadium there, on the water, for water shows. There were about ten other boats anchored with us. We had a beautiful view of Miami with its lights and Christmas decorations.

CHAPTER 63
The Bahamas

On December 16 we crossed the 40-mile-wide Gulf Stream to the Bahamas. The winds were light and directly on our nose, so we motored all the way in relatively calm seas. We arrived at Gun Cay at 4:30 p.m. We were tired and happy to be there at last. This really was the destination for the year. All year long people would ask, "Where are you going?" I always said, "The Bahamas for Christmas!"

The next day we motored across the Great Bahama Bank. With light winds, we motored all day in water that was seldom more than ten feet deep. We were still on the bank when we dropped our anchor at 5:15 p.m. for the night. There was nothing to be seen in any direction on the great expanse of water. We arrived at Chub Cay Marina early the next afternoon and moved to the dock. There we cleared Bahamian customs and received a six-month permit for the boat for only $20.

Later, *Imagine This* arrived in the harbor, towed by a single-handed Dutch sailor, Ron, on *Canada Goose*. Don and Tonya had continued to have all kinds of trouble because of their lack of knowledge about boat handling and sailing. Their old Swan was showing its age, with things wearing out and giving up. Tonya was just about ready to give up and fly home from Nassau after they met the children. Ultimately, Ron led them all the way to Nassau.

Three days before Christmas we motored for five hours across the Yellow Bank to Allen's Cay, in the northern Exumas. After we had anchored, we took our dinghy to the nearby Greenleaf Cay to visit the iguanas. The minute our dinghy touched the beach on this tiny uninhabited key, a dozen or so large iguanas came out of the brush toward us, expecting to be fed some sort of leafy greens. I just took some close-up photographs. We stayed at Allen's Cay for the holiday weekend.

On December 24 we strung Christmas lights on our lifelines and hooked them up to our little Honda generator. I stopped at each of the boats anchored in the harbor and invited the crew to the *Mary Constance* at 5:00 for a Christmas Eve get-together. There were finally nine of us aboard. I think everyone enjoyed the gathering because we were all so far away from our homes.

Christmas 1995, in the Bahamas, was certainly different from any we have had before or since. We exchanged gifts after breakfast, earrings and two books for Mary and new binoculars for me. She reminded me that the coffee grinder, which we had been using since South Carolina, was to be considered a gift for me. We visited Bob, Helen, and Susan on *Merry Way* because Mary wanted to give them a fruitcake. Then we dinked over to look at the German vessel *Carpe Diem*. A crewmember, with the captain's permission, invited us aboard for a tour. People on large chartered catamarans sailed and slept aboard their boats, but had their breakfast and dinner aboard the mother ship, *Carpe Diem*. They were going to have a big Junkanoo party that evening.

Junkanoo is celebrated in many of the Bahaman Islands on the day after Christmas. It originated when the slaves, deprived of the Christian celebrations, held their own the next day, hidden from their masters. Today they hold parades with bands and costumes similar to the Mardi Gras.

After lunch, we used our dinghy to reach a wonderful coral reef and snorkeled for 45 minutes above this beautiful coral garden with a multitude of colored tropical fish. Back in the boat, Mary prepared a dinner of chicken with cranberry sauce, dressing, peas and sweet potatoes. Because we felt it was wrong for Laurent, a single-handed sailor from Quebec, to be alone on Christmas night, we asked him to join us. He brought wine and dessert, Bananas Flambé, which he cooked on our stove. It was a Christmas Day to remember!

The next day the winds shifted and the harbor got rough so, one by one, the boats left. We left at 12:30 for a ten-mile sail south to Norman Island. The next day we went ashore with our trash, then walked all around and looked at the ruins of the "drug cartel" headquarters. Things had just deteriorated even more since we last visited in November 1989. We did learn that three homes on the north end of the island had been repaired. From our boat we saw three small planes take off from the runway.

We had just put on our sail covers at Staniel Cay when a boat came by and the couple on board called out to us, "We last saw you in Port aux Basques, Newfoundland." It was Monty and Betsy, who had been on *Little Haste* in 1993. Now they were on a different boat, named *Salsa*. We discovered that they had cruised most of the Caribbean while we were sailing in the north. After they anchored and settled in, they invited us aboard their boat. We spent all afternoon aboard *Salsa*. We were not talked out, so Betsy prepared some scrambled eggs for the four of us. After supper, Mary Kay and Ron from *Rag Time* came aboard and we all watched a VCR movie together. This type of chance encounter with other sailors occurred repeatedly during our cruising years. Sometimes they occurred in very unlikely places.

Sunday morning, December 31, New Year's Eve, we went to a Sunday service at a small Baptist church on the island. A week after Christmas, they were still singing Christmas carols: we sang at least seven of them to a foot-stamping beat, different than we had ever heard before.

We decided that it was about time to return to the United States. We had previously arranged to leave our boat on a dock in front of a private home, on a canal off the New River, in Fort Lauderdale. After all, I was still working! With an overnight stop at Norman Cay, we arrived and anchored in Nassau harbor on January 3. We had planned to stay there only a few days, but the weather changed our plans and it was almost a week before we could resume our trip.

I kept a single side-band radio schedule, most of the time on our Bahamas trip, with Herb on "Southbound II," a land-based operator in Toronto, Ontario. Herb was a highly skilled amateur meteorologist, who would give weather advice tailored specifically to the location of a boat. He had been doing this quite a few years and was highly regarded. There was no charge for his service. He warned me that there was a fairly strong cold front due to pass through the Bahamas, followed by strong northerly winds over the Gulf Stream. He advised that we wait out the cold front in Nassau.

We put out another anchor and more chain on a beautiful calm day, but at sunset the winds started. It blew hard all that night and the next day. Our preparations paid off. We stayed put, while some other boats in the harbor dragged their anchors and in at least one case, a boat lost her dinghy.

Following Herb's weather advice, we stayed one more day in Nassau and then left for our trip to Ft. Lauderdale. We had a rough crossing of the Tongue of the Ocean that stirred up some sediment in our port fuel tank, so we made a quick stop at Chub Cay for fuel and topped off our large starboard tank. We had very light headwinds, so we once again motored across the Grand Bank and dropped our anchor in the middle of nowhere at 10:00 p.m. We were under way again at 5:30 a.m. The next day we crossed a calm Gulf Stream and anchored in Lake Silvia, Fort Lauderdale, at 5:15 p.m. We had traveled 160 nautical miles. We were asleep by 8:00 that evening, grateful for Herb's weather forecast.

After several days preparing the *Mary Constance* for storage at Mrs. Halvorson's dock, we flew home on January 18, 1996. Two weeks later we left in the motorhome on our business trip. I had greatly reduced my territory to only Alabama and the northern half of Florida, so we completed our calls in less than two months.

CHAPTER 64

Cuba

We flew back to Fort Lauderdale on April 27 and rented a car. We found the boat in good shape, except for the need of a thorough wash. There are more marine facilities in Fort Lauderdale than almost any other location on the East Coast of the United States. We took advantage of them to get our VHF radio repaired and purchased a number of things that we needed for the boat. The Seven Seas Cruising Association (SSCA) has their office in Fort Lauderdale, and we visited it a number of times.

At the SSCA office, we met some live-aboard sailors who had recently visited Cuba. We had thought that this trip was impossible because of the strict Treasury Department restrictions prohibiting spending any money in Cuba. We learned that the Clinton administration was prosecuting only the most blatant violations of this rule. All we would have to do would be to secure United States Coast Guard permission to cross the restricted zone, which was in force to prevent Cuban refugees from reaching the United States. We filled out a form available at the SSCA office and faxed it to the Coast Guard. We purchased a cruising guide and charts for a trip to Cuba. The faxed permit arrived the next day.

We sailed to Key West, which is only 90 miles from Cuba. We left the anchorage at Key West on May 15 at 6:30 p.m. for an overnight passage to Cuba. It took us 21 hours to reach the

Marina Hemingway, the only entry point permitted for pleasure craft. We sailed during the night with a reefed mainsail, plus a staysail and mizzen, a safe combination in case of unexpected squalls. The waves were 6 to 8 feet. After sunrise, we hoisted our large genoa jib and furled our staysail.

Our arrival in Cuba was anything but auspicious. We were still some distance from Marina Hemingway when we received a call from the Cuban harbor control. We identified ourselves as the American vessel *Mary Constance,* headed to their marina. They cleared us for arrival. Our trouble began when we tried to furl our genoa jib. It jammed and we were not able to roll it up. This meant that we had to loosen the halyard and drop the whole jib out of its track in the forestay. I had to gather this very large sail as it came down and stuff it into a sail bag. This was a slow and time-consuming process. In the meantime, we let the boat drift. Unfortunately, the strong Gulf Stream current was moving us in the direction of the Havana harbor. We received several increasingly urgent calls from the harbor control telling us that we were not headed toward the Marina Hemingway. Each time we responded that we had a problem and would change our course as soon as we had fixed it. I suspect that they just did not understand enough English.

The calls stopped after we had started the engine and headed toward the marina entrance. We entered through a narrow, relatively shallow pass between vicious-looking coral on either side. At the marina a man directed us to a dock.

We had ten different officials aboard the *Mary Constance* before we were cleared to stay in the country. Officials from customs, immigration, health, port control, and agriculture all arrived in pairs. All were very friendly. Communist Cuba tried to provide everyone with a good education and a job. Sometimes the job did not fit the education. We learned later that one of the men aboard our boat was a qualified medical doctor.

The pleasure boat marina, built by president and dictator Batista for his son before the Castro revolution, was named after Ernest Hemingway. It had suffered from years of neglect. Our electrical connection to the shore had been cobbled together by a yard worker using amazing, dangerous-looking wires and splices. When the marina did have power, our connection also worked. Water was available, if you had a long enough hose to reach the faucet.

We were tired from the crossing, and both of us slept most of the day. After supper, I walked the dock and was amazed to find *Salsa,* with Monty and Betsy aboard. We had no idea that they had any plans to visit Cuba. They were equally surprised to find us there.

We expected to find many pictures of Fidel Castro in Havana but were surprised to find there were an equal number—perhaps more—of two other heroes, Che Guevara and Ernest Hemingway. The first did not surprise us; the second did. Hemingway had permanent residences in Key West and Cuba in the 1930's and 1940's and was greatly respected by the Cuban people. Our friend Monty bore a remarkable resemblance to Hemingway, with a very similar white beard and hair. Several times, when we were visiting Havana, small children pointed to him and said, "Papa, Papa," their way of recognizing one of their heroes.

We stayed in Cuba for only one week. Early in our stay we had two days of very heavy rain and high temperatures that confined us to our boat. Then we discovered that the refrigeration compressor on our engine was not working. We needed a new compressor, and it just was not available in Cuba. We were able to buy some ice for our refrigerator, but we had to start to use the frozen things in our freezer immediately. We had thought that we would cruise west along the south coast of Cuba, but it was obvious that we would not be able to purchase ice anywhere along this less populated and more primitive coast. We just did not have provisions for more than a few days without refrigeration.

On two nicer days we took a taxi into Havana. It was an interesting drive to a beautiful old city. The taxi was a 1960 American automobile, which, like many of the cars that we saw, was maintained by sheer perseverance and ingenuity. Some of the beautiful old buildings, with balcony facades reminiscent of those seen in New Orleans were being repaired with a United Nations grant. Unfortunately, many others were just crumbling away. Everywhere there were police and guards and begging children. We discovered that the Cuban people really liked Americans, in spite of our government's tough embargo.

The night before Monty and Betsy were due to leave, we walked a mile to have dinner cooked at Pedro's Restaurant, located on the roof of his house. There were only four tables, a limit set by the government which discouraged all private enterprise. Pedro cooked a large fish on his outdoor grill. The delicious fish with trimmings cost us only $3.00 US each. This was more than the average Cuban earned in a month. We learned later that the Cuban government had imposed a large tax on this type of enterprise.

On Monday, May 27, we checked out at the government-owned marina, paying our $200 dock bill and $15 for each of our visas. Obviously, the Cuban government liked American dollars. It took us two hours to clear through the Cuban bureaucracy. We finally departed at 5:45 p.m. and had a great sail back. The water was smooth, and we flew all four sails all the way. We anchored in the harbor at Key West at 9:00 a.m. the next day, after 15 hours of almost perfect sailing.

CHAPTER 65

Change of Plans

We learned that our grandson Bob was going to be married to Amelia Rodd on July 27 in West Virginia, and we wanted to attend. We both felt that we had had enough of sailing in the tropics and decided to move the boat north, perhaps to the Chesapeake, where we could leave it for the winter. We also agreed that we would rather make at least one long offshore passage north to avoid some of the winding shallow channels in the southern Intracoastal Waterway.

After a day's rest in Key West, we sailed to Boot Key Harbor in Marathon. There we had our refrigerator fixed by a supposed "refrigerator expert," who was living aboard a boat in the harbor. We had to wait for the repairs for three days. When we arrived in Fort Lauderdale, we discovered that once again the refrigerator was not functioning, so we had it repaired again by Marine Refrigeration Repair Service. We also had another mechanic change the impeller on our engine's fresh water system pump.

On Friday, June 14, we topped off our diesel tanks and headed north, offshore in the Atlantic. In the next four days we sailed 527 nautical miles in 80 hours, at an average of 6.6 knots. We had wonderful wind most of the time and received a boost from the Gulf Stream. We would have had a better average if I hadn't goofed and left the Gulf Stream for several hours. We arrived in Beaufort, North Carolina at 4:30 p.m. on Monday. I was 75 years old and Mary was almost 74.

We stayed in Beaufort for three days waiting out the first tropical storm of the season, forecast to pass our area the next day with possible heavy winds and rain. Neither amounted to anything. However, while we were there, we picked up our voicemail messages from home. Among them was a message from Kate, relaying the message that Kelly said we would be welcome as unpaid crew on the *Tree of Life* in Tahiti from August 1 to August 27. This meant we would be flying to Tahiti with Kate, who was coming home for her brother Bob's wedding. We decided to lay up the boat in Annapolis, Maryland. We started north again, this time on the inland waterway.

On June 24 we arrived at Great Bridge, Virginia to find *Ariel III,* with our friends Alex and Diane aboard. We had a long visit with them aboard their boat, and then we all went to dinner at the "Ho Ho Chinese Restaurant," where we celebrated our 52nd wedding anniversary.

We arrived in the Annapolis, Maryland harbor on July 3, where, in spite of the holiday weekend, we were able to pick up a town mooring. Early in the morning of the Fourth of July, we "dressed ship" with all of our signal flags. I believe we were the first boat to do this, and as the day progressed, we watched flags blossom all over the harbor like colorful flowers. Son David and his wife Charlotte arrived in the *Merry Sea,* a small 14-foot sailboat, and tied alongside us on the *Mary Constance.*

It was a beautiful day, with good sailing winds in the harbor, so Dave and I decided to take the small sailboat for a spin among the anchored boats. We had not been sailing very long when a puff of wind caught us unawares and we capsized. I came up under the sail but had no difficulty swimming out from under it. It was not until later that I realized that I had been totally submerged and was wearing my hearing aid! It did not take us long to right the boat, climb aboard, and start bailing. In the meantime, every loose object on the boat was drifting away, with the exception of the anchor, which had not been tied to the boat and had gone to the bottom. A man in a small powerboat collected our floating belongings and brought them to us. In all the years we had sailed the *Merry Sea,* neither of us had ever capsized it! We were a sorry wet mess when we climbed aboard the *Mary Constance.* Soon there were drying clothes hanging everywhere. Fortunately, it was a good drying day. After a fresh water rinse and a day's drying time, the hearing aid started working again.

Our friends Ridge and Kathy offered us the use of their dock at the sailing club that Ridge managed. We moved there the next morning and were quite grateful because his dock was free. That same morning Mary slipped while crossing into the cockpit. With one foot on the bridge deck and the other foot on the seat, she did a very painful spread-eagle. She was in agony. Kathy was able to drive her to an orthopedic surgeon that afternoon, and he confirmed what we had guessed: she had pulled her hamstring muscle. He complimented us for using hot and cold compresses and told her that all she could do was to take some painkillers and rest. I think it was soon after this experience that Mary said she thought I should go alone to the South Pacific.

We decided to lay up the boat, on land, in Steve's boat yard. His wife Audrey drove us to BWI Airport for our flight home. We didn't return to the boat until late in May 1997. On July 27 Bob and Amelia were married in a garden wedding at her parents' vacation farm in West Virginia.

CHAPTER 66

The South Pacific

Four days after the wedding, I left to join the *Tree of Life* in Tahiti. My granddaughter Kate left one day later to rejoin the boat and her husband. In deference to my age, I spent one day in San Diego resting before the long South Pacific flight. Therefore we arrived on the same day, but on different flights.

Sailing aboard the large schooner was a new experience for me. My quarters were to be in the sumptuous owner's cabin with its own private bathroom. For some of the trip, I would share the king-size double bed with another man. The bed had a bundling board running down the center. There were seven of us in the crew. In addition to the captain and owner Kelly, there were first mate Frederick and his wife Kate; two young women, who were a couple and shared a cabin; and my roommate and me. I was the oldest person aboard. Each of us was expected to stand daily watches and cook the meals one day a week. The idea of preparing three meals for seven people really frightened me. As it turned out, my granddaughter Kate helped me out planning and preparing my meals. In addition, all of us were assigned chores aboard the boat. My job consisted of scraping and applying many coats of finish to the brightwork on top of the cabin hatches and railings.

We only spent one day in Tahiti, after Kate and I arrived, before we left on our first passage. The schooner was a big boat, 70 feet long with a beam of almost 19 feet. She could be steered from inside a large deckhouse or from a wheel located just forward of the deckhouse which gave an unobstructed view of the sails. I found the boat difficult to steer because it had hydraulic steering, which was very sensitive to small movements of the wheel. We were required to hand-steer the boat. Even when we were powering, we were not allowed to use the autopilot.

After several days at sea, our first port of call was Bora Bora, considered to be one of the most beautiful tropical islands in the South Pacific. We sailed through a passage in the coral reef which circles the island and anchored in the lagoon. That night the captain took us all ashore for dinner at a very expensive tropical restaurant. Kelly never asked us to share in the cost of any of our excursions ashore.

A photographer from *National Geographic* magazine joined us for a period on the *Tree of Life*. She and another photographer were photographing the French Polynesian islands. She chartered a small boat so that she could photograph the schooner entering Bora Bora. I asked her if I could join her. She agreed, and both of us took pictures as the crew sailed the schooner before us, over and over again. When the story in *National Geographic* was published, none of the boat's pictures was included, but I got a good one which is still hanging on our wall.

The biggest difference I experienced in sailing on the big boat was my loss of independence. All the time that Mary and I sailed, we decided where to go, when to go ashore, how long to stay, and with whom we could visit and spend time. I found it very difficult to get to know the people of the islands or any of the boats in the harbor. We did have people aboard our boat from other boats, but often they were invited in large numbers for a party, where I found it almost impossible to get to know any one person. Part of the problem was my age because the people that the captain liked to socialize with were very much younger than I.

Certain wonderful events stand out in my memory of this trip. Frederick was an avid fisherman and always trolled a lure behind the boat. When he hooked a fish, everything stopped aboard the boat; we backed the sails to slow it down as he rushed back and forth on the deck, fighting to bring the fish aboard. One day in particular, I recall he brought aboard a particularly large tuna that resulted in some wonderful meals on the boat. I vividly remember the absolutely calm day when we were motoring and Kelly called for a "skinny dip" for the crew. I was very careful to avoid watching my beautiful 21-year-old granddaughter strip down for the event. I didn't participate because I didn't think I could make the climb back aboard the boat after the swim.

I have almost no recollection of the time we spent in Tonga. Samoa was different! I remember the day when the boat was anchored in a lovely protected lagoon. I swam off the boat as much as I could that day because not more than 50 feet from the boat was a gorgeous coral reef. I snorkeled, in the clear warm water, over amazingly beautiful types of coral. Over, through, and among the corals were more different types of colorful coral-dwelling fish than I had ever seen before. Each time I returned, I saw at least one new fish.

The kingdom of Samoa, when we visited it, differed greatly from American Samoa, a United States protectorate.

It was one of the few Polynesian archipelagoes which had never been colonized. It had unique democratic government. Landownership was protected; property could only be sold to other Samoans. They could lease their land to others.

I was fortunate to be able to spend two days ashore on my own. The first day ashore, I just wandered around talking to people. As a result, I was asked to attend a Samoan funeral and burial ceremony. It was a moving experience. Later that day I had an hour-long conversation with a Samoan gentleman about my own age. Tape-recorded movies had just reached the island, and he was greatly concerned about their influence on the younger generation. Many of Western Samoa's old traditions still remained. European Christian missionaries had reached the islands, and the very conservative women's dresses were the result. Dresses reached the ankles, and even when they went swimming or bathing, their attire remained the same.

A Polynesian Islands Festival was under way, and I was able to move close to the stage to photograph dance programs presented by people from all over Polynesia. They varied greatly, from foot-stamping, heavyset, chanting Samoans to a beautiful, bare-breasted dance by young Fiji women. I am not sure which island they represented, but one group featured dancing men in weird masks, accompanied by a surprisingly beautiful melody produced by several men on bamboo panpipes.

I left the schooner in Samoa, but when preparing for my departure from the boat, it was discovered that Kelly, who had collected all our passports to check us into the island, had somehow returned without mine and it was now missing. I was fortunate that there was an American Consul in Samoa. I spent many hours in the consulate waiting room, waiting while my paperwork flew back and forth to the American Embassy in New Zealand. Finally I received a letter under the seal of the United States documenting the fact that I was, indeed, an American citizen. I was free to thank Kelly for my experience aboard the *Tree of Life* and to say goodbye to the crew.

I flew home by way of Hawaii, where I stopped for a 24-hour rest in Honolulu. I never saw anything of the island except the inside of my hotel room and a Burger King that was located conveniently to the hotel. I was back in Chagrin Falls on September 25.

In mid-October my brother Bob made a quick three-day trip to Cleveland and stayed with us. He came for a ceremony where he was inducted into the Shaker Heights High School Honor Roll of Distinguished Alumni. He had already received almost every award possible in his academic field, of vision. I believe that the honor he received from his high school meant more to him than many of the others. Only one day after he returned to San Diego, his wife of 50 years, Alice, died. She had been in hospice care for some time and urged my brother to go and accept the award. I felt it was her final gift to her husband. Mary and I flew to San Diego to attend her memorial service in November.

CHAPTER 67

Back to Maine

On May 13, 1997 we arrived at Steve's boat yard in Annapolis. With the help of a young man, I removed the cover from our boat and started the somewhat tedious dismantling of the wooden framework. The boatyard applied a new coat of anti-fouling paint the next day. Things were going well until the boatyard lifted the *Mary Constance* in slings to let the centerboard down and paint it. The centerboard cable broke, and we discovered the pulley on the top of the board was frozen and rusty along with the fittings. The whole top of the centerboard needed to be rebuilt. With the boat back on land I was able to finish almost all of the chores needed to get it back to go sailing with the exception of the sails and rigging.

On our trip north we stopped in familiar anchorages. We had one long offshore passage. We left Cape May at 6:30 a.m. for a 200-mile trip to Block Island, Rhode Island. We anchored in the Great Salt Pond, July 2, at 2:00 p.m., 31 hours after we left Cape May. We averaged 6.45 knots. We spent the Fourth of July weekend there, along with hundreds of other boats. The fireworks were great.

We stopped in Fairhaven, Massachusetts, where we had our rusty 16-year-old Espar heater replaced with a newer and better version. Fairhaven shares a harbor with New Bedford. A large hurricane breakwall protects the harbor. We continued into the harbor and through the swing bridge over Route 6, and we anchored in a quiet spot behind Pope's Island. The next day we took our dinghy across the harbor to visit New Bedford.

Two places in the city stand out in my mind. The Seamen's Chapel was immortalized as the "Whaleman's Chapel" by Herman Melville in his classic novel *Moby Dick*. With its pulpit, shaped as the bow of a boat, it stands to this day as the house of prayer and memorial to New Bedford whalemen and to fishermen who have lost their lives at sea. The Whaling Museum, located in a wonderful building, is fascinating. It is the largest museum of its kind, and we spent several hours there.

We found Alex and Diane on *Ariel III*, anchored in Onset Bay. We had dinner together ashore that evening. When we told them that we thought we would leave the boat in Maine for the winter and perhaps base there in following years, they urged us to visit their homeport in Belfast, on Penobscot Bay. It is amazing how conversations such as this can change your life for years.

Two weeks later, we picked up a mooring in Belfast harbor. We liked what we found there. Almost everything was easily accessible on foot from the harbor, including the library, the post office, a supermarket, and a very good hardware store. The town had undergone quite a transformation since the days when I called on the funeral director in town. A large credit card processing facility had opened up just outside of town and brought an influx of people to the sleepy village. Many of the beautiful old ship's captains' houses had been renewed. There were no vacancies for stores on the main street.

There were some problems with Belfast harbor. It was located at the mouth of the Passagassawakeag River with 15-foot tides. When strong southeast winds blew against a falling tide, they could create large nasty waves in the harbor. We solved this problem by watching the weather forecasts and moving our boat a short distance across Penobscot Bay, to a lovely protected anchorage in Smith Cove.

The *Mary Constance* was beginning to show her age. The paint job that we received from the Fort Lauderdale yard after Hugo was not holding up. We got estimates for hull repairs and painting from two of the most respected yards in the Penobscot area. In both cases the cost was prohibitive for us. One of them was actually more than we paid for the boat. Alex and two other men told me that the painter at the Belfast Boatyard did excellent work. When we received an estimate from the yard for painting our boat and repairing the necessary cracks in the hull, it was within reason. There was only one catch: the painter was going south for the winter and would have to do the boat almost immediately, before he left. We decided to cut our summer short.

I had previously told Jack that I would attend the sales meeting on September 1, so I made a quick four-day flight to Chagrin Falls. The day after I arrived back, the yard removed both of our masts and their rigging. Later the same day, at high tide, they pulled the *Mary Constance* out of the water on a very large trailer designed for the purpose. The next day, Mary and I worked hard removing all of the contents of the *Mary Constance* to the motorhome. Steve, the painter, insisted that everything that did not need painting be removed from the exterior of the boat. The bowsprit and wind vane were already in storage. I spent two days helping the painter remove all the rest of the through-hull and through-deck hardware. We watched as the boatyard trailer backed our boat into the large paint shop area. We arrived home on September 12.

CHAPTER 68

The Big Mistake

1988 turned out quite differently than we had anticipated. In January and February we made our business calls in Alabama and Florida for the last time. I had already told Jack that this would be my last trip representing the directory. At age 77, I thought it was time to quit. I felt it was important to tell my customers this, so that they would be prepared to receive someone new the next year.

In the last days of May we arrived at the Belfast boatyard in the motorhome towing our small Toyota Corolla. The newly painted *Mary Constance* was still in the large storage shed at the boatyard. The painter had done a superb job of correcting the fiberglass faults and painting. She looked wonderful with her soft yellow hull. There was much work to be done, since the fastenings that we removed had to be reinstalled. I helped Ed, from the boatyard, to install the chain plates and numerous other fittings. Mary and I put new name letters on the transom.

Yard workers loaded the boat on the big trailer and took it to the boatyard in preparation for stepping the masts. I always liked to run the engine on land at least once, to be certain it would start before launching. I checked the engine oil and the transmission oil. Next I ran a garden hose to the fresh water intake on the engine to supply it with cooling water. The engine started quickly, and while it was running I turned on the refrigeration system to see if it was working. It did not seem like it was functioning properly. In the next two days the yard worker reinstalled the bow pulpit and Aries wind vane and installed the masts and rigging. Finally it was time to launch the *Mary Constance,* and once in the water, they towed her to a nearby dock.

On June 24, the next day, the refrigeration man arrived to check the system. I started the engine for him, and he said that it seemed to be cooling okay. At almost the same moment, the engine stopped and would not turn over again. It didn't take very long to discover the problem; all of the lubricating oil had drained out of the engine through a new crack in the oil pan. It had never occurred to me to check the oil before we started the engine, since I had done this only two days before. All this happened on our 54th wedding anniversary! It takes a special kind of woman to maintain our marriage all these years.

The yard mechanic and another experienced mechanic both agreed that the engine was irreparably damaged and would have to be replaced or rebuilt. I decided to have the yard mechanic rebuild our engine. He would send the main part of the engine to an engine rebuilder. The yard mechanic's job was to disassemble the engine and later reassemble it. This job took two full months, to the day. Our boat was ready to sail again on August 24.

Fortunately, the *Mary Constance* was designed so that the cockpit sole (floor) was removable, to make it possible to lift the engine directly out of the boat. Even this was not simple, because the steering pedestal and engine controls had to be removed before the floor. It is amazing how many things are attached to an engine. Finally, they towed the *Mary Constance* to the Tugboat Dock, where a large crane lifted the engine out of the boat and on to the shore. The yard forklift picked it up the engine and took it to the new work shed.

I took my time cleaning up the engine compartment and painting it. I discovered the cockpit floor was deteriorating under the teak grating, so I had the opportunity to apply a new fiberglass coating to the cabin sole, and paint it while it was out of the boat. Randy, the yard mechanic, began disassembling the diesel, and soon its parts were spread all over the work area. When this was finished, he sent the block, complete with its internal parts, to the engine rebuilders. It took weeks and weeks before the rebuilders could round up the necessary parts for our 22-year-old Westerbeke diesel.

We had a different summer, but a pleasant one. We had the motorhome to live in and our small car for transportation. Much of the time we parked the motorhome in the boatyard storage lot outside of town. It was a quiet spot because most of the boats stored there in the winter were in the water. We were able to get electricity and to set up our DirecTV dish so that we could watch television and movies in the motorhome.

For a very reasonable amount, we purchased permits to dump our motorhome holding tanks in the village sewage facility. We had already become friends with a number of people living in Belfast. Mary became very active in the 12-step program in the area. Many nights, while she was at a meeting, I watched TV movies. We purchased a post office box, so we could have our mail from home forwarded directly to us. We attended Sunday services at the Congregational Church, and new Unitarian friends invited us to their home for a special outdoor service and luncheon.

In mid-July we drove the motorhome to the beautiful Sugarloaf Mountain Ski Resort, for an extended weekend, to attend Mary's program's 21st Annual Maine Round-Up. One night, we watched the "Belfast Days" parade and fireworks over the harbor. We really felt like Belfast residents.

On August 1, we drove to Lincolnville, Maine where we left our car and took the ferry to Islesboro to attend the Seven Seas Cruising Association's annual Maine Gam. There were almost 70 cruising boats anchored opposite the house of our friends Dick and Kathy. Their large beautiful yard served as a meeting place for all of the visiting sailors. Many of our cruising friends were there.

A few days later we drove to Buck Harbor to watch the community steel drum band, Flash in the Pans. This remarkably good large band gave an outdoor performance for a street dance. A music teacher who lived in Blue Hill, Maine started it. On a trip to Trinidad he had become enamored of steel drums and learned how to make them. Today the band has approximately 35 members, many of whom had little or no prior musical background. They ranged in age from teens to over 70. Their repertoire included an eclectic mix of traditional Calypso, pop, swing, blues, and classical pieces. Mary and I became "Flash groupies," and in subsequent years, followed them whenever we could.

We moved aboard the boat with all of the things from our motorhome on August 27. The next morning I left for Chagrin Falls in the motorhome, towing our little car. Mary stayed aboard the boat. I flew back on September 1 to learn that she had had a very difficult and distressing weekend in my absence.

All of the electricity on the boat had stopped functioning. This meant that the only light she had at night was from candles, and that she could not start the engine to cool down the refrigerator and freezer. On Saturday, Mary was able to reach Alex, the yard owner, and he came to the boat but was not able to find the cause of the problem. His wife Bitsa took all of the frozen food from the boat to store in her home freezer. It was not until the day after I returned that an electrician discovered the nature of the problem, a bad cable that should have been replaced when the engine was rebuilt. During the next two weeks, we discovered several other small problems that resulted from the installation of the engine. Among them were a leak in the manifold, which allowed exhaust gases to escape into the engine compartment, and a loose connection on the engine diesel return, which was dripping diesel oil into the bilge.

CHAPTER 69

South Again

Finally, on September 17, we left Belfast on our voyage south toward the Bahamas. Over the next two weeks we stopped at our favorite harbors and anchorages. We stayed several days in the harbor at Newport, Rhode Island waiting for the weather to become less boisterous, and then on Saturday sailed to the Great Salt Pond at Block Island. Shortly before we arrived there, I discovered that our engine generator was not producing electricity. I diagnosed the problem as a faulty regulator. I reported our problem to the harbormaster on our VHF radio.

We were amazed when, on Sunday morning, a mechanic arrived at our boat with a new regulator that he quickly installed. It was a beautiful day, and we decided to make the 36-hour off-shore trip to Cape May, New Jersey. Mary cooked some food for the trip, and we left Block Island at 2:00 p.m. It was a calm day with no wind, so we motored for hours. We really enjoyed our new rebuilt engine, which the yard had aligned perfectly so it ran smoother than it had for years. Mary said it was great not to have rattling pans on the stove.

We were still motoring along in calm seas at 2:00 a.m. when the engine oil pressure alarm went off. I shut down the engine and discovered that we were losing lubricating oil through some old hoses on the engine. I didn't have enough oil aboard to operate the engine under these conditions. We hoisted the sails, but there just was not enough wind to move the boat. We were about 30 miles off the coast of Long Island. I was able to get a Boat US Towing Service dispatcher on our cell phone. She was asleep in bed, somewhere in Mid-America, when her telephone rang. I gave her our latitude and longitude, and she said she would get back to us. After awhile, the Coast Guard at Shinnecock Bay, Long Island, called us on our radio to get the particulars of our problem. They went through their usual checklist, and when they were assured that we were in no immediate danger, they told us that a towboat was on its way. We furled our sails and waited.

About two hours later the towboat arrived and took us in tow. It would take the operator longer to make the return trip because he couldn't move any faster than our 7.5-knot hull speed. He called to us and said it would be perfectly all right if we wanted to sleep while we were being towed. It was amazing how quiet it was in our aft cabin; in calm seas with no engine running, all we heard was the gentle swish of the water against the hull. We slept until 7:00 a.m. while he towed us into Shinnecock Bay and then way back across the bay to the Jackson Marina. We were certainly happy that we had bought towing insurance, which cost us $85. Our tow was billed to the insurance company for over $900.

The marina mechanic arrived on our boat at 8:00 a.m. and replaced all of the defective oil hoses. I was able to buy an automotive type regulator to replace the one that we had installed only the day before at Block Island. It was already not functioning. We left Shinnecock Bay the next day at 7:00 a.m., to continue our overnight sail to Cape May. We anchored there the next morning.

Because the winds and tides were favorable for a trip up Delaware Bay and the Chesapeake and Delaware Canal, we were able to catch only a few hours of sleep before we left at 2:00 p.m. As a result of our departure time, we would be making much of the trip after dark. We had made the passage in daylight several times and felt confident that we could handle it in the dark.

The passage up Delaware Bay was fast, because the current was with us. It became more difficult as the last of the daylight faded from the sky. We had to be very careful to separate the proper channel lights from the many lights along the shore, and also to distinguish them from the fast-moving lights of large vessels. Most of the trip we had been motoring with our mainsail up to steady the motion of the boat. We finally reached the entrance to the C&D Canal and were maneuvering to give the right of way to a tugboat, with a large barge in tow, when our engine overheat alarm went off. I shut off the engine, and with the help of a few puffs of wind, we drifted off the entrance channel to a spot with only 15 feet of water. We dropped the anchor and let out a lot of chain. The river current pulled the chain taut and set our anchor for us. I turned on the anchor light and we went to bed. Neither of us felt adequate to cope with this problem until we got some sleep.

We awoke that morning to find ourselves alone in a vast expanse of calm water well outside one of the canal entrance markers. It took me only a few minutes to discover the nature of our problem. The steel shaft connecting our salt-water pump to the engine had broken in half. Once again, I called Boat US Towing Service. When I gave the dispatcher our position and predicament, she asked me somewhat plaintively, "Are you having battery problems or something?" I assured her that these were unrelated occurrences and she said a towboat from Delaware City would come and get us. We could see the city from our boat.

That morning, when he arrived, the towboat captain said that on his way to work he had noticed us and wondered what we were doing anchored out there. He towed us into the Delaware City Marina, where the mechanic removed the old pump and ordered a new one from Westerbeke. I was able, because of my experience when they were rebuilding our engine, to tell a mechanic who to call and what to say to get quick service.

Friday, October 9, the next day, our daughter Connie called to tell us the bad news that Mary's brother Parker had died in his sleep the night before. It was a shock because we had all thought he was in excellent health.

At 10:00 a.m. the replacement water pump arrived. At 2:00 p.m. we paid our bill and left for our trip down the C&D Canal to the Chesapeake. After an overnight stop anchored in the Sassafras River we anchored in Back Creek, opposite the Port Annapolis Marina. It was difficult to find the spot into a very crowded anchorage. The SSCA Annapolis Gam was being held at the Marina, and the very large Annapolis Sailboat Show was taking place in the harbor. We attended both.

Almost two weeks later we rented a car and picked up our son David, to drive to Cleveland for Parker's memorial service. It was amazing how many lawyers spoke about their experiences of Parker mentoring them in their careers. He had been a highly respected trial lawyer and partner in a prominent law firm.

As soon as we returned to the boat, we resumed our trip south on the Intracoastal Waterway. In November we tied up at the 68th Street Marina in Jacksonville, Florida. We agreed that it would be nice to take a vacation from our vacation, and return home for the holidays in December. We arranged to leave our boat at the marina in our absence. When we flew home, we had no idea that it would be a long time before we would return to the boat.

CHAPTER 70

Health Problems

Once we were home, we began a series of doctor's appointments. I had a PSA test and Mary had a mammogram. A week after that, she received a call from her doctor saying that they had found a very tiny suspicious lump which had not been there in her previous mammogram. At his recommendation she had a biopsy in which they found cancer cells, so he went ahead and performed a lumpectomy to remove the tiny tumor. This was finished just four days before Christmas, which we celebrated with Connie in her new house. Three days after Christmas the doctor performed a second operation to remove and biopsy a number of Mary's lymph nodes. On New Year's Eve he called to assure us that he had found no cancer cells. He recommended that as a precaution, she have a series of pinpoint radiation treatments. She was referred to a radiation oncologist, who explained that she would have one treatment a day, five days a week, for six weeks. She was able to drive herself to the hospital for treatments and had very little discomfort, aside from what looked like slight sunburn. She started taking the drug Tamoxifen and agreed to be part of a study comparing it with other treatments. She would take the drug for five years.

We flew back to the boat in Jacksonville, Florida on March 9, 1999. We discovered that due to yard negligence, part of our rub rail had been damaged. The marina agreed to fix it. As a result, we were still tied up at the marina a week later when I experienced an irregular heartbeat, which I learned later was atrial fibrillation. A man from a neighboring boat took me to the Jacksonville University Hospital emergency room. They told my neighbor that they would keep me overnight to medicate the irregularity. It turned out that the fibrillation stopped while they were examining me later, so they discharged me. I arrived back at the boat in the middle of the night by taxi. The hospital doctor said he could not see any reason why we should not continue our boat trip south.

On St. Patrick's Day the Marina finished our rub rail repairs, so on March 18, my 78th birthday, we once again started our trip south on the Waterway. We had a strong current to buck, so we stopped about 20 miles from St. Augustine in a little cove at Pine Island. That night, all alone in this very isolated cove, I experienced more irregular heartbeats.

The next morning we continued to St. Augustine, where we anchored in the harbor, and I started my search for a cardiologist. After trying two other cardiologists who could not see me for more than a month, I discovered a cardiologist who came to St. Augustine on Mondays, where he maintained a small office. He agreed to see me the next Monday. When he examined me, he said that I should have an echocardiogram at the Jacksonville Hospital. We rented a small car for a week so we could drive back and forth to Jacksonville. I had the recommended procedure two days later in Jacksonville and wore a heart monitor for several days.

The next Monday, the doctor said that I had had an abnormal stress test and he would like to perform an angiogram at the

Jacksonville hospital the next day, and if he found a blockage he would fix it right then. I had the procedure done at 2:00 on Tuesday, March 30. In the recovery room I learned that the doctor had found one of my arteries 75% blocked and performed an angioplasty to clear the blockage and inserted a stent. As far as I can determine, my fibrillation had nothing to do with the blockage. I had never had any of the symptoms associated with the blocked artery. Had I not had the fibrillation, I might not have been aware of the blockage until I had a heart attack.

Wednesday morning the surgeon came into the room with another doctor. He explained, "I have been your plumber, now I would like to have you talk with our electrician." The second cardiologist explained that some types of fibrillation could be cured by a procedure called ablation. He felt that in my case, the chances were quite good it could be successful. I agreed to have the operation. It was scheduled for Friday. Mary picked me up and we went back to the boat.

On Friday, April 2, we arrived back at the hospital at 10:00 a.m., and at about noon I was rolled back into surgery for my second procedure of the week. So at 4:00 the doctor told Mary that he thought the procedure had been successful. Friday was Good Friday, so Mary went to the hospital chapel and had communion.

I think Mary was quite remarkable during this whole time. Staying on a boat in a harbor is not easy: each time she went ashore she had to climb from the boat into the dinghy, start the engine, take it to shore and tie it up, climb up to the dock, and walk to the car wherever she had parked it for the night. Several times she made the 20-mile drive to Jacksonville and back. Spending all night alone on a boat anchored in a strange harbor would have terrified many women.

After the year's medical experiences, we thought that it would be wise to stay in United States territorial waters and so decided to head north to Maine. Our boat had been almost stationary for a long time in the warm Florida waters. As result, an amazing amount of growth had formed on the bottom. We thought it would be wise to have the boat lifted and scrubbed off and a new coat of anti-fouling paint applied. We found only one boat yard in the area that said they could do this, but when they tried to lift the *Mary Constance* out of the water, they discovered that their equipment was just not up to the job. We learned about a scuba diver, who scrubbed the bottom of the boat clean. We felt that it would suffice until we got to Maine.

On our way north we went offshore to avoid the miles of tedious motoring through the grasslands of Georgia. The rest of the time we traveled the inland waterway, and then once more we had an overnight sail offshore, from Cape May to Atlantic Highlands, New Jersey. When we arrived in Belfast, Maine on July 16, Mary said, "Now we can start our vacation."

For the rest of the summer we spent leisurely days cruising in Penobscot Bay, exploring many of the beautiful harbors and anchorages. In the grocery store Mary met a woman who was a member of the steel drum band that we liked so much. She told Mary that she had an extra mooring at Buck Harbor that we were free to use any time. Just about every time the Flash in the Pans performed at Buck Harbor, we were there, often with friends. We were able to anchor with all of the other boats at Islesboro and participate in all the activities at the SSCA Maine Gam.

We had planned to leave the boat with the Belfast boatyard, but we learned that the cost would be almost prohibitive for us. Because the boats had to be towed through the village to the storage yard, it was necessary to remove the masts and store them separately. We had an excellent framework and three-part cover for our boat that was designed to leave the masts and rigging up. A new friend told us that he left his boat up the Penobscot River at Winterport. The estimate from this boatyard was just a little more than half of what we would have paid in Belfast.

I flew home on August 13 and returned in the motorhome with the boat cover. The yard hauled the *Mary Constance* out of the water on September 7. After our usual winter preparation and covering the boat, we drove home to Chagrin Falls in the motorhome, towing the little Toyota Corolla.

In early November we made a quick automobile trip to Windsor, Ontario to purchase Mary's cancer drug Tamoxifen, which she took daily. It cost almost $3.00 a pill in the United States. We bought it in Canada for 17 cents a pill. Shortly after that on November 8, we left in the motorhome for a trip south. We stayed in a campground at Melbourne, Florida for four days while we attended the Seven Seas Cruising Association annual meeting. It was a wonderful time to renew old acquaintances and make new friends. We were also able to hear a talk by Herb, the Canadian meteorologist who had been so helpful to us on the radio in the Bahamas. He received the Association medal and a $500 stipend for his service to cruising sailors.

After the meeting we drove south to Marathon, in the Florida Keys, for a visit with friends Ridge and Kathy, who were now permanent residents there aboard their boat in a marina. They had been so helpful and kind to us in Annapolis.

We visited with Ann and Phil Hermann at Shell Point Village. They had just moved into a beautiful new apartment. We were very impressed by what this total care retirement community had become since we first visited my father and mother there. The village was only seven years old when we first visited it.

We drove north and arrived at Manassas, Virginia to spend three days with David and Charlotte. We went with them to a very enjoyable Thanksgiving potluck dinner at their Langley Hill Friends Meeting.

CHAPTER 71

Moving

The long periods together while driving in the motorhome have resulted in several life-changing decisions. On our trip home from Manassas, Mary and I agreed that we would like to move to Shell Point Village if we could handle it financially. After a few days at home we asked Bebe, the realtor who had handled all of our real estate transactions during our years in Chagrin Falls, if she could come up with an estimate of the value of our home. A week later she conducted a walk-through of our house and grounds with several of her associates. They came up with varying estimates, but we felt even the most conservative of them would be sufficient to make it possible for us to move to Shell Point.

Early in January 2000 we sent a sizable deposit to Shell Point Village to secure our place on the waiting list for a two-bedroom, two-bath apartment in one of the midrise buildings. This was a major turning point in our lives. We decided to put the house on the market in May, with the expectation that it would sell sometime during the summer.

It is difficult to leave the house in which you have lived for 41 years. Almost all of our children had left things in our large attic. I had a workshop and built-in photographic darkroom in the basement. We had been in constant touch with our children, and they all agreed to come to Chagrin Falls in late February for five days. David said he would like our large artificial Christmas tree, which was going to be too big for our apartment, so we left it up. When our children arrived, we made up lists: the things we were going to take with us; the things they could take home with them; the things that they would like but we could not give up until we finally moved; finally, the list of the items each person would like to have when the estate was broken up after our deaths.

When they arrived, they browsed through the books that they would like to have. We had set up card tables with all kinds of things that we no longer wanted. They drew lots and took turns selecting items from the tables. We all enjoyed the process.

Our realtor, Bebe, created a marketing plan to sell our house. On May 10 she put a "For Sale" sign in the front yard. On May 11 she ran ads in the two local newspapers. On the 12th she had an open house. By the end of the next week she had sold the house twice! The first people backed out. The second people purchased the house for the entire asking price. The final settlement and their occupation of the house would not take place until late July.

I called the Shell Point sales office and told them that our house had sold much more quickly than we had expected, and asked if they could have anything for us sometime in the summer. They advised us they would not have any two-bedroom, two-bath apartments available by that time, but in early August they could put us in a one-bedroom, one-bath apartment in Macoma Court. This would put us at the top of the waiting list for a larger unit when it became available. We accepted the offer.

We decided to go to the boat and return to the house in time to complete removing everything, except those things that the movers were going to pack for Florida. We spent almost a month in Maine before returning to Chagrin Falls. Once again our children were a great help in preparing to move. The local public television station had an annual fund-raising auction, so we donated a painting and two prints to that affair. A book dealer came and purchased a number of books. We donated all the rest, with the exception of those we were going to take with us, to the local library book sale. A library volunteer arrived to pick them up in her large luxury car and filled the trunk, the back seat, and the passenger seat. She returned for a second load that filled her trunk again.

Finally we discovered a man who would remove everything left in our house that we did not plan to move, free of charge, for just what he could glean. Good to his word, he removed a truckload of things from the attic to the basement and left a clean barren house.

The United Van Line packers arrived on July 26. We watched as they packed everything that we were taking south. It was probably the least strenuous day that we had in a week. We spent the night and the next day in our motorhome, parked in our driveway, connected to an electrical outlet that I had installed there years before. After a day of waiting, the big van arrived and loaded our belongings. We left early in the morning for Florida, in the motorhome towing our car. After 44 years, we were no longer residents in Chagrin Falls.

Tuesday, August 1, 2000 we signed the final papers and took possession of our apartment in Shell Point Village. We moved our motorhome into the Groves Campground, which was very convenient to Shell Point. We ate and slept in the motorhome. We were very busy during the week before the moving van arrived. We purchased and assembled two bookcases and an entertainment center that would hold our TV and all of our other electronics. The telephone man came and installed our new phone. We had a two-hour orientation trip in a golf cart, as well as a sit-down briefing in the administration building, to explain all the services at Shell Point. We walked to the Island Café for a very good sandwich and fruit luncheon and then checked out some books and videos at the Shell Point Library. We were beginning to discover how very convenient Macoma Court was to everything.

It was apparent that we could not fit everything we had planned to bring with us into this small apartment. There was nowhere for our dining room table and six chairs. At a nearby Kiwanis thrift shop we discovered a small round table with a large leaf. It came with four chairs with casters. I purchased it with the understanding that they would hold it until our furniture arrived, then deliver it to the moving van and take away our old dining room furniture. When the moving van finally arrived, the exchange took place exactly as I had planned it.

It took us only ten days after the furniture arrived until we had the apartment completely furnished. We even had pictures on the walls. We never moved out of the motorhome, since we felt it would be silly to move everything into the apartment and then back to the motorhome, because we planned to go north again, to the boat, for the balance of the summer.

On August 14, Mary and Ann Hermann celebrated their birthday together. They had been celebrating the occasion since they were just toddlers whose mothers knew each other. Over the ensuing years they had very few opportunities to be together on their birthday, so it was particularly nice that they both were going to be living at Shell Point.

We returned to the boat and our cruising on Penobscot Bay. After about a month we received a call from Shell Point Village, telling us that they would have the type of apartment that we had requested available around Christmastime. Between us, we made one of those nonverbal decisions. I told him that we had not eaten or slept in our apartment and we thought we would like to try living in it before we committed to another place. We never did move. As I write this, we are happy in the smaller apartment. Actually, we were experts in small space living. Even a one-bedroom, one-bath apartment was bigger than the space we had in either the motorhome or the boat. Every time we receive our monthly maintenance bill, we are grateful that we made this decision.

CHAPTER 72

Where We Were When It Happened

Our year 2001 was noteworthy for two events, the first personal, the second national. On June 7 while I was working in the boatyard getting the *Mary Constance* ready for the water, I felt something on the back of my leg. I reached down and pulled off a fully engorged tick. Lyme disease was prevalent in New England, and so I had Mary take me to the emergency room at the hospital in Bangor. The doctor there said that it did not look like a tick bite. I assured him it was, because I had pulled it off myself. He agreed to draw some blood to check if any Lyme disease titers were present. About a week later the hospital called to say my test had turned out negative. On July 7 I began to run a low-grade fever. Two days later, when I was able to see the doctor, he ordered another blood test for Lyme disease. On Friday the 13th, of all days, the doctor called to tell me the test had turned out positive and I had Lyme disease. He started me on a course of high-powered antibiotics. I think we caught the disease in time, because I have not had a noticeable reoccurrence.

We had some wonderful cruising days in early September. The weather was beautiful, and the trees had begun to change to their fall colors. Most of the other boats had been laid up on shore or had headed south, so we had anchorages almost to ourselves. On September 10 we sailed up the beautiful Soames Sound and anchored at the head of the fjord for the night. There was only one other small sailboat in the anchorage. The next morning we watched the early TV news as usual, then turned it off and tuned into the "cruisers' net." Just shortly after that, Chris, from the Cal 27 anchored near us, came over in his dinghy and asked us if we had heard the news. We had not, so we turned on the TV and saw the pictures, again and again, of the two planes crashing into the towers of the World Trade Center. At our suggestion Chris brought his wife back to our boat and the four of us watched the small television for hours, as the tragic events unfolded and the two great towers collapsed in a heap, changing the New York skyline forever.

It was after this event that we decided to have our boat hauled out for the winter a week earlier than we had originally planned. We arrived back at our apartment in Fort Myers on September 30.

By this time Mary was once again very active in her program and attended several meetings a week in the greater Fort Myers area. I had found that Shell Point did not have a photographic club. With the approval of the activities department, I started one and we were soon having monthly meetings during the winter months.

Shell Point did have computer club meetings, conducted by Mike, who had a computer service that had grown originally from service to customers at the village. Someone in management discovered that he was running the club. This was against Shell Point rules, because a resident had to be the president of a club. I volunteered to take over the club, maintain its mailing list, and handle the publicity for upcoming meetings, as long as Mike provided the programs. He said he thought this was great and he would not charge anymore. He was being paid $50 a meeting. No one in management realized that he was being paid. I solved the management's problems and saved them money. I was a hero for a day.

In April 2002 we flew to our son David's house and then drove to a Quaker summer camp facility, in the Maryland Catoctin Mountains, to attend the wedding of our granddaughter Betsy and Ben Mathis. Ben elected to take Betsy's last name and legally change his name to Ben Boynton. When our first great-grandchild arrived a month later, his name was Caspian Boynton.

CHAPTER 73

Penobscot Bay Cruising

In late May 2002 we left Shell Point in the motorhome for Maine. Five days later we arrived in Winterport, Maine, to find the boat and the Toyota Corolla under cover in the boatyard. Both were in excellent condition. Just a week later we moved aboard the *Mary Constance* for the summer. We rented a boatyard mooring in Belfast harbor for the summer.

We had a high point and a low point that summer. The low point occurred on July 2: when we were sailing briskly up Penobscot Bay, I was on the foredeck adjusting sails and Mary was at the helm, when she misjudged how far off a buoyed reef we needed to pass. We were sailing fast when we hit the bottom. We bumped hard two or three times, and passed right over the obstacle. We continued sailing until we reached Belfast harbor and picked up our morning. That night I awoke to the sound of the boat's bilge pump running at least twice. In the morning I removed floorboards and discovered water in the bilge; the boat was definitely leaking.

The nearest marina with a Travel Lift able to lift our boat directly out of the water was in Rockland, Maine. When I called them and explained our problem, the yard manager said, "Come right down, we will be waiting for you." As we approached the yard docks, we found two men waiting in the Travel Lift slip. They motioned us to come right in. The lift slings were already in place. Once on land, we found several gouges in the hull, one of which looked like it had slightly penetrated through the fiberglass. The next day was the Fourth of July, a yard holiday, but they assured us that it would not take long to fix the problem the day after the holiday. We slept aboard the boat. It was very hot on the Fourth, so we spent a good part of the day in the very interesting, air-conditioned Farnsworth Museum.

At 8:00 the next morning, workmen started grinding on the hull. Then, with this finished, they applied layer upon layer of fiberglass and they sanded the final layer smooth. Finally they painted the patch with bottom paint. By early afternoon the job was completed and the *Mary Constance* was back in the water.

The high point of the summer was when Mary got her new dinghy for her birthday. For some time we had often been thoroughly wet down trying to get ashore in the choppy Belfast harbor. When I asked Mary what she would like for her birthday, she said, "I would really like a new dinghy." It was all that I needed to hop in the car with Mary and drive to Hamilton Marine where we ordered a new hard bottom dinghy, with the stipulation that they had to deliver it inflated to the dock at Belfast.

We had resisted owning a rigid fiberglass bottom, inflatable dinghy for years, because we would not have been able to store it inflated on deck. Now that we were not going offshore anymore, we usually towed the dinghy; it was much easier than hauling it on deck and launching it when needed. A hard bottom dinghy would tow just as easily as our old soft bottom one.

We celebrated Mary's 80th birthday on August 14, 2002 with friends at the Dockside Restaurant. She received two identical birthday cakes, both decorated with "Happy Birthday Mary," because I had ordered one to be delivered ahead of time to the restaurant from the local supermarket, and unbeknownst to me, our friends Alex and Diane had done the same thing! Later when we got back to the dock, Mary gave one of her cakes to the dockmaster to take home to his family.

The next day we were anchored in the harbor when the dockmaster called us on the ship-to-shore radio saying "Mary's dinghy has arrived." By the time we arrived at the city boat-launch ramp, several of our friends from the harbor were already there to help us put Mary's Dink in the water from the delivery truck. It turned into a festive affair. Harbor VHF conversations are just like an old-fashioned phone party line. There is a humorous saying, "Old sailors never die; they just get a little dinghy." Mary got her dinghy for her 80th birthday. With a used 9.9 hp outboard, which I purchased from a friend, I realized one of my dreams. I had finally acquired a very fast dinghy that would get up and plane across the open water.

CHAPTER 74

A Year of Transition

The year 2003 was one of transition for us. We decided that the time had come to sell the *Mary Constance*. I was 82 years old, and Mary would turn 81 that summer. We still had no difficulty sailing the *Mary Constance*. We could still clamber aboard, directly from our dinghy, and the sail handling did not seem difficult for me. The problem was maintenance. I no longer had the energy or the flexibility to do the things I had always done. The turning point occurred the day that I spent two hours in the engine compartment, in a fetal position, changing the engine starter. When I crawled out, my body told me that I should not ever do that again. We couldn't afford to have the boat maintained for us by a boatyard.

We had a great summer aboard the boat in Penobscot Bay, doing all the things we like to do best and anchoring in favorite anchorages with favorite people. On July 16 we listed the *Mary Constance* with a brokerage firm in Camden, Maine that seemed to do a good business with older boats. Our contract stipulated that if we found a buyer and sold the boat, they would receive no commission.

We had a lovely cruise in late August when we explored several anchorages we had not seen before and finally arrived in Soames Sound, which is located in Acadia National Park. Once anchored in the harbor, we took the dinghy ashore and walked a short distance to the street, where we caught one of the free Park Service buses. They circulate throughout the park stopping at the most interesting places. The same buses took us to Bar Harbor, where we had luncheon at our favorite small restaurant.

When we laid up the boat for the winter in Winterport on September 12, we were discouraged because the yacht brokerage representative had not even visited the boat himself and had not provided one prospect. We anticipated that next year we would have to once again commission the boat and keep it in yacht condition, to show it to prospects. We could not have been more wrong.

Our boating friend Jim Hammond helped us put the cover on the boat, and we left it in the yard along with the dinghy for the winter. Our yacht broker did call to say that he had a prospect that would like to look at the boat in October and asked if we could have somebody uncover it. Nothing came of this. We heard nothing more from the broker.

Anchored Off A Bahamas Beach

Boat Hauling At Winterport Marina

Our Motorhome In Maine Campground

Raft-Up at SSCA Maine Gam

The Family at our 60th Anniversary Party

Macoma Court

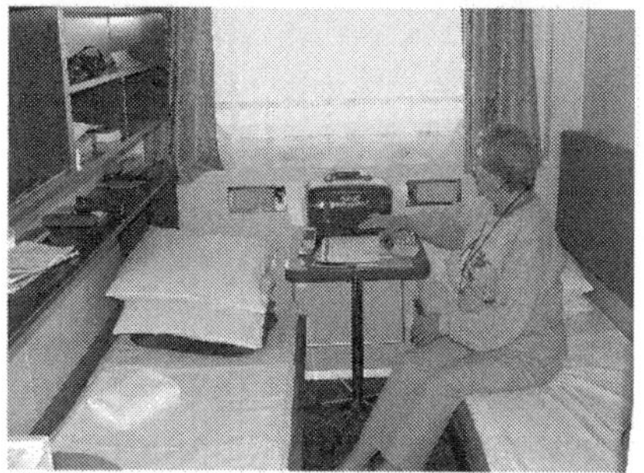
Our Cabin on the Russian Canal Boat

African Guides help me up a Steep Hill

CHAPTER 75

Goodbye Mary Constance

The year 2004 started with what was one of the most incredible occurrences that we have experienced in our lives. On January 2 the yard manager where the boat was stored called to say that he had a couple of men who would really like to look at our boat. I was incredulous; I could not imagine that anybody really interested in a boat would want to look at it in the middle of winter when it was covered with snow. The yard manager was adamant that they really were legitimate prospects. I called our friend Jim, who was living aboard his boat in the Belfast harbor, and asked him if he would be willing to come and meet these people, fold back a corner of the tarp, and insert a ladder so that they could climb aboard. He said that of course he would help us.

That afternoon, after the prospects had examined the boat and he had replaced the cover, Jim called me and said that he felt they were very interested in buying my boat. That evening Guy, one of the two men, called and said "I want your boat." He asked me how much I wanted for it. He obviously had not seen the brokerage listing, so I quoted the asking price we had set in the listing and then to that, added a commission for the yard manager. He said, "Fine, I'll take it."

I asked him when he would plan to have the boat surveyed, and he replied that he had had a lot of boating experience over the years and did not need a survey. I could not believe what

I was hearing; surveyors almost always find something that needs to be repaired or replaced, which would have been at my expense.

I found a purchase agreement on the Internet and customized it to specify the terms of our agreement. The *Mary Constance* was owned by Tema Inc., a Delaware corporation that we had formed because Delaware had no sales tax. The boat was built in Delaware and we purchased her in Delaware. I sold her as president of Tema Inc. For the first time, I was able to use the official Tema Inc. embossed seal on the notarized agreements that I sent to Guy. He returned his duly signed and notarized copy in about ten days. We received our first payment on February 10.

I had promised Guy that Mary and I would help him commission the boat in the spring. In April he called to ask if it would be all right to uncover the boat so he could do some work on it before we arrived. I gave him permission. He called again in May, to ask if it would be all right if he paid us cash for the next large installment. I assumed he meant he would give us a personal check instead of the bank draft specified in the agreement. I said that would be okay.

When we arrived at the boatyard in May, we discovered that Guy had indeed been working on the boat. He had put a beautiful smooth varnish finish on the teak cockpit grating that we had always kept bare to provide a nonskid surface.

We saw nothing of Guy until he arrived two days later and knocked on the motorhome door to make his next sizable payment on the boat. As he said he would, he paid us in cash. He presented us with $35,000 in $100 bills! After the initial shock wore off, we sat in the motorhome with Guy and counted the money. Once we finished, Guy left and Mary put the money in a canvas bag. We wondered what we were going to do with that much cash; we were in Maine and our bank was in Fort Myers. Then I remembered that Mary had a small savings account in Key Bank, headquartered in Cleveland. For some reason they had a small branch office in Belfast, Maine. We drove to Belfast, with the car doors locked and Mary gripping the canvas bag tightly in her lap, and presented the cash to a startled cashier. Once again, the cashier had to count all the money. We left with the bank receipt, greatly relieved.

Once again I went to work preparing the boat for the water. I expected Guy to help me do this, so he could learn the idiosyncrasies of the boat. But he didn't arrive often, and when he did, he seemed to spend most of his time chatting with the people in the boatyard office. Finally I drew up a list of things that needed to be completed before the boat was launched and presented it to him. I told him that my time was limited and he would have to do anything that we did not finish on the list. This seemed to energize him some.

The boatyard workers lifted me to the top of the mainmast in their man-lift, so I could install all of the running rigging. I used the bosun's chair, with a four-purchase block and tackle, to reach the top of the mizzenmast. We had a quiet morning one day, with practically no wind, so we were able to reeve all the sails. Guy was attaching one of the genoa sheets to the sail when Mary realized he was using an ordinary knot. She suggested that he use a bowline instead, because it would be much easier to remove after it had been under tension for a long time. He asked Mary, "What is a bowline?" The bowline is probably the most widely used knot on boats.

We left the boatyard two days later on June 7. We moved to a campground close to Belfast, where we had rented a site for a month. We were not present when the *Mary Constance* was launched. We really moved into the campground. After about one week we had our own local telephone, as well as the usual water, sewer, and electrical connections. Directly across the street, within easy walking distance, was a large fitness center that we joined. We were campers, not sailors.

On June 24 Mary and I celebrated our 60th wedding anniversary. We drove to Bucksport for our celebration dinner. Just before we left, we received a call from Guy to tell us that the *Mary Constance* was docked in Bangor. The news added to our celebration. We were free at last.

CHAPTER 76

Our 60th Wedding Anniversary

For some time our children had wanted to celebrate our 60th wedding anniversary and suggested that we all meet at our daughter Beth's house in Billerica, Mass. on July 10. This date was selected because our Quaker children planned to attend the Friends General Conference (FGC). It was being held on the campus of the University of Massachusetts in Amherst, an easy drive from Beth's house. After we had agreed to this, our son David called and asked Mary if she would be willing to speak at one of the AA meetings being held during the conference. So on the 8th, we drove the motorhome and car to Beth's house. The next day we drove the car to a bed and breakfast in Amherst. Mary spoke at the meeting. Then we joined our family at the conference and attended a lecture together in the evening. We spent the night at the B&B, and after a delicious breakfast there, we drove back to Billerica for the big day.

Beth and Tony had pruned and mown their back yard and set up a 10 x 20 foot screened room. There were enough chairs for all and a beautifully decorated table across one end. There were six cars, with five different state license plates, parked in various spots, plus the motorhome. Three assorted sleeping tents were erected in the spacious backyard. All four of our children and their spouses, and our grandsons, Bob McPeak and Thomas Boynton, were there. Beth had the foresight to rent a fancy Porto-let. We all used it because it was close to the activities in the yard.

Beth and Connie planned the meal, and purchased it all from a high-quality food store. This way they did not have to be in the kitchen preparing the food while we were all visiting in the screened room. I thought it was a very good idea. The beautiful luncheon was laid out on the table decorated with white roses and pink flowers with several different salads, bowls of fruit compote, and an assortment of breads and rolls. The centerpiece was a great yellow cake, with thick chocolate frosting. They served it with ice cream.

Bob had to leave before supper, but everyone else was there when Beth came back from the store, once again with three different soups that we had with the leftover salad and more fruit. It was another delicious meal. Thomas had to leave after supper, but the rest of us stayed and visited well into the night. It was a great time. Mary and I had a chance to talk with each of our children and grandsons separately during the day.

The clan broke up the next day and went their separate ways. We returned to our campground site. A few days later we received a brochure from a travel agency in the Fort Myers area, describing a two-week canal trip in Russia, from Moscow to St. Petersburg. They were offering a considerable discount to anyone who could leave in late August. We had been frustrated in our attempts to sail the *Mary Constance* to St. Petersburg, and I had always wanted to see the great Hermitage Museum. We decided to go. We had valid U.S. passports, and the travel company would take care of securing our Russian visas. Our airfare was included in the price, and we discovered that the flight departed from Boston.

CHAPTER 77

Russia

On August 22 we checked out of the campground and drove to Beth and Tony's house, where we left the motorhome and the car while we took our cruise. Beth took us to Logan Airport the next morning and met us when we returned. We transferred planes in Frankfurt and were surprised to find two attractive young women from the travel agency, who joined a fairly large group of us on the flight to Moscow. We went directly from the Moscow airport to our ship, where we found our luggage already in our stateroom. The vessel was one of dozens of long narrow boats, only two stories high, designed to navigate the waters. We went on conducted tours of all of the tourist sites in Moscow before our boat left for the trip down the waterway. Everywhere on the trip we were shown the opulence of the czars' furnishings and buildings. We always had English-speaking, highly knowledgeable guides.

The high point of the trip for me was our visit to the Hermitage Museum, where the travel company had arranged for us to arrive a full hour before the normal opening. Tour companies assume that one of the main interests of tourists is shopping for souvenirs. The Hermitage guide stopped with our group at a large museum gift shop. Mary and I took advantage of this and walked ahead alone to find ourselves in a large gallery devoted exclusively to Impressionist painters. There was one other lady in the room; she departed soon after we arrived and we had the gallery to ourselves, with not even a guard. Almost every Impressionist painter was represented on the walls, with excellent examples of their work. We could have touched them with our fingers. But of course, we didn't.

One of our tour incentives was a train ride to Helsinki, Finland. We had a night in a nice hotel and a day to go sightseeing before we flew home. We spent the night at Beth's house. The next day we started our trip to Florida in the motorhome towing our car.

In February 2005, my brother Bob underwent bladder surgery and was advised that he had a malignancy that had metastasized. He elected to use alternative medicine instead of drastic chemotherapy. I was able to visit him twice in San Diego before his death on September 4, 2006. He continued his fast morning walks almost to the end. Mary and I attended his memorial service on September 16. In July 2006 we sold our motorhome, ending another chapter in our life.

CHAPTER 78

Africa

In the spring of 2007 I received a brochure in the mail describing a photographic safari in Tanzania. I told Mary that this was something that I had always hoped to do, and she said "I think you should go." When I called Thomson Safaris, they assured me that they would provide a roommate so I would not have to pay the single person premium. When I arrived in Tanzania in June, I discovered that my roommate held degrees in zoology and was a professional-grade photographer. Not only all that, he was a wonderful person and looked after me for the whole trip. There were 15 of us in the group, evenly divided between men and women. At 86 I was the oldest person in the group by at least 20 years. I soon discovered that the Tanzanian guides had a great respect for old age and helped me whenever I needed it.

I had the least sophisticated cameras of anybody on the trip. In spite of this, I came back with pictures of every animal that I wanted to photograph, plus some wonderful video of the wildebeest migration and monkeys in the trees. After I returned, I produced a one-hour DVD of the trip that I showed in the Shell Point auditorium.

On August 22, 2007 Mary had a laminectomy performed on her lower back. She was in the hospital for two days and then the Shell Point Pavilion (nursing home) for two and a half weeks of rehabilitation. We were so grateful to be here at Shell Point, where our health needs are taken care of.

CHAPTER 79

A Son's Death

On December 27, 2007 we received the shocking news that our 62-year-old son David had died suddenly. Only two days before, on Christmas Day, I had talked to him for some time on the phone and he told me he had a cold that seemed to be getting better. Two days later he woke up in the middle of the night complaining of being cold. His wife Charlotte tried to warm him, but it suddenly became apparent he was in great trouble. She called 911. By the time the medics arrived, he was unconscious. He never regained consciousness. A virulent virus, which had destroyed most of his bodily functions, had attacked his body.

We reached the hospital in Manassas, Virginia in time to say our goodbyes, but he was already gone and was on life support. All his family was with him when the life support was disconnected.

David's Quaker memorial service was held in the Sandy Spring Friends Meeting House in Sandy Spring, Maryland, because the Langley Hill Meeting House was too small. Over 300 people attended. We all gathered in silence for several minutes before the clerk of his meeting rose and read this eulogy.

David Merrill Boynton

April 2, 1945 – December 29, 2007

David was born on April 2, 1945, the first child of Ted and Mary Orr Boynton. Four months later, his country became the first and only nation to use nuclear weapons on a human population. It seems that David had his work cut out for him from the beginning.

All of his life, David worked for peace, not only on a national and global scale, but in his day-to-day relationships with others. Through his life, David exemplified that peace which takes away the occasion for war. He believed in honesty and truthfulness even when it might be costly to him. He valued people and relationships over material things and reached out to that of God in every person he met. He had a quiet but intense spirituality, cultivated through years of prayer and reflection, which shone through every aspect of his daily life.

David had many roles and lived each to the best of his ability. He was a husband, father, son, brother, grandfather, dancer, CPA, friend, peace activist, cyclist, salesman, chef, conscientious objector, sailor, financial manager, Quaker, publisher, committee clerk, systems analyst, mentor, and much more.

Honesty and kindness were as natural to David as breathing. When he saw others doing wrong, he confronted them so humbly and gently that they rarely took offense. When he applied for C.O. [conscientious objector] status during the Vietnam War, he insisted on declaring his affiliation with the United Church of Christ, not his more recent affiliation with Quakerism. He believed that all persons should be able to refuse military service on grounds of conscience and didn't want to take unfair advantage of his own association with a traditional peace church.

After majoring in chemistry at Earlham College and completing his alternative service at the National Institutes of Health, David spent a year traveling, including a five-month voyage by sailboat from the East Coast through the Panama Canal to San Francisco. Then he went to work for his uncle, and together they founded a successful publishing company. He lived for a while in Chicago, attending 57th Street Meeting, and there he met Charlotte Montel. They were married under the care of the meeting on January 15, 1972. Shortly thereafter, David and Charlotte moved to Northern Virginia and joined Langley Hill Meeting. Over the course of the next 35 years, David served on almost every committee of the meeting, clerking several. He was also the meeting's treasurer and later bookkeeper. He served on the Finance Committee and Peace and Social Concerns Committee of Baltimore Yearly Meeting, as well as the Camp Facilities Committee for Camp Catoctin.

Eventually he left publishing to work for the Friends Committee on National Legislation, where he became Associate Secretary for Finance and Development. He brought his background in business and his passion for peace and justice to FCNL and used both to advance the goals of the organization. He never hesitated to place his expertise in computer systems and financial management at the service of organizations he believed in. At various times he served as financial steward for, among others, Catoctin Quaker Camp, Northern Virginia Coalition for a Nuclear Weapons Freeze, the Folklore Society of Greater Washington, Bikes for the World, and even his children's pre-school.

During the last 13 years of his life, David worked as Director of Institutional Research at the National Science Teachers Association, a non-profit organization dedicated to promoting excellence and innovation in science teaching and learning. There he was responsible for accounting, financial modeling, and systems support. Here is what a colleague at NSTA had to say about David: "There was not a day that staff were not at his door asking for help in solving problems—he loved problem-solving. His intellect and open manner made him a wonderful colleague and confidant. He was my anchor and my friend. I will miss him a lot."

David was a friend and confidant to many others as well. He was one of those rare individuals who could really listen to others. He listened to friends vent their frustrations. He listened to people who had different political views. He listened to people who were hurting because of some tragedy in their life. He listened to friends who just needed a sounding board, or advice. When David listened, you felt heard. He rarely stopped listening so that he could tell his own story. For this reason, even those who knew him well were often surprised to learn about new aspects of his life that they had not known about before.

One of David's most cherished roles was that of father to Tom and Betsy, and later of grandfather to Caspian. The times spent with his children and grandchild were among the happiest in his life. Throughout his life he remained close to his parents and to his siblings (Connie, Jim, and Beth) and their families. David loved to dance, and he and Charlotte were regular attendees at contra dances on Friday and Sunday nights, as well as dance weekends at Buffalo Gap. Towards the end of his life he became an avid cyclist. He rode to work. He rode at Friends' gatherings. He rode summer and winter, rain or shine. He rode for exercise and transportation and fellowship, but mostly for the sheer joy of being out in God's creation.

At Langley Hill, David and Charlotte were always ready to welcome newcomers. They cherished the fellowship of the meeting community and participated actively together in every aspect of its life, from potlucks to retreats, to committee meetings, to service. David was always ready to help someone move, or drive someone who needed a ride, or deliver something that needed delivering. He did this for the pleasure he got from helping others.

Recently, David was especially active in two important leadings of the meeting, the weekly peace vigil at the U.S. Capitol, now into its fifth year, and the monthly vigil against torture in front of the CIA. The latter vigil was started and nurtured by David, and he was always careful to alert the CIA to our coming and treat their employees with respect. Thanks largely to David, we have always been treated respectfully in return.

David never hesitated to speak God's truth as he understood it, even when he was in the minority. But he did so with such simplicity, kindness, and humility, that his message was always well received and often helped the Meeting to reach unity on difficult issues.

David talked from time to time about what he believed about the afterlife. He had obviously given it considerable thought. He was very clear that we should not wait for heaven after we died, but rather live as though heaven were right here with us on earth. That was how David lived his life, and in so doing, he showed us the power of the simple prayer that meant so much to him: "Lord, make me an instrument of thy peace."

After a few moments' silence, people stood and expressed their feelings about David and his life. It was a wonderful, heartwarming experience for Mary and me to hear how many people had loved and respected him. Even though he died young, he had a successful and fulfilling life.

There was a reception in an adjoining hall served by the meeting. We were delighted that two of his college friends were there. I created a PowerPoint presentation of his life, in pictures, for the occasion.

CHAPTER 80

Alaska

In June 2008 the Shell Point Activities Department sponsored an eight-day cruise up the Alaskan Inside Passage. The all-inclusive fare was very reasonable, and we decided to try it. This time, we were not the oldest Shell Point people on the trip. Our luggage was picked up at the door and delivered to our apartment at the end of the trip. We flew to Seattle, where we spent a night in a nice hotel and then boarded a Holland America cruise ship for the voyage. The weather was beautiful for the entire trip. We stopped and visited in some interesting towns. The scenery was gorgeous, especially so when our cruise ship entered into breathtaking Glacier Bay.

Mary and I took a side trip one afternoon on a whale-watching vessel, where I achieved two of my objectives for the trip. I photographed orca whales in the wild and captured a picture of a breaching humpback whale.

CHAPTER 81

Life at Shell Point

Alaska was our last trip away from home. Since then we have been full-time residents in our apartment at the Shell Point Retirement Community. All during our residence here, up until the present time, we have continued to be active. Mary sorts mail every Thursday morning at the Pavilion, to be delivered to the residence patients, or redirected, as needed, to a person responsible for their financial affairs. Mary is still very active in her program and attends four meetings a week. I go to one of these with her. We are both still able to drive our car. We have a golf cart for our community transportation.

I have continued to pursue my photographic hobby in several ways. A few years ago I was responsible for converting part of our regular darkroom into a digital darkroom. The darkroom was no longer being used for film-based photography. We installed two computers with two scanners, along with the software to convert slides and pictures into digital format. I created illustrated flipcharts explaining how to use the equipment. I still personally train people in the use of the scanners.

After I acquired my video camera, I produced several short programs for Shell Point TV. For one of them I photographed every activity offered to Shell Point residents, using pictures only of their hands in action.

Our second-floor apartment has always overlooked the side of the Pavilion (nursing home). After fundraising was completed and the permits granted for a new rehabilitation building and medical center, I decided it would be fun to video the construction from beginning to end. I was able to photograph some of it directly through our living room window. I produced nine eight-minute programs for Shell Point TV. Because I really knew nothing much about construction, I called my programs "The Sidewalk Superintendent." In these programs I tried to describe, as much as possible, how things were done, rather than what had been done. They proved to be very popular with our residents.

In 2005, with club members' approval, I suggested that the Photographic Club take over the annual Shell Point Photographic Contest, which previously had been run by the marketing department. This was a major project because it usually drew as many as 250 entries, all of which had to be matted and mounted on display boards. I was responsible for this, as well as many club activities, until about two years ago, when I cleared my schedule to write these memoirs.

CHAPTER 82

Family Christmas Cards

Over the years we have created and printed photographic Christmas cards. These are a few from our early years.

One day, not long ago, I said to myself, "In spite of my advanced age (91), I am a really happy man." When I told Mary, age 90 about this experience, she said, "I have had the same experience; I am a really happy woman." Our life together has been a wonderful adventure and still is.

Not The End

1953

1955

Boynton
Favorite
Christmas Cards

1958

1961

1967

Acknowledgments

I would like to thank Carolyn Bartholet, for editing my manuscript. She generously volunteered to take on the task. My wife Mary, read my writing over and over again. Without her encouragement and help I do not think that I would have been able to finish the project. My son in law, Tony Parkes, professionally proofread the manuscript. My thanks go out to him. My Daughter Beth did a final reading and caught several of my mistakes. Thanks Beth.

I am very aware that memories are often subject to change over the years. If anyone who reads this book remembers an event in a different way, I hope he or she will forgive me.

17062740R00265

Made in the USA
Charleston, SC
24 January 2013